THE BRITISH POLITICAL TRADITION

EDITED BY ALAN BULLOCK AND F. W. DEAKIN

BOOK SEVEN

THE CHALLENGE OF SOCIALISM

ALSO IN THE

BRITISH POLITICAL TRADITION SERIES

THE DEBATE ON THE AMERICAN REVOLUTION, 1761-1783
Edited by Max Beloff
Professor of Government and Public Administration, Oxford

THE DEBATE ON THE FRENCH REVOLUTION, 1789-1800
Edited by Alfred Cobban
Professor of French History, London University

BRITAIN AND EUROPE: PITT TO CHURCHILL, 1793-1940
Edited by James Joll
Fellow of St. Antony's College, Oxford

THE CONSERVATIVE TRADITION
Edited by R. J. White
Fellow of Downing College, Cambridge

THE ENGLISH RADICAL TRADITION, 1763-1914
Edited by S. Maccoby

THE LIBERAL TRADITION: FROM FOX TO KEYNES
Edited by Alan Bullock
Master of St. Catherine's College, Oxford
and Maurice Shock
Fellow of University College, Oxford

THE CONCEPT OF EMPIRE: BURKE TO ATTLEE 1774-1947
Edited by George Bennett

THE CHALLENGE OF SOCIALISM

EDITED BY

HENRY PELLING, PH.D.

FELLOW OF ST. JOHN'S COLLEGE, CAMBRIDGE

SECOND EDITION

ADAM & CHARLES BLACK
LONDON

FIRST PUBLISHED 1954
SECOND EDITION 1968

4, 5 AND 6 SOHO SQUARE LONDON W.1

PRINTED IN GREAT BRITAIN
BY JOHN DICKENS & CO LTD
NORTHAMPTON

GENERAL PREFACE

One of the unique contributions the English people have made to civilization has been the discussion of political issues which has been going on in Britain continuously since the sixteenth century. It is a discussion which has ranged over the whole field of political thought and experience. It began with the relation of the State to the individual in religious matters; for the last half century it has been increasingly preoccupied with the relation of the State to the individual in economic matters. The strength of the tradition, the right of rebellion; the demand for equality, the rights of property; the place of justice and morality in foreign policy, the relations between Britain and her overseas territories; the claims of minorities, the value of civil and religious freedom; the rule of law, the Rule of the Saints; the rights of the individual, the claims of the State—all these have been the subject of passionate and incessant argument among Englishmen since the time of the Reformation.

This debate has never been of an academic character. There are, it is true, masterpieces of political philosophy in the English language: Hobbes' *Leviathan* is an obvious example. But the true character of this debate has been empirical: the discussion of particular and practical issues, in the course of which a clash of principle and attitude is brought out, but in which the element of abstract thought is always kept in relation to an immediate and actual situation. The riches of British political thought are to be found less in the philosophers' discussions of terms like "The State", "freedom" and "obligation"—important though these are—than in the writings and speeches on contemporary political issues of men like Lilburne, Locke, Bolingbroke, Burke, Tom Paine, Fox, the Mills, Cobden, Disraeli, Gladstone, and the Fabians. No other literature in the world is so rich in political pamphlets as English, and the pages of *Hansard* are a mine not only for the historian of political events but also for the historian of political ideas. It is in the discussions provoked by the major crises in British history—the Civil War, the Revolt of the American Colonies, the Reform Bills of the nineteenth century—that our political ideas have been hammered out.

One unfortunate result of this is that much of the material which anyone interested in English political ideas needs to read is inaccessible. Pamphlets and speeches are often only to be found in contemporary publications hidden away on the more obscure shelves of the big libraries. Even when the reader has secured a volume of seventeenth-century pamphlets or of Gladstone's speeches, he may well be deterred by the large amount of now irrelevant detail or polemic through which he has to make his way before striking the characteristic ideas and assumptions of the writer or speaker. It is to meet the need of the reader who is interested in English political ideas but has neither the time, the patience, nor perhaps the opportunity, to read through a library of books to find the material he is looking for that this present series of books is designed. Its aim is to present from sources of the most varied kind, books, pamphlets, speeches, letters, newspapers, a selection of original material illustrating the different facets of Englishmen's discussion of politics. Each volume will include an introductory essay by the editor together with sufficient explanation of the circumstances to make each extract intelligible. In some cases it has seemed best to make a particular crisis the focus of the discussion: this has been done with Mr. Beloff's volume, *The Debate on the American Revolution*, and with Dr. Cobban's *The Debate on the French Revolution*. In other cases the development of a particular view has been traced over a long period of years: this is the case, for instance, with the volumes on the Conservative, the Liberal, and the Radical Traditions. In a third case, that of the volume on "Britain and Europe", our idea has been to single out a recurrent problem in English politics and trace its discussion from Pitt's day to our own.

To begin with, we have concentrated our attention on the period between the Revolt of the American Colonies and the Great War of 1914. When that has been covered we hope to treat the earlier period in the same way, notably the political discussions of the seventeenth century.

We do not believe that any one of these facets can be singled out and labelled as in some particular way more characteristic than others of the British Political Tradition: the rebels have as great a part in our political tradition as those who who have argued the case for the claims of prescription and established authority. The wealth of that tradition is that it includes Lilburne, Tom Paine, Richard Cobden and the Early English Socialists as well as Locke, Burke and Disraeli.

We have tried to hold the balance even. In no sense do we wish to act as propagandists or advocates. While each editor has been given complete freedom to present his material as he wishes, we have been concerned as general editors to see that equal representation is given to different views in the series as a whole. Only in this way, we believe, is it possible to display the British Political Tradition in its unequalled richness, as built up out of a variety of political opinions and out of the clash between them, as the great and continuous debate of the nation to which, in its very nature, there can be no end.

ALAN BULLOCK
F. W. DEAKIN

Oxford

CONTENTS

ACKNOWLEDGEMENTS

I WOULD thank the following authors and owners of copyright material for their kind permission to use extracts from these works:

Messrs. Adprint Ltd. (*The English People* by George Orwell, published in Messrs. Collins' Britain in Pictures Series).

Messrs. George Allen & Unwin Ltd. (*Roads to Freedom* by Bertrand Russell; *Equality* by R. H. Tawney; *Parliamentary Government in England* by H. J. Laski; *The Evolution of Modern Capitalism* by J. A. Hobson).

The Rt. Hon. C. R. Attlee and Messrs. Victor Gollancz Ltd. (*The Labour Party in Perspective*).

Messrs. G. Bell & Sons Ltd. (*The Acquisitive Society* by R. H. Tawney; *Self-Government in Industry* by G. D. H. Cole).

Professor G. D. H. Cole (*Self-Government in Industry* and *A Simple Case for Socialism*).

Dame Isobel Cripps and Messrs. Victor Gollancz Ltd. (*Problems of a Socialist Government* by Sir Stafford Cripps).

The Fabian Society (*The Progress of Socialism* by Sidney Webb; *Twentieth-Century Politics* by Sidney Webb; *This Misery of Boots* by H. G. Wells; *The Way Forward* by James Griffiths; *International Government* by Leonard Woolf; *Socialism and the Welfare State* by Kingsley Martin).

Messrs. Victor Gollancz Ltd. (*A Simple Case for Socialism*).

Independent Labour Party (*The Living Wage* by H. N. Brailsford; *Socialism for Today* by H. N. Brailsford; *White Capital and Coloured Labour* by S. Olivier; *The Meaning of Socialism* by J. B. Glasier; *Socialism and Society* by J. Ramsay Macdonald).

Messrs. Lawrence & Wishart Ltd. (*Serving My Time* by Harry Pollitt).

Messrs. Jarrolds Ltd. and Mr. Fred Henderson (*The Case for Socialism*).

Mr. Kingsley Martin and Messrs. Victor Gollancz (*Harold Laski*).

Messrs. Longmans, Green & Co. Ltd. and The Passfield Trust (*A Constitution for the Socialist Commonwealth of Great Britain* by Sidney and Beatrice Webb).

Messrs. Macmillan & Co. Ltd. (*Self-Government in Industry* by G. D. H. Cole).

Oxford University Press (*The Modern Democratic State* by Lord Lindsay).

Messrs. Routledge & Kegan Paul Ltd. (*Practical Socialism* by Hugh Dalton).

Messrs. Selwyn & Blount Ltd. (*My England* by G. Lansbury).

The Society of Authors and the Public Trustee (*The Intelligent Woman's Guide to Capitalism and Socialism*, an article in *National Reformer*, by George Bernard Shaw; also his contribution to the *Report of the Industrial Remuneration Conference*).

H.M.S.O., The Publishers of *Hansard* (speeches by Mr. J. T. W. Newbold and Mr. Aneurin Bevan; extract from Memorandum: The Commonwealth of India Bill).

The Rt. Hon. John Strachey and Messrs. Victor Gollancz Ltd. (*The Theory and Practice of Socialism*).

The Turnstile Press Ltd. (*New Fabian Essays* by R. H. S. Crossman).

Messrs. A. P. Watt & Son (*New Worlds for Old* by H. G. Wells).

Should any extracts from works still in copyright be included inadvertently without acknowledgement the publishers should be notified so that such acknowledgement may be made in future editions.

H.M.P.

INTRODUCTION

BRITISH Socialism has been defined by R. H. Tawney as "the effort, partly critical, partly constructive, at once aspiration, theory, prophecy, and programme, which has as its object to substitute for the direction of industry by the motive of personal profit and the method of unrestricted competition some principle of organization more compatible with social solidarity and economic freedom".

It would be quite possible to trace aspects of this ideal back into British history much earlier than has been done in this volume—back, for instance, to Winstanley and the Levellers, to Harrington and to More. But, as is emphasized in Professor Tawney's definition, the modern Socialist movement is so largely a reaction to the industrial developments of the last two centuries that it seems practical and convenient to start with the years when the Industrial Revolution was just beginning to change the face and character of the country. At that time, we find Socialism emerging from the Radical tradition, which was already established not only here but also in America and France. This selection of documents therefore quotes first from the Radical critics of property who appeared at the end of the eighteenth century.

From similar premises different thinkers drew different conclusions. Just as Paine's *Agrarian Justice* was based on the natural law theory of Locke's *Civil Government*, which to other writers provided the foundation for a defence of existing property rights; so Godwin and many of the early Socialists—Owen, Thompson, Hodgskin—started from the principle of utility to build a political philosophy very different from that of Bentham. Godwin himself cannot be described as a Socialist : but it is in his work that we find most strongly emphasized the optimistic psychology which Owen accepted in constructing his theory of Socialist co-operation. Following the empiricism of Hume and Helvetius, Godwin believed that human nature is entirely shaped by environment, and that a rational education will produce the perfect man. The influence of Godwin's ideas upon Owen, by way of their mutual friend Thomas Holcroft, was profound. Owen devised his co-operative schemes to provide a remedy for the distress produced by the industrial system in which as a factory-master he participated; and he had no doubt that in the new environment that he proposed to establish the character of the co-operators would be transformed. It is with Owen that we are first and most clearly in touch with British Socialist thought: though it was not until 1827 that the word "Socialist" appeared for the first time—in an organ of the Owenite movement, the *Co-operative Magazine*.

From the same philosophical premises the Benthamites drew strikingly different conclusions for economic policy. For them, as for Adam Smith, the path of reform lay in removing the hindrances to a free economy, on the principle of the "invisible hand" that identified the self-interest of the individual with that of the community. Benthamite Radicalism consequently became the ethos of the rising commercial and industrial classes who sought to destroy the privileges of the old land-owning aristocracy. Constitutional reform and an attack upon landownership became the goal and the limit of Radical political aims. The Socialists, on the other hand, were separated from Radicalism, and at odds with it, in that they rejected the idea that the individual self-interest of unregenerate man could lead to the welfare of the community. The difference, as it worked out in practice, is illustrated by the contrast between the Benthamite view of the Poor Law and that of the Socialists; between the 1834 Act and the Minority Report of 1909; between the principle of Less Eligibility and the concept of Social Responsibility.

But this is to anticipate. We must beware of thinking that there was any continuous tradition of Socialist thought in Britain until the last quarter of the nineteenth century. It is true that Owen himself was never forgotten, for he did not merely write about Socialism, but founded colonies and encouraged co-operative societies and trade unions, some of which survived with his principles written into their rules. But the Owenite ideal was rejected in the Victorian age, and the able Socialist economists who were his contemporaries were almost completely ignored until the end of the century, when they were rediscovered through the researches of Dr. Menger and Professor Foxwell.[1] The Chartist Left, undoubtedly Socialist as it was, found its inspiration abroad—in the leaders of the first French Revolution, in Baboeuf and Buonarotti, and in the contemporary continental agitators such as Louis Blanc and Karl Marx. Even the Christian Socialists derived their knowledge of Socialism from the study of the French experiments made by their leader, J. M. Ludlow, during his education in Paris. The tenuous links between these thinkers and the revival of British Socialism in the eighteen-eighties were maintained almost entirely by the little group of exiles led by Marx and Engels. Even in the present century, foreign ideas and movements have contributed largely to British Socialist thought, as is clear when we recall the impact of Industrial Unionism, of Syndicalism, and of Leninism. Indeed, Socialist thought appears as a continuous development from the beginning of the nineteenth century only if it is regarded as an international movement rather than as a

[1] A. Menger, *The Right to the Whole Produce of Labour*, with introduction by H. S. Foxwell (1899).

permanently active element within the boundaries of any one country.

It is in this sense that Socialism represents, in its early manifestations, a challenge to the British political tradition rather than an integral part of it. It is true that the Socialist analysis of society was based, in the first place, on an examination of industrial change in Britain, the country at that time most advanced in the application of the new techniques. When, as in the eighteen-twenties and at the end of the two following decades, this industrial change resulted in serious distress and widespread unemployment, the denunciation of capitalism rapidly increased in volume and intensity. But when the progress of industrialization was comparatively smooth, the challenge died away into silence so far as Britain was concerned. The Socialist movement continued to exist because it was not less cosmopolitan than capitalism itself; and the nature of its analysis, emphasizing as it did the universality of economic laws, was such as to discourage any recognition of national political characteristics.

This may help to explain the remarkable way in which the early anti-capitalist economists were ignored by the immediately following generations, in the mid-Victorian era of capitalist prosperity. If any mention of them is to be found at all, it is in the work of exiles from other lands —in an occasional footnote in the volumes of Marx and Engels. Even before he started work in the British Museum Marx had read many of the British critics of capitalism, and in his early work *The Poverty of Philosophy* he examined the thought of one of them, J. F. Bray, at some length. He realized their importance : basing themselves on the labour-value theory of Ricardo, the statistics of Patrick Colquhoun and the contemporary evidence of popular distress, they had rapidly developed the conceptions of surplus value and capitalist exploitation. Indeed, it is a striking fact that all the main ideas of Marxist economics are to be found in the work of these early British Socialists, though none of them, not even Thompson, in any way approached Marx as a master of economic analysis and constructive thought.

Marx's *Capital* was not translated into English until 1887, though originally published in German twenty years before; and in the meantime John Stuart Mill's *Principles of Political Economy* was the textbook of economics in this country. Mill, though he discussed Socialism in this volume, chose to ignore the Ricardian Socialists: and so they passed into oblivion. Their standpoint was adopted by Ruskin, who followed them in accepting Ricardo's dictum that " labour determines value ", and using it as a stick to beat the rest of classical economics: but Ruskin's views resembled theirs by coincidence rather than by direct or even indirect influence, for there is no evidence that he had ever heard of them, although he knew some of the Christian Socialists.

There was no question of Ruskin's views ever being forgotten in the same way. He was no theoretical economist, but his commonsense contributions to the definition of terms such as " wealth " and " value ", and his scorn for the conception of " over-production " in a world of almost universal poverty and scarcity, had a profound influence in the later nineteenth century: perhaps most notably on J. A. Hobson, the " economic heretic " who, in his turn, propounded ideas which have been of primary importance in shaping recent Socialist thought.

Ruskin provided another important and constructive line of criticism of the existing industrial system in his suggestion—partly derived from Carlyle—that the guilds of the Middle Ages might be revived in order to restore a sense of independence and dignity to the producers and craftsmen of the present day. This idea was to develop further in the distinctively Socialist propaganda of William Morris, and in the twentieth-century movements of Syndicalism and Guild Socialism.

It is only in the last two decades of the nineteenth century, with the growth of permanent political organization, that we can say that Socialism began to exert a definite and continuous influence on British political thought. The delayed impact of Marx's *Capital,* with its special stress on the theory of value, was transmitted to the English public through the propaganda of the Social-Democratic Federation and the Socialist League. Hyndman and Morris, the respective leaders of these two bodies, affixed the stamp of their own personalities to the doctrine they were advocating. Hyndman's Marxism had an element of what Marx himself regarded as chauvinism; Morris, though free from blame on this score, was an anti-parliamentarian and inclined to favour anarchist ideas.

But both Hyndman and Morris regarded themselves as interpreters, and not as revisers, of Marx's ideas. The Fabians were the first to take an eclectic attitude towards Marxist thought. They were influenced to some extent by Comte: indeed, in many ways they resemble the followers of Comte's master Saint-Simon. In the face of the growing threat to Britain's commercial supremacy caused by industrial development in Germany and the United States, they came to regard Socialism as a policy of national efficiency adapted to the requirements of a new mercantilist age. They held that a policy of this sort could be separated from the various political issues with which Socialism had become involved in the past, especially on the continent—such as anti-clericalism and republicanism. They argued, too, that Socialism could do without the labour theory of value, and could be based just as well on the Jevonian concept of Final Utility. Above all, they maintained that their type of Socialism could dispense with the tactics of violent revolution: that the machinery of the new state could be evolved

—in fact, already was being evolved—without any violent transformation of society. Some of the leading Fabians, indeed, had no great respect for democratic government. They sought to win their ends by the permeation of the governing class and the bureaucracy: and they made little attempt to win working-class recruits for their own society.

Many of these conservative elements of Fabianism were absent from the working-class Socialism that developed in the early eighteen-nineties in the Independent Labour Party, and that formed an important element in the Labour Party from its foundation in 1900. Working men accepted readily enough the idea of gradual evolutionary progress towards Socialism, for the threat of revolutionary action had little attraction save for the unemployed, and not often even for them. The fight for the suffrage had made their leaders into convinced Liberal-Radicals, and they carried with them the old internationalist tradition that was a continuous element in working-class politics in the nineteenth century. The Labour Party, indeed, did not even in theory become a Socialist party until 1918; both before that date and afterwards it inherited a considerable legacy of ideas from the Liberal Party which it gradually dispossessed from its parliamentary position; and these ideas came to it almost as much from those who called themselves Socialists, such as Keir Hardie, Ramsay MacDonald and Philip Snowden, as from those who refused to accept the denomination of the new political creed.

The history of Socialist thought must not be identified with the history of the Labour Party, although it is true to-day that the vast majority of British Socialists are members of that party. But the fact that since 1900 there has always been a high proportion of Socialists actually participating in a political association run on trade union funds has undoubtedly had a moderating influence on the Socialist movement as a whole, linking it with a series of established interests holding accumulated privileges and property. In a moment of depression less than two years after the party was founded, Keir Hardie, its very architect, could admit publicly that "the keen edge has been taken off our Socialist propaganda by our growing connection with the Trade Union movement". Yet he did not advocate withdrawal from the association, and the proportion of the Socialist movement which has chosen to work inside the Labour Party has increased steadily since that time.

This does not mean that British Socialism has stood still in the last half-century, or simply retreated still further from the Marxist position to something more in accord with its Liberal inheritance. On the contrary, there has been a richness of debate and controversy on distinctly Socialist lines that has been an invigorating influence throughout the political life of the country. This would never have taken place if Marxism had been accepted as a dogma, to be interpreted but never to be challenged; nor could it have happened, on the other hand, without a framework of ideas created by many writers, Marx among them, within which the present-day Socialist has moved in response to the events and circumstances of his time. This framework, it should be explained, is wide enough in all conscience, and carries with it no necessary philosophical implications. Idealists and materialists, Catholics, Anglicans, nonconformists and freethinkers can all be Socialists if they wish. Strict Marxists there still are, of course, in Britain: those of the old Hyndmanite type, represented by the teaching of the National Council of Labour Colleges; and those of the Leninist type who belong to the Communist Party; to mention only the most important groups. But also there are the Fabians, the latter-day Christian Socialists (no longer an exclusively Anglican group), the philosophical idealists like A. D. Lindsay who have transformed the Liberal concept of the State by the acceptance of fresh social responsibilities. All of these groups have had their contribution to make; and between the extremes of dogmatism and pragmatism, British Socialism has found a fair freedom of manoeuvre. Looking back over the issues of the last half-century, it seems remarkable how much the movement has been swung by the impact of events both at home and abroad; and yet—apart from its remarkably undogmatic nature—there are certain features which have emerged in the last half-century and which can perhaps be regarded as characteristic of it.

The most important of these features is the general acceptance of the view that it is practicable in this country to achieve a transfer of power without resort to violence. It must be remembered that this was a possibility that Marx and Engels themselves did not rule out. As we have seen, the bulk of the British Socialist movement accepted the Fabian view that a gradual evolutionary transformation of social institutions was likely to take place. In the years before the 1914 war we find the parliamentary leaders of Socialism, especially Ramsay MacDonald, defining their task as simply the replacement of the Liberal Party and the absorption of its remnants. It is true that the uprush of violence in Europe caused by the war and the revolutions that accompanied it led to the growth of a more uncertain attitude, and to the foundation of the Communist Party along Marxist-Leninist lines. But the Communist Party remained comparatively uninfluential in the 1920's, and gained little strength even in the following decade, when the same issue arose once more as a result of the world economic crisis and the rise of Fascism. It is a matter of contrast with the Socialist movements of most Continental countries and of America, that the British Socialist tradition explicitly rejects the idea that its objectives can only be attained by force.

This, then, is the most distinctive feature of British

Socialist thought in the present century. It determines the attitude of the large majority of its adherents to the ideal of political liberty and to the practical problems of constitutional government. The Socialist believes that political liberty does not guarantee economic liberty: but the conception of the dictatorship of the proletariat has made little appeal to him, and he has rarely felt inclined to challenge the authority of Parliament. The gloomy prophecies of Professor Laski represented a popular point of view only in the bitter reaction to the events of 1931. The most interesting controversies of Socialist theory in this century have taken place on the basis of an acceptance of constitutional action to attain power. Thus on the one hand the "expropriation of the expropriators" was modified into a programme of compensated nationalization on Fabian lines: and on the other hand revolutionary Syndicalism was transformed into the Guild Socialism of Cole and Tawney.

The issue between these two points of view—Fabian nationalization or Guild Socialism—stimulated some of the ablest propagandist writing of the present century. This was largely because it raised questions of morals and aesthetics as well as of politics and economics. What are the relative advantages of centralization and decentralization? Which is more desirable, the satisfaction of the consumer or the freedom of the craftsman? What are the real incentives to the production of wealth? And what in any case is wealth? The debate outstepped the boundaries of Marxian and Jevonian economics and brought a new generation back to Carlyle, Ruskin and Morris.

Still, the British Socialist movement, even in these years when it grew rapidly and developed the characteristics of an important element in the national political tradition, could not fail to be deeply influenced by the events that ended for ever Britain's position of independence from the affairs of the continent. It was no accident that the Guild

Socialist movement disintegrated in the final years of the Great War and in the controversies aroused by the Russian revolution. Thenceforward world politics were never far outside the discussions of Socialist thought. The irregularities of the British economy were seen to be linked closely with the growing difficulties of world trade in general. Socialists therefore took a keen interest in foreign affairs, not only for the sake of the preservation of peace, but also in the belief that the future stability of the world's economy depended on international co-operation. J. A. Hobson's work on imperialism had first been written at the time of the Boer War, but it was in the 1920's and 1930's that his views, coupled with Lenin's development of the same theme, had their most profound influence on Socialist thought. Capitalist states were forced to expand territorially, and thus the basic cause of war was the economic rivalry of the great powers. This was the simple thesis which was accepted by a majority of Socialists in this period, and which encouraged the growth of pacifism in the Labour Party.

The collapse of the second Labour Government in 1931 was an important event in the history of Socialist thought, and this too was due to what was primarily an international crisis. It was suddenly realized that no Socialist government could expect to retain control of the country's economy unless it took immediate measures to safeguard the international stability of sterling. Because of this, and partly also under the influence of the Russian Five Year Plan, the idea of economic planning—until this time a curiously neglected aspect of Socialist thought in this country—began to develop rapidly. The success of the largely empirical methods employed by Roosevelt's New Deal led to a general acceptance of the underconsumption theory of which J. A. Hobson had for many years been the only prominent exponent. It was along these lines that in 1936 J. M. Keynes formulated his General Theory, which showed how full employment could be achieved in a capitalist or mixed economy. The measure of the development of economic thought in these years is provided by the fact that an economic policy which even the Labour Government of 1929 did not dare to adopt was accepted by all parties in the wartime coalition some fifteen years later.

Meanwhile the Nazi persecutions in Germany had rallied the great bulk of the Socialist movement to a policy of collective security, and to a fuller realization of the advantages of the political democracy which was at stake. The war that ensued saw the mobilization of the country's resources to a higher degree than that achieved by any other country, with the possible exception of Russia. At its conclusion the Labour Government which had triumphed at the polls was able to take over power with all the essential economic controls already in existence. The problems of the transfer of power which had been debated with such anxiety in the 1930's were thus immeasurably eased. The Labour Government did what it was expected to do by nationalizing some of the country's basic industries and expanding its social services; and it also achieved some redistribution of the national income by budgetary methods. But, rather unexpectedly, its principal difficulty turned out to be the country's external trading situation, and it was for this purpose that many of the wartime controls were retained and in some directions even extended.

Led by Stafford Cripps as Chancellor of the Exchequer, British Socialism linked up once more with the policy of national efficiency which Sidney Webb had advocated half a century before. The old Fabian ideal was now largely achieved: the government was taking charge of the drive for more industrial production, encouraging the growth of scientific management, furthering technical education, and controlling capital development even in the sphere of private enterprise. The system of placing the nationalized industries under independent public corporations, in accordance with plans worked out by Herbert Morrison, was one which made the fewest possible concessions to the temporarily dormant ideas of Guild Socialism. But this was not the last word on the subject: even before the 1945 Government had finished its term, there were grumblings in the trade union movement and among the Labour backbenchers which indicated that there might be attempts to remedy the shortcomings of nationalised industry along Guild lines.

The disappointments of the postwar world situation have been felt severely by Socialists, partly because they expected to be able to find a basis of co-operation with the Soviet regime, and partly because they hoped for a wider success of their own democratic Socialist creed in other countries. The troubles of the last few years have shown that international friction cannot be regarded as primarily due to the economic rivalries of capitalist states. The most that the Socialist can now say is that only the existence of an international authority with overriding powers of government can prevent the danger of war, and that even then the existing serious economic inequalities among different peoples must be eliminated before the world can hope for lasting peace. In the absence of such a world state, even the old colonial relationship must be maintained in some form in the case of peoples not yet capable of self-government: and the Labour Government of 1945 did what it could, with the assistance of the valuable preparatory work of the Fabian Colonial Bureau, to devise a policy to bring the dependent territories to a position where they could reasonably claim the self-government which was readily ceded to India, Pakistan, Burma and Ceylon.

The present is a time for stocktaking on the part of Socialists. The differences of opinion inside the Labour movement, while not always differences of principle, are yet symptomatic of the need for re-adjustment to the fresh problems created by recent successes and failures. Many illusions have had to be cast aside as the movement has developed; many more are on their way out at the moment. Owen believed that men's motives are entirely shaped by environment: this view, though valuable in part, has long since been abandoned as a comprehensive explanation. Marx expected the development of capitalism to lead to the increasing misery of the working class: yet although many of the factors that he analysed continue to have the tendency that he observed, it cannot be maintained that his general prophecy has been justified. Hobson and Lenin saw in expanding capitalism the primary cause of war: this is now seen to be an explanation of only some of the conflicts of this century. Like Newtonian physics, the old postulates have had their value in the past, but can no longer be considered to be adequate in their original form.

How is the Socialist going to reformulate his theories? And—if he can solve the problem of Britain's external relations and international trading position—what is his future programme of reform to be? The answers to these questions remain still hidden in the future. But at least it is noteworthy that the attempt to reformulate is in fact taking place; that groups of Socialists such as the Fabian Society and the Socialist Union are busy trying to find a fresh basis for their beliefs; that the great bulk of the British Socialist movement is not hindered, like the German Social-Democrats early in the century, by the need to conform to beliefs which they have in practice abandoned. If we refer back to the definition of Socialism by Professor Tawney with which this essay began, we can see that there is still a long way for the Socialist to go to the realisation of his ideal. In many ways, indeed, he may seem further away from it than ever. Yet even if, in the face of twentieth century facts, he loses his belief in continual universal progress—the old

Liberal illusion of the eighteenth century—he will still continue, with Charles Kingsley, to be "discontented with the divine discontent, and ashamed with the noble shame". He will not accept, as the conservative may, that "men sail a boundless and a bottomless sea" with "neither starting-place nor appointed destination" (Oakeshott). Whatever the setbacks of storm and tempest, he will still be setting his course in a definite direction; for otherwise, to his mind, it would not be worth while having a ship of state at all.

It remains to say a word about the method in which the collection of documents in this volume has been compiled. In Part I, "The Repeated Challenge", I have isolated the various Socialist or socialistic groups of the nineteenth century, and of the first quarter of the twentieth century, and endeavoured to illustrate their various distinctive features. I have not hesitated to include thinkers who were not definitely Socialist, where I felt that they had made a real contribution to Socialist thought. I have also taken a broad view of the term "British", so as to include the more important foreigners who, while living in this country, have exerted a direct influence on the native movement.

In Part II, "Aspects of the Tradition", I have attempted a different task—to analyse the more continuous development of Socialist thinking in the present century. This part of the book overlaps chronologically with the previous one. It deals with Socialism as an accepted element in British political life—as a movement not of sects but (at least in part) of a parliamentary party moving towards the responsibility of government. I have tried to illustrate the major controversies of this period, as well as the present general attitude of British Socialism. I have reluctantly been forced to omit or to deal very cursorily with many important issues, such as, for instance, the Socialist view of Local Government. If, in the same process of restriction, I have ignored the opinions of various small Socialist minorities of the present day or the recent past, I can only plead that this is inevitable in a volume of this size.

Finally, as an epilogue I have quoted a passage from a work by the Socialist propagandist Bruce Glasier, who is little remembered now outside the ranks of the older members of the movement, to show how Socialism, as a human faith, has given its followers not only an ideal to dream of but also a stimulus to sustained social activity. The impact of Socialism in Britain has been enormously increased by the enthusiasm and energy of its supporters. For many of them, the Socialist movement in itself has provided a measure of the principle of association which they seek to extend to the wider community. Even to-day, when Socialism has become almost a "respectable" creed in this country, this is a factor which, in our search for the elements of the British political tradition, we would do well not to ignore.

The Queen's College, Oxford 1953

PART I

THE REPEATED CHALLENGE

I

CRITICS OF PROPERTY

The writers quoted in this section were not strictly Socialists, but their criticism of property was the starting-point from which the constructive ideas of Socialism developed. Thomas Spence was a school-teacher in 1775 when he read to the Newcastle Philosophical Society the lecture that was later published under the title of *The Whole Rights of Man* (a). This lecture, which advocated the re-organisation of the land under the ownership of parochial communes, was republished in 1882 by H. M. Hyndman, the leader of the Socialist revival of that time, under the somewhat misleading title *The Nationalisation of the Land.*

William Godwin, now regarded as the father of Anarchism, published his *Enquiry concerning Political Justice* (b) in 1793, when the alarm and fear aroused in this country by the excesses of the French Revolution were at their height. The high cost of the book, which was lavishly produced, and the apparently unpractical character of the speculations it contained, no doubt explain why it was able to escape suppression by the government. Tom Paine, a much more popular Radical author best known for his *Rights of Man,* dealt with the problems of landownership in his *Agrarian Justice* (c), but as will be seen from the concluding paragraph of the extract here quoted, his reform programme is much more moderate than that of Spence.

Charles Hall was a physician, but little else than this is known of him. Although his reform proposals do not amount to much, his analysis of social evils is penetrating, and in one remarkable passage he anticipates the surplus value theory of Karl Marx. The quotations given below are from this passage (d) and from his discussion of the causes of war, which foreshadows another important Socialist criticism of capitalist society (e).

The final extract in this section is taken from Thomas Evans, librarian of the Society of Spenceans. Evans follows Spence's proposals for agrarian communes, and appeals to " true Christianity " in support of his arguments (f).

(a) THOMAS SPENCE. *The Whole Rights of Man*

1775

THAT property in land and liberty among men in a state of nature ought to be equal, few, one would be fain to hope, would be foolish enough to deny. Therefore, taking this to be granted, the country of any people, in a native state, is properly their common, in which each of them has an equal property, with free liberty to sustain himself and family with the animals, fruits and other products thereof. Thus such a people reap jointly the whole advantages of their country, or neighbourhood, without having their right in so doing called in question by any, not even by the most selfish and corrupt. For upon what must they live if not upon the productions of the country in which they reside? Surely, to deny them that right is in effect denying them a right to live. Well, methinks some are now ready to say, but is it lawful, reasonable and just, for this people to sell, or make a present even, of the whole of their country, or common, to whom they will, to be held by them and their heirs for ever?

To this I answer, If their posterity require no grosser materials to live and move upon than air, it would certainly be very ill-natured to dispute their right of parting with what of their own, their posterity would never have occasion for; but if their posterity cannot live but as grossly as they do, the same gross materials must be left them to live upon. For a right to deprive anything of the means of living, supposes a right to deprive it of life; and this right ancestors are not supposed to have over their posterity.

Hence it is plain that the land or earth, in any country or neighbourhood, with everything in or on the same, or pertaining thereto, belongs at all times to the living inhabitants of the said country or neighbourhood in an equal manner. For, as I said before, there is no living but on land and its productions, consequently, what we cannot live without we have the same property in as in our lives. (*pp.* 5*f.*)

(b) WILLIAM GODWIN. *Political Justice*

1793

WHAT is the criterion that must determine whether this or that substance, capable of contributing to the benefit of a human being, ought to be considered as your property or mine? To this question there can be but one answer—Justice. Let us then recur to the principles of justice.

To whom does any article of property, suppose a loaf of bread, justly belong? To him who most wants it, or to whom the possession of it will be most beneficial. Here are six men famished with hunger, and the loaf is, absolutely considered, capable of satisfying the cravings of them all. Who is it that has a reasonable claim to benefit by the qualities with which this loaf is endowed? They are all brothers perhaps, and the law of primogeniture bestows it exclusively on the eldest. But does justice confirm this award? The laws of different countries dispose of property in a thousand different ways; but there can be but one way which is most conformable to reason.

It would have been easy to put a case much stronger than that which has just been stated. I have an hundred loaves in my possession, and in the next street there is a poor man expiring with hunger, to whom one of these loaves would be the means of preserving his life. If I withhold this loaf from him, am I not unjust? If I impart it, am I not complying with what justice demands? To whom does the loaf justly belong?

I suppose myself in other respects to be in easy circumstances, and that I do not want this bread as an object of barter or sale, to procure me any of the other necessaries of a human being. Our animal wants have long since been defined, and are stated to consist of food, clothing and shelter. If justice have any meaning, nothing can be more iniquitous, than for one man to possess superfluities, while there is a human being in existence that is not adequately supplied with these.

Justice does not stop here. Every man is entitled, so far as the general stock will suffice, not only to the means of being, but of well being. It is unjust, if one man labour to the destruction of his health or his life, that another man may abound in luxuries. It is unjust, if one man be deprived of leisure to cultivate his rational powers, while another man contributes not a single effort to add to the common stock. The faculties of one man are like the faculties of another man. Justice directs that each man, unless perhaps he be employed more beneficially to the public, should contribute to the cultivation of the common harvest, of which each man consumes a share. This reciprocity indeed, as was observed when that subject was the matter of separate consideration, if of the very essence of justice. How the latter branch of it, the necessary labour, is to be secured, while each man is admitted to claim his share of the produce, we shall presently have occasion to enquire. . . .

But it has been alledged, "that we find among different men very different degrees of labour and industry, and that it is not just they shall receive an equal reward." It cannot indeed be denied that the attainments of men in virtue and usefulness ought by no means to be confounded. How far the present system of property contributes to their being equitably treated it is very easy to determine. The present system of property confers on one man immense wealth in consideration of the accident of his birth. He that from beggary ascends to opulence is usually known not to have effected this transition by methods very creditable to his honesty or his usefulness. The most industrious and active member of society is frequently with great difficulty able to keep his family from starving.

But, to pass over these iniquitous effects of the unequal distribution of property, let us consider the nature of the reward which is thus proposed to industry. If you be industrious, you shall have an hundred times more food than you can eat and an hundred times more clothes than you can wear. Where is the justice of this? If I be the greatest benefactor the human species ever knew, is that a reason for bestowing on me what I do not want, especially when there are thousands to whom my superfluity would be of the greatest advantage? With this superfluity I can purchase nothing but gaudy ostentation and envy, nothing but the pitiful pleasure of returning to the poor under the name of generosity that to which reason gives them an irresistible claim, nothing but prejudice, error and vice.

The doctrine of the injustice of accumulated property has been the foundation of all religious morality. The object of this morality has been, to excite men by individual virtue to repair this injustice. The most energetic teachers of religion have been irresistibly led to assert the precise truth upon this interesting subject. They have taught the rich, that they hold their wealth only as a trust, that they are strictly accountable for every atom of their expenditure, that they are merely administrators, and by no means proprietors in chief. The defect of this system, is, that they rather excite us to palliate our injustice than to forsake it. (*pp.* 789–91; 794*f.*)

(c) TOM PAINE. *Agrarian Justice*

1797

THERE could be no such things as landed property originally. Man did not make the earth, and, though he had a natural right to *occupy* it, he had no right to *locate as his property* in perpetuity any part of it; neither did the Creator of the earth open a land-office, from whence the first title-deeds should issue. From whence then arose the idea of landed property? I answer as before, that when cultivation began, the idea of landed property began with it, from the impossibility of separating the improvement made by cultivation from the earth itself upon which that improvement was made. The value of the improvement so far exceeded the value of the natural earth, at that time, as to absorb it; till, in the end, the common right of all became confounded into the cultivated right of the individual. But they are nevertheless distinct species of rights, and will continue to be so as long as the earth endures.

It is only by tracing things to their origin, that we can gain rightful ideas of them; and it is by gaining such ideas that we discover the boundary that divides right from wrong, and which teaches every man to know his own. I have entitled this tract *Agrarian Justice,* to distinguish it from *Agrarian Law.* Nothing could be more unjust than Agrarian Law in a country improved by cultivation; for though every man, as an inhabitant of the earth, is a joint proprietor of it in its natural state, it does not follow that he is a joint proprietor of cultivated earth. The additional value made by cultivation, after the system was admitted, became the property of those who did it, or who inherited it from them, or who purchased it. It had originally an owner. Whilst, therefore, I advocate the right, and interest myself in the hard case of all those who have been thrown out of their natural inheritance by the introduction of the system of landed property, I equally defend the right of the possessor to the part which is his.

Cultivation is, at least, one of the greatest natural improvements ever made by human invention. It has given to created earth a tenfold value. But the landed monopoly that began with it, has produced the greatest evil. It has dispossessed more than half the inhabitants of every nation of their natural inheritance, without providing for them, as ought to have been done, as an indemnification for that loss; and has thereby created a species of poverty and wretchedness that did not exist before.

In advocating the case of the persons thus dispossessed, it is right and not a charity that I am pleading for. But it is that kind of right which, being neglected at first, could not be brought forward afterwards, till heaven had opened the way by a revolution in the system of government. Let us then do honour to revolutions by justice, and give currency to their principles by blessings.

Having thus, in a few words, opened the merits of the case, I proceed to the plan I have to propose, which is,

To create a National Fund, out of which there shall be paid to every person, when arrived at the age of twenty-one years the sum of Fifteen Pounds sterling, *as a compensation in part for the loss of his or her natural inheritance by the introduction of the system of landed property; and also the sum of* Ten Pounds per annum *during life, to every person now living of the age of fifty years, and to all others as they shall arrive at that age.* (*pp.* 6*f.*)

(d) CHARLES HALL. *The Effects of Civilization on the People in European States*

1805

It might be said, that if the workman receives the wages for his work, that he receives the fruit of his labour: but it is to be considered, that the wages of the labourer are not the fruit or produce of his labour, that is, the things his labour actually makes; but the price the master has agreed to give, and what the workman, in most instances, is compelled to take for or in lieu of the whole produce of his labour: this is sometimes rendered evident, as when the labourer has his wages, as it were, in kind, by receiving a part of the wheat or the potatoes, etc. which his labour has raised: the small part he receives of the whole is then seen.

It may, notwithstanding, seem difficult to be understood, how it happens, that the poor man receives so small a part of the fruits of his own labour, as the one-eighth or one-ninth, since we know of no master tradesman or manufacturer who has so large a profit on any article made by the poor man.

But it is to be remembered, that there are many more people than one, who take a profit on almost every single thing that is turned out by the workman or workmen; for instance, in a coach, there is, first, the master coach-maker, then the master painter, the master colourman; there is the tanner, the currier, the glass plate maker, the draper, the timber merchants, the master smith, the master harness maker, the silver and plate-furniture maker. . . .

If the poor did receive and make use of a greater proportion of the produce of their labour, than is stated to be received by them; how could the rich enjoy and consume so many things, as it is evident they do; and who, it is equally evident, contribute nothing to the production of them. (*pp.* 121–3.)

(e) CHARLES HALL. *Ibidem*

1805

The rich of most of the different civilized nations of Europe, all coveting the same things, the countries producing those things are the continual objects of contests and wars between these different powers. These wars are easily excited by the rich, who are either themselves the persons with whom lies the power of making war and peace; or are the persons who have great influence with those who have that power.

These are the chief motives on which foreign and other conquests are attempted, and of course of most of the wars of modern times. If property was equally divided, and there were no rich, the inhabitants of a parish would seldom be led out of their parish for any thing wanted; every place would produce everything that there was a real occasion for.

The objects of all wars, whether near or distant, are to increase trade, or to extend territory; or the wars are occasioned by the ambition or irritability of the rich. As to the first cause: although the wars, entered into on this account, are often said to be undertaken for the benefit of the people, they have really no other effect than the obtaining of the insignificant things above mentioned. As to the second object: this is desired only by the aggressors, in order to place a greater number of people, the inhabitants of their intended new acquisitions, under their subjection; whose labour they may employ to the same purposes as they do that of the poor of their own country. (*pp.* 171*f.*)

(f) THOMAS EVANS. *Christian Policy, The Salvation of the Empire*

1816

For the stagnant industry, and to prevent the ruin of the country by giving an opportunity for the exercise of its full powers, in the adoption of true and genuine Christian policy; to elevate it to that superior situation its superior organization, intelligence, native industry, and unbounded talent, so pre-eminently entitle it to hold in the rank of nations.

To effect which I propose, that all feudality be abolished, and the territory of these realms be declared to be the people's farm; that there be no other tenure, but leasehold; that the mortgage or national debt shall cease; that there be no more taxation; that no alteration be made in the established forms of government; that a written constitution be drawn up and established, defining the forms and powers of government, the rights of the people, the security of their persons and properties, that may be referred to on all occasions; and that all the relative classes of society continue undisturbed. Great as this undertaking may appear, it can be easily effected without detriment to so much as one individual, and will establish for ever the fame and glory of the government; the liberty of the world through its means; the permanent strength, wealth, security, and happiness of all classes of the people of these realms.

The means to accomplish this, is by transferring all the land, waters, mines, houses, and all feudal permanent property to the people to be held in parochial (or other small) partnerships, which (in my view of the subject) may be administered as follows. Each parish to be the proprietor of this property, or part of the general national estate, within its boundary, as a body corporate. . . .

This policy, once established in any nation as state policy, would destroy war, and soon make all mankind, brothers and Christians. The pagan authorities of the world were so sensible of this, that they used all manner of means, to destroy and exterminate these worshippers of justice; these Christian votaries of Astraea. Wherever they have appeared, they have been chased and hunted down with fire and sword; no where would they be tolerated unless they consented to relinquish their opinions, and became the servants, the corrupted tools of power; and in this situation we find them at this day. Christianity does not consist in forms, or ceremonies, or fastings, or prayers, or psalm-singing, or preaching, but in justice. Men in our own day have been persuaded such public exhibitions are pleasing to God; and so were the pagans; but what do the Greeks tell you was the instruction of Joshua, the son of Joseph and Mary: "Do not exhibit yourselves like the Pharisees, praying ostentatiously in public, but withdraw into your closet, and having shut the door, say 'our Father, etc.'" And let the reader turn to the nineteenth chapter of Matthew, and the tenth of Mark; and then, judge if mine be Christian policy or not. The young rich man that had large possessions could not become a follower, no, *equality did not suit,* it would not do to serve God at that rate. *"But it is easier for a camel to go through the eye of a needle, than for a rich man to enter the kingdom of heaven."* And why; he is a robber, he is a monopolizer of the earth, he dispossesses his brothers, he seizes on the gift of the common Father, he declares war and defiance to the advocates of justice. O! what an admirable fable is this! Look at and consider it reader, not spiritually, but naturally, rationally. (*pp.* 25–7)

2

THE CO-OPERATIVE IDEAL

To Robert Owen, the cotton manufacturer, we can clearly attach the name of Socialist. His successful experiment in establishing a model village at New Lanark led him to the view that character was entirely formed by environment, and that all ills were due to the existing economic system (a). Proceeding from Ricardo's statement in his *Principles of Political Economy* that " the value of a commodity depends upon the relative quantity of labour which is necessary for its production ", Owen suggested that the value of goods should be measured by the amount of manual labour put into producing them : this should be the basis of exchange (b). He advocated the establishment of co-operative colonies in which this basis of exchange should prevail (*c*), and proceeded to found one at New Harmony in Indiana. This, however, proved to be a failure, as did that at Orbiston in Lanarkshire financed by his disciple the Edinburgh businessman Abram Combe (d).

In spite of these failures, many co-operative societies were founded in the late eighteen-twenties and early eighteen-thirties, and Owen went on to establish a National Equitable Labour Exchange at which the products of co-operative societies could be exchanged at labour value (for which see 4b, below).

(a) ROBERT OWEN. *A New View of Society*

1813

HITHERTO, indeed, in all ages and in all countries, man seems to have blindly conspired against the happiness of man, and to have remained as ignorant of himself as he was of the solar system prior to the days of Copernicus and Galileo.

Many of the learned and wise among our ancestors were conscious of this ignorance, and deeply lamented its effects; and some of them recommended the partial adoption of those principles which can alone relieve the world from the miserable effects of ignorance.

The time, however, for the emancipation of the human mind was not then arrived: the world was not prepared to receive it. The history of humanity shows it to be an undeviating law of the Great Ruler of the Universe, that man shall not prematurely break the shell of ignorance; that he must patiently wait until the principle of knowledge has pervaded the whole mass of the interior, to give it life and strength sufficient to bear the light of day.

Those who have duly reflected on the nature and extent of the mental movements of the world for the last half-century, must be conscious that great changes are in progress; that Providence in its wisdom is about to permit man to advance another important step towards that degree of intelligence which he may ultimately desire him to acquire. Observe the transactions of the passing hours; see the whole mass of mind in full motion; behold it momentarily increasing in vigour, and preparing ere long to burst its confinement. But what is to be the nature of this change? A due attention to the facts around us, and to those transmitted by the invention of printing from former ages, will afford a satisfactory reply.

From the earliest ages to this day, it has been the practice of the world to act on the supposition that each individual man forms his own character, and that therefore he is accountable for all his sentiments and habits, and consequently merits reward for some and punishment for others. Every system which has been established among men has been founded on these erroneous principles. When, however, they shall be brought to the test of fair examination, they will be found not only unsupported by any ascertained fact, but in direct opposition to all experience, and to the evidence of our senses. This is not a slight mistake, which involves only trivial consequences; it is a fundamental error of the highest possible magnitude; it enters into all our proceedings regarding man from his infancy; and it will be found to be the true and sole origin of evil. It generates and perpetuates ignorance, hatred, and revenge, where, without such error, only intelligence, confidence, and kindness would exist. It has hitherto been the Evil Genius of the world. It severs man from man throughout the various regions of the earth; and makes enemies of those who, but for this gross error, would have enjoyed each other's kind offices and sincere friendship. It is, in short, an error which carries misery in all its consequences.

This error cannot much longer exist; for every day will make it more and more evident that *the character of man is, without a single exception, always formed for him; that it may be, and is chiefly, created by his predecessors; that they give him, or may give him, his ideas and habits, which are the powers that govern and direct his conduct. Man, therefore, never did, nor is it possible he ever can, form his own individual character.*

The knowledge of this important fact has not been derived from any of the wild and heated speculations of an ardent and ungoverned imagination; on the contrary, it proceeds from a long and patient study of the theory and practice of human nature, under many varied circumstances, it will be found to be a deduction drawn from such a multiplicity of facts, as to afford the most complete demonstration.

Had not mankind been misinstructed from infancy on this subject, making it necessary that they should unlearn what they have been taught, the simple statement now given would render this truth instantly obvious to every rational mind. Men would know that their predecessors might have given them the habits of ferocious cannibalism, or of the highest known benevolence and intelligence; and by the acquirement of this knowledge they will soon learn that, as parents, preceptors, and legislators united, they possess the means of training the rising generation to either of those extremes; that they may with the greatest certainty make them the conscientious worshippers of Juggernaut, or of the most pure spirit possessing the essence of every excellence which the human imagination can conceive; that they may train the young to become effeminate, deceitful, ignorantly selfish, intemperate, revengeful, murderous,—of course ignorant, irrational, and miserable; or to be manly, just, generous, temperate, active, kind, and benevolent,—that is, intelligent, rational, and happy. The knowledge of these principles having been derived from facts which perpetually exist, they defy ingenuity itself to convict them of error; nay, the most severe scrutiny will make it evident that they are utterly unassailable and secure from attack.

Is it then wisdom to think and to act in opposition to the facts which hourly exhibit themselves around us, and in direct contradiction to the evidence of our senses? Inquire of the most learned and wise of the present day, ask them to speak with sincerity, and they will tell you that they have long known these principles to be true. Hitherto, however, the tide of public opinion, in all countries, has been directed by a combination of prejudice, bigotry, and fanaticism, derived from the wildest imaginations of ignorance; and the most enlightened men have not dared to expose those errors which to them were offensive, prominent, and glaring.

Happily for man this reign of ignorance rapidly approaches to dissolution, its terrors are already on the wing, and soon they will be compelled to take their flight, never more to return. For now the knowledge of the existing errors is not only possessed by the learned and reflecting, but it is spreading far and wide throughout society; and ere long it will be fully comprehended even by the most ignorant.

Attempts may indeed be made by individuals, who through ignorance mistake their real interests, to retard the progress of this knowledge; but as it will prove itself to be in unison with the evidence of our senses, and therefore true beyond the possibility of disproof, it cannot be impeded, and in its course will overwhelm all opposition.

These principles, however, are not more true in theory than they prove beneficial whenever they are properly applied to practice. Why, therefore, should all their substantial advantages be longer withheld from the mass of mankind? Can it, by possibility, be a crime to pursue the only practical means which a rational being can adopt to diminish the misery of man, and increase his happiness?

This question, of the deepest interest to society, is now brought to the fair test of public experiment. It remains to be proved, whether the character of man shall continue to be formed under the guidance of the most inconsistent principles, the errors of which for centuries past have been most manifest to every reflecting rational mind; or whether it shall be moulded under the direction of uniformly consistent principles, derived from the unvarying facts of the creation of principles, the truth of which no sane man will now attempt to deny.

It is then by the full and complete disclosure of these principles, that Providence now evidently designs to effect the destruction of ignorance and misery, and firmly to establish the reign of reason, intelligence, and happiness. (*Essay Third, pp.* 14–21)

(b) ROBERT OWEN. *Report to the County of Lanark*

1821

The great object of society is, to obtain wealth, and to enjoy it.

The genuine principle of barter was, to exchange the supposed prime cost of, or value of labour in, one article, against the prime cost of, or amount of labour contained in any other article. This is the only equitable principle of exchange; but, as inventions increased and human desires multiplied, it was found to be inconvenient in practice. Barter was succeeded by commerce, the principle of which is, to produce or procure every article at the lowest, and to obtain for it, in exchange, the highest amount of labour. To effect this, an artificial standard of value was necessary; and metals were, by common consent among nations, permitted to perform the office.

This principle, in the progress of its operation, has been productive of important advantages, and of very great evils; but, like barter, it has been suited to a certain stage of society. It has stimulated invention; it has given industry and talent to the human character; and has secured the future exertion of those energies which otherwise might have remained dormant and unknown.

But it has made man ignorantly, individually selfish; placed him in opposition to his fellows; engendered fraud and deceit; blindly urged him forward to create, but deprived him of the wisdom to enjoy. In striving to take advantage of others he has over-reached himself. The strong hand of necessity will now force him into the path which conducts to that wisdom in which he has been so long deficient. He will discover the advantages to be derived from uniting in practice the best parts of the principles of barter and commerce, and dismissing those which experience has proved to be inconvenient and injurious.

This substantial improvement in the progress of society may be easily effected by exchanging all articles with each other at their prime cost, or with reference to the amount of labour in each, which can be equitably ascertained, and by permitting the exchange to be made through a convenient medium to represent this value, and which will thus represent a real and unchanging value, and be issued only as substantial wealth increases. The profit of production will arise, in all cases, from the value of the labour contained in the article produced, and it will be for the interest of society that this profit should be most ample. Its exact amount will depend upon what, by strict examination, shall be proved to be the present real value of a day's labour; calculated with reference to the amount of wealth, in the necessaries and comforts of life, which an average labourer may, by temperate exertions, be now made to produce.

It would require an accurate and extended consideration of the existing state of society to determine the exact value of the unit or day's labour which society ought now to fix as a standard of value: but a more slight and general view of the subject is sufficient to show, that this unit need not represent a less value than the wealth contained in the necessaries and comforts of life which may now be purchased with five shillings.

The landholder and capitalist would be benefited by this arrangement in the same degree with the labourer because labour is the foundation of all values, and it is only from labour, liberally remunerated, that high profits can be paid for agricultural and manufactured products.

Depressed as the value of labour now is, there is no proposition in Euclid more true, than that society would be immediately benefited, in a great variety of ways, to an incalculable extent, by making labour the standard of value. By this expedient all the markets in the world, which are now virtually closed against offering a profit to the producers of wealth, would be opened to an unlimited extent; and in each individual exchange all the parties interested would be sure to receive ample remuneration for their labour. (*pp.* 20–2)

(c) ROBERT OWEN. Letter to *The Economist*

1 September 1821

The proposed change may be made by means of competing for a short time with the existing commercial system, indeed no other mode of relieving society from its present difficulties appears practicable, and by these means the change becomes not only natural, but irresistible.

To accomplish the change in this manner it is necessary to create labour of a superior quality, and cheaper than can be now brought to market; for all cost resolves itself into labour, and it is evident that those arrangements which can produce the most skilful labour at the least expence, and at the same time support the labourer in the best health and most comfort, will, upon common commercial principles, put all other methods out of the market.

The inferior methods will be superseded by the superior, as human labour has been replaced by the steam engine,—as the single-thread spinning-wheel has been by Arkwright's superior mechanism,—and as the common hand printing-press is now being replaced by the new power printing machinery.

From these, and a thousand other instances, which might be easily adduced, of the extensive and rapid application of the sciences, (however ill directed,) to manufactures, commerce, agriculture, and the common purposes of life, a necessity has arisen for other corresponding changes among the working classes, in order to permit society *to benefit* by the scientific improvements which have been so extensively, but (from the want of proper arrangements in society) hitherto injuriously introduced. The changes proposed for this purpose consist of new arrangements derived from science.

1st. TO ERECT, HEAT AND VENTILATE LODGING APARTMENTS for the working classes, *better and cheaper* than can be effected by any of the plans now in practice.

2nd. TO FEED them *better and cheaper.*

3rd. TO CLOTHE them *better and cheaper.*

4th. TO TRAIN AND EDUCATE THEM *better and cheaper.*

5th. *To secure to them* BETTER HEALTH *than they* now enjoy.

6th. TO APPLY THEIR LABOUR *to Agriculture, Manufactures, and all the purposes of society,* WITH SCIENCE BETTER DIRECTED *than heretofore.*

And lastly, *To make them* IN ALL RESPECTS *better members of society.*

Every one must acknowledge that these will be important improvements, if they can be obtained.

It is now to be shown that they are easily attainable, and that all the means necessary to give them permanence now superabound.

The most difficult problem to solve was, "to ascertain what number of persons could be associated together so as to give to each the most advantage with the least inconvenience." . . .

The arrangements best adapted for the improvement and happiness of the working classes, and which must at the same time render their labour superior to, and cheaper, than that of all other labourers are as follows:—

From about 500 to 1,500 individuals, or (supposing four to a family) about 300 families, are to reside in habitations in the country, on which much foresight and science have been exercised in devising their erection and combination, and in which an attempt has been made to unite, in these buildings, every domestic advantage and comfort of which the dwellings of the working classes are now susceptible.

They comprise spacious sitting and bed-rooms, extensive public kitchen and eating-rooms, schools for different ages, church, places of worship for Dissenters, infirmary, library, lecture-room and inn for the accommodation of the friends and visitors of the inhabitants.

These buildings are to enclose an extensive play-ground for the younger children; space for gymnastic exercises for the elder children, and of recreation for adults.

They are to be surrounded by gardens, which are to be chiefly cultivated by females and elder children, and to be placed in the midst of about 600 acres of land; the arable part of which will be principally cultivated by the spade.

(d) ABRAM COMBE. *Metaphorical Sketches of the Old and New Systems*

1823

Of course, we often see "*triumphant refutations*" given, of opinions, which have no existence out of the brain of the person who refutes them.—Exactly of this nature was the assertion which the Reverend Andrew Wilson is reported to have made, in his introductory lecture to the Edinburgh School of Arts, when he contended, "that the Dreams of Equality, which some had indulged in, could never be reduced to practice." Now, I have never heard of any Individuals, or class of Individuals, who entertained the notion, that it was possible to make even two Individuals equal.—To do so is physically impossible. A great portion of the happiness which one Individual enjoys above another, is derived from superior habits and attainments. Though these will always command respect or esteem; yet this respect or esteem, and the pleasure it gives, are both beyond the controul of the Individuals. The one has no power to increase or diminish this feeling of respect; and the other has as little over the feeling of pleasure, which he derives from it.

To entertain the notion of putting all men on a footing of equality in these respects would, indeed, be a dream. It would be an idea which no rational being could entertain for a moment; and I am not aware of any Individual having ever promulgated such a notion. Yet, to secure general Esteem or Respect, seems to be the summit of Human ambition.

If it is practicable, by proper arrangements, to create a superabundance of all that is either requisite or desirable for supplying the wants of human nature, nothing will be easier than to place all men on a footing of equality in these respects. To give all an equal share of that, of which there is a superabundance, is very different from making all Individuals equal, or exactly alike. Air is a first requisite to human existence, and the wants of all are equally supplied in this respect; yet the mere circumstance of supplying equally our bodily wants, has no tendency to make us all alike.—Napoleon Bonaparte and Louis XVIII were on a footing of Equality, as far as the command of personal comfort was concerned; yet these outward circumstances had no effect over their natural formation or acquired habits.—So will it be while Nature remains the same.—Superior talents and good conduct will always command our esteem; and this esteem or respect is their natural reward. Ask the poet, the painter, or the actor, if the consciousness of giving pleasure to the public, is not their highest reward. The money that they receive, beyond what is necessary to supply their daily expenditure, is nothing to compare with it.

It is a law of our nature, that we *must respect* that which gives us pleasure, even while we know that the talents, or power which the Individual possesses for giving us this pleasure, is a gift, bestowed on him by Nature, or by circumstances over which he had no controul. We may share his pleasure with Individuals so gifted, or we may sympathize with and pity those who are more unfortunate; but it is the essence of irrationality to praise one, and to blame another, upon account of the mere possession, or want, of talents, which no one has the power of bestowing upon himself.

While Mankind continue to follow their imagination under the guidance of Ignorance and Inconsistency, there can be no equality even in their moral feeling. As soon as the general and immutable Law of Right and Wrong, shall be impressed upon their minds, in its natural simplicity,—and as soon as men shall be taught that every thing which promotes the general happiness of Mankind is Right, and that every thing which produces a preponderating share of misery is Wrong,—then there will be as much unison in their moral feelings, as there is in their natural feelings of happiness or misery. All the inequalities in man, *which Nature has made*, will always continue, and these inequalities will have no *great tendency* to injure the happiness of a single individual. All the present inequalities which Ignorance has made, in opposition to Nature, may be removed, without injuring the happiness of a single human being; because daily experience shews us, that those Individuals, whom we suppose to be thus highly favoured, are often more unhappy than the lowest in the throng.

When our children shall be taught that it is honourable

to promote the comfort of their species, even by performing the meanest offices of domestic drudgery, they will naturally be as anxious to seek approbation in this way, as they are now to do so, by means of fantastic dress, grand furniture, titles, rank, or the accumulation of money. The children of Ignorance will smile at this; but if their reasoning powers had not been destroyed, they would at once have perceived, that such a mode of Education, is a thousand times more rational, than any which is in practice in the World at present. It is, indeed, true, that if the "Arch Fiend himself" had devised a system of Education for promoting Vice, Misery, and Disappointment, he could not have pitched upon one, more suited to his purpose, than the one which is, now, general throughout the World. And the worst feature in this erroneous Education is, *that which promotes irrational and unnatural distinctions.* (*pp.* 156–60)

3

ANTI-CAPITALIST ECONOMICS

There were several able economic writers in the eighteen-twenties who developed on the Ricardian labour-value basis a detailed criticism of the capitalist system. One of the ablest was the anonymous author of a pamphlet addressed to the young Lord John Russell, who had himself ventured a few criticisms of orthodox political economy. As Marx and Engels both realized, its importance lies in its anticipation of the theory of Surplus Value—here found in a form much more precise than Charles Hall was capable of—and in its deduction therefrom of something closely akin to Marx's laws of Capitalist Accumulation and Increasing Misery (a). The author bases much of his argument on the statistics provided by Patrick Colquhoun, whose *Treatise on the Wealth, Power, and Resources of the British Empire* was published in 1814.

William Thompson, an Irish landlord, was a utilitarian and not a convinced Owenite when he wrote his *Inquiry into the Principles of the Distribution of Wealth.* His work, which for sustained argument and power of analysis is unsurpassed in the literature of the period, contains a discussion of one possible weakness of Owenism—the lack of incentive in an egalitarian society (b). A more optimistic author was John Gray, a commercial traveller. He shared the Owenite belief in the unlimited possibilities of wealth opened out by the Industrial Revolution, and looked forward to the early arrival of the Socialist millenium (c). Thomas Hodgskin, a former naval officer and a deeper thinker than Gray, lectured on political economy at the London Mechanics' Institute, which he helped to found. His *Labour Defended against the Claims of Capital* is full of vigorous polemic, but has little constructive to offer beyond a system of free and competing small producers (d). The last work quoted in this section was written rather later than the others: *Labour's Wrongs and Labour's Remedy,* by J. F. Bray, an American-born compositor of Leeds, synthesizes Owenism and the class-conscious politics of the eighteen-thirties (e). It proposes a sort of National Joint-Stock scheme as a transitional stage on the path to full Communism. Bray returned to the United States in 1842 and was an active member of the American Socialist Labour Party in the later years of his life.

(a) *The Source and Remedy of the National Difficulties, deduced from* Principles of Political Economy, *in a letter to Lord John Russell*

1821

It is admitted that the interest paid to the capitalists, whether in the nature of rents, interests of money, or profits of trade, is *paid out of the labour of others.* If then capital go on accumulating, as it would naturally do, the labour to be given for the use of capital must go on increasing, interest for capital continuing the same, till all the labour of all the labourers of the society is engrossed by the capitalist. This consequence is logically correct. There is, however, one objection, and only one objection to it, that it is a consequence *impossible to happen;* for whatever may be due to the capitalist, he can *only receive* the *surplus* labour of the labourer; for the labourer *must live;* he must satisfy the cravings of nature before he satisfies the cravings of the capitalist. But the reader will observe that the objection is only untrue in *this extreme case.* It is perfectly and entirely true, that if capital does not decrease in value as it increases in amount, the capitalists will exact from the labourers the produce of every hour's labour beyond what it is *possible* for the labourer to subsist on; and however horrid and disgusting it may seem, the capitalist may eventually speculate on the food that requires the least labour to produce it, and eventually may say to the labourer, " You shan't eat bread, because barley meal is cheaper; you shan't eat meat, because it is possible to subsist on beet root and potatoes." *And to this point have we come!* and *by this very process have we arrived at it!* . . . .

" It is a curious and interesting fact ", says Colquhoun, " that an acre of potatoes will produce four times the sustenance of an acre of corn "; and he strongly urges the legislature in consequence to encourage its cultivation.

Why, if the labourer can be brought to feed on potatoes instead of bread, it is indisputably true that more can be exacted from his labour; that is to say, if when he fed on bread he was obliged to retain for the maintenance of himself and his family the labour of Monday and Tuesday, he will, on potatoes, require only the half of Monday; and the remaining half of Monday and the whole of Tuesday are available for the service of the state or the capitalist. And this is an " interesting fact "? Great God! is it to be endured that a man, offering a huge volume in proof of the growing prosperity of the country, of its unbounded wealth and resources, is to offer such an insult to our better feelings, as to connect it with the distressing facts, " that butcher's meat has almost become inaccessible to the labouring classes ", and that it is a foolish luxury to leave them bread, because human nature may exist on potatoes? (*pp.* 23–6)

(b) WILLIAM THOMPSON. *An Inquiry into the Principles of the Distribution of Wealth*

1824

Were food and all other objects of wealth supplied to man, like light, air, and in most places water, in such quantities as to be abundant for all, without the necessity of any human effort for their production; and were it proposed, *in order to make them produce more happiness,* to limit their consumption by the greater number of individuals of the community, that the remainder might have more than they could consume; who is there that would not exclaim against the absurdity of such a proposal? Or, were they only in such quantity, but still unconnected with human exertion, as to afford by a limited supply to all, enough for mere necessary use but not for superfluity; would not the person, in this case also, be deemed irrational who should propose to increase the sum total of the happiness of the community, by any inequality of distribution, taking from some what was merely necessary, in order to load others with satiety? The absurdity and the mischief in the latter case would be the greatest: for those who had at best but merely necessaries, would suffer more pain in being deprived of them to add to the superfluities of others, than those who previously possessed abundance. Suppose a third case, that a given supply, any how obtained, but without the intervention of human exertion, that would give but a treat to all, were every year, every month, or every day, acquired by a community; the enjoyment of any individual using at the same time 500, 1,000, or any other number of those portions, would scarcely, from the laws of our organization, double the enjoyment of any one of those from whom one of the single shares was taken or withheld. This, it is hoped, has been already made evident and will be further proved when we inquire into the effects of *excessive* inequality of wealth on the happiness of a community.

In all cases then, whether of a large or small supply, where human effort has not been concerned in the production, equality of distribution is the rule of justice. Let the reader pause, reflect, and speculate, and assign if he can any other justification amongst beings similarly constituted, capable of equal degrees of happiness, of a departure from the law of equality in distribution, than the necessity of human exertion for the production. There can be no other justification of a departure from equality of distribution. Its blessings are so transcendently great, so productive of immensely increased agreeable sensations, peace, and benevolence, that never but when justified by the necessity of continued production should they be departed from. To this superior *necessity,* and to this alone, must they yield; and to this necessity must they be strictly limited.

What is the circumstance which distinguishes the objects of wealth as means of enjoyment, from other means of enjoyment which come not under the name of wealth? The necessity of *labor* for their production. In nothing but in being the creatures of human labor, do they differ from other sources of enjoyment. Without labor they could not exist. Without security—which means the exclusive possession by every man of all the advantages of his labor—labor would not be called forth. Therefore in the distribution of such articles where labor is employed, called articles of wealth, and in these alone, equality must be limited by security, because in no other case are equality and production incompatible with each other. What is the reason of this? that equality is not, wherever attainable, to be desired? is it that equality itself is not founded in justice and productive of happiness? Far from it. But because its paramount blessings cannot be obtained, when applied to one particular class of objects of desire, those which are produced by labor, called objects of wealth, without destroying the source, the supply of such objects. Were it possible to ensure a reproduction by labor of the articles equally consumed, all the advantages of equality would be as fully derivable from the equal distribution of objects of wealth, as of any other objects of desire or materials of happiness whatever. A celebrated practical as well as philosophical inquirer, conceives that he has demonstrated *experimentally* that reproduction and equality are *not* incompatible even when applied to objects of wealth, produced, as they all are, by labor. He conceives that he has proved that other motives, besides *individual* necessity and the love of the factitious pleasures of superiority of wealth, can be found, and made to operate with sufficient energy, to ensure a constant reproduction of abundant wealth, for the equal use of the whole community. As *almost* all falsehood and violence, and as *all* stealing proceeds from inequality of distribution of wealth; *he* would certainly be no mean benefactor to his species, who could demonstrate the practicability of thoroughly eradicating, by removing the causes of, these the most numerous by far of human miseries and vices. The mischiefs arising from the mis-regulation of our appetites, passions, and desires, and from the want of knowledge and loss of the pleasures of intellectual culture, would be the only ones to which the attention of society would be then anxiously directed; and the whole attention being concentrated on these, the prospects of indefinite improvement would be captivating indeed. . . .

In the course of our argument in this inquiry, we have, however, all along reasoned on the supposition of labor by *individual competition,* and taken it for granted, in opposition to Mr. Owen, that the reproduction of wealth and security were incompatible with equality of wealth. By no scheme or combination affecting a whole community, have these discordant principles been ever yet in human practice reconciled. But to assert that they could not, as moral wisdom improved, be found reconcileable, would be as presumptuous reasoning from ignorance, in morals, as to assert, in physics (and not many years ago the writer heard the assertion made by an experienced naval officer, who now owns a steam-vessel and practises what he pronounced impracticable), that it would be impossible to apply steam navigation to the ocean or to strong river currents. No part of our argument is built even on the practicability of reconciling these two hitherto rival principles of security and equality; or rather of reproduction and equality; for although equality might leave every one secure in the possession of his equal share by taking away the motives of plunder, it would remain still, under such circumstances, to *supply motives to production.* This is the real difficulty; which Mr. Owen conceives he has solved. Conceding therefore so much on the one hand, we must strictly guard, on the other, against the abuses and false inferences that may be drawn from this concession. Wherever inequality is not called for by the clear necessity of security, not of that false security which is partially applied to soothe the imaginary alarms of the rich, protecting mere possession however acquired, while it overlooks violence applied to the very means of existence of the poor; but of that equal and just security which is alike to all; *equality* is to be pursued as the means of the greatest happiness derivable from distribution. Quite opposite to this has been the current philosophy, in order to uphold the enormous practices everywhere in operation, and outraging equally the principles of security and equality. There is scarcely a violation of the principle of security, for which the maintenance of that principle has not served as a pretext. The word, security, once laid hold or by the lovers of exclusive privileges and possessions, and but partially understood or wilfully misrepresented, has been reserved for the protection of the rich and powerful alone, to guard their possessions, however acquired, though at the expense not only of equality but of the security of the rest of the community, and has been by the rich used as a cover for every oppression, nay as a justification of the most atrocious cruelty, the worst species of vice. (*pp.* 144–7)

(c) JOHN GRAY. *A Lecture on Human Happiness*

1825

WE are for ever being told that we have already more produce than we want. Strange and foolish error! Let those who entertain such a thought understand their own words. They *say,* we have more produce than we *want.* They *mean,* we have more produce than there is a *demand for.* When every human being has everything his heart can wish, then, and not till then, we shall have as much produce as we want. But dreadful is the contrast to this in society as it now is. Go see your wretched fellow-creatures, of which there are thousands in this country, hungry, houseless and in rags, and enquire of them, whether THEY have a superabundance of wealth! Go to your manufacturing towns, and see the wretched producers of your wealth, ye who roll in luxurious profusion, ask of them, whether THEY have more than they have need of; and blush when ye tell us of superabundance! We have frequently more produce than we have a demand for—a great deal more: but demand is limited by competition: abolish IT, and demand shall be equal to production though it be increased a thousand fold!

It is competition then, and nothing but competition, which limits the annual income of the country. From this arises poverty, by which man is driven to acts of desperation for the commission of which, poverty, by introducing him into a world of wretchedness, and surrounding him from his infancy with vicious circumstances, has prepared his mind. And as competition necessarily arises from the division of the interests of men in the employment of capital, and in the distribution of the produce of labour, it is certain that nothing less than an *entire change* in the commercial arrangements of society can be productive of any essential benefit to mankind.

Now here we would, as it were, make a full stop, and appeal to the judgment of every rational being whether this be true. We would enquire alike of every class, of every sect, of every party, whether it be true, that competition in the employment of capital is the circumstance which limits production! Is it not true, that the enjoyments of life are produced by human labour? Is it not true, that there must ever be two natural limits to those enjoyments, viz: the exhaustion of our productive powers, and the satisfaction of our wants? Is it not true, that with these limits we have at present nothing to do? Have not the institutions of society raised up a third limit? and is not the name of it competition? And if this be true, was there ever a truth of so much importance to the commercial interests of society? Is not attainment of wealth the object of commerce? Is it not the great business of us all, or at least of most of us? Are we not panting after it with eager anxiety, and are not the chief energies, both of our bodies and of our minds devoted to the pursuit of it? Let us then abolish this third limit to production, and *everything that deserves the name of wealth shall instantly become accessible to all*: for we should then have as much wealth as we have the POWER OF CREATING!!! Measure it who can: it is impossible; for every week, every Mechanics' Magazine is pouring forth some new invention, which, under the NEW SYSTEM, would become an advantage equal to the labour it would save.

But can this limit be abolished? We answer, it can be done at any time, without the slightest difficulty, without the slightest violence, without the slightest real injury to a single individual.

The governors of this country could abolish it at home in a few years, and with it all the miseries of poverty. The governors of this country ought to do this, for human misery and blood, and crimes unnumbered are the cost of its continuance. They might as well effect this mighty change:

they might as well have, what they would term, the merit of setting an example to all the civilized world, which would be followed with an unexampled rapidity: for the governors of this country *cannot prevent it from being done.* They cannot, as rational men, have a wish to prevent it, but if they had, they might as well attempt to take the sun in one hand and the moon in the other: and if they do not do it, and that immediately too, individuals will.

The day is fast approaching when the sun of truth shall shed his rays amongst those countless thousands who endure their chains with patience now, because they know not whence they come, nor how they can be free; and because, as all exist in bondage, each in his brother sees a fellow slave, and cries, alas! " it is the lot of man ". But show them freedom; give them but a sight of human bliss, tell them it is within the reach of all, and prove it so; they will not longer live in slavery, nor bear their chains at all. That sun has not yet risen; but his rays are just appearing: twilight has appeared, and ere a term of twenty years shall pass, its mighty influence shall bring on man a greater change than man has yet beheld! (*pp.* 67–9)

(d) THOMAS HODGSKIN. *Labour Defended Against the Claims of Capital*

1825

A ROAD is made by a certain quantity of labour, and is then called fixed capital; the constant repairs it needs, however, are a continual making, and the expense incurred by them is called circulating capital. But neither the circulating nor the fixed capital return any profit to the road-makers unless there are persons to travel over the road or make a further use of their labour. The road facilitates the progress of the traveller, and just in proportion as people do travel over it, so does the labour which has been employed on the road become productive and useful. One easily comprehends why both these species of labour should be paid—why the road-makers should receive some of the benefits accruing only to the road-user; but I do not comprehend why all these benefits should go to the *road* itself and be appropriated by a set of persons who neither make nor use it, under the name of profit for their capital. One is almost tempted to believe that capital is a sort of cabalistic word, like Church or State, or any other of those general terms which are invented by those who fleece the rest of mankind to conceal the hand that shears them. It is a sort of idol before which men are called upon to prostrate themselves, while the cunning priest from behind the altar, profaning the God whom he pretends to serve, and mocking those sweet sentiments of devotion and gratitude, or those terrible emotions of fear and resentment, one or the other of which seems common to the whole human race, as they are enlightened and wise, or ignorant and debased, puts forth his hand to receive and appropriate the offerings which he calls for in the name of religion.

A steam-engine also is a most complete instrument, but alas! for the capitalist it does not go of itself. A peculiar skill is required to make it and put it up, and peculiar skill and labour must afterwards direct and regulate its movements. What would it produce without the engineer? To the stranger who did not possess the engineer's skill, only misery, death and destruction. Its vast utility does not depend on stored-up iron and wood, but on that practical and living knowledge of the powers of nature which enables some men to construct it, and others to guide it.

If we descend to more minute instruments, and consider such as are guided by the hand, the necessity of skill and labour, and the utter worthlessness of capital by itself, will be still more obvious. It has been asked, what would a carpenter effect without his hatchet and his saw? I put the converse of the question, and ask what the hatchet and the saw could effect without the carpenter? Rust and rottenness must be the answer. A plough or a scythe may be made with the most cunning art, but to use either of them a man must have an adroit turn of the hand, or a peculiar species of skill. The shoemaker who can thrust awls through leather with singular dexterity and neatness, cannot make any use of a watchmaker's tools; and the most skilful and dexterous maker of plane, saw, and chisel-blades, would find it difficult to construct with them any of that furniture which the cabinet-maker forms with so much dispatch and beautiful effect. Almost every species of workman, however, from having acquired a certain dexterity in the use of his hands, and from having frequently seen the operations of other workmen, would learn the art of another man much better than a person who had never practised any kind of manual dexterity, and never seen it practised. But if a skilled labourer could not direct any kind of instruments so well as the man who has been constantly accustomed to use them, it is plain that the whole productive power of such instruments must depend altogether on the peculiar skill of the artizan and mechanic, who has been trained to practise different arts.

Fixed capital, of whatever species, then, is only a costly production, costly to make, and costly to preserve, without that particular species of skill and labour which guides each instrument, and which, as I have before shown, is nourished, instructed, and maintained by wages alone. The utility of the instruments the labourer uses can in no wise be separated from his skill. Whoever may be the owner of fixed capital —and in the present state of society he who makes it, is not, and he who uses it, is not—it is the hand and knowledge of the labourer which make it, preserve it from decay, and which use it to any beneficial end. (*pp.* 16–18)

(e) J. F. BRAY. *Labour's Wrongs and Labour's Remedy*

1839

The subject of exchanges is one on which too much attention cannot be bestowed by the productive classes; for it is more by the infraction of this third condition by the capitalist, than by all other causes united, that inequality of condition is produced and maintained, and the working man offered up, bound hand and foot, a sacrifice upon the altar of Mammon.

From the very nature of labour and exchange, strict justice not only requires that all exchangers should be *mutually,* but that they should likewise be *equally,* benefited. Men have only two things which they can exchange with each other, namely, labour, and the produce of labour; therefore, let them exchange as they will, they merely give, as it were, labour for labour. If a just system of exchanges were acted upon, the value of all articles would be determined by the entire cost of production; *and equal values should always exchange for equal values.* If, for instance, it takes a hatter one day to make a hat, and the shoemaker the same time to make a pair of shoes—supposing the material used by each to be of the same value—and they exchange these articles with each other, they are not only mutually but equally benefited; the advantage derived by either party cannot be a disadvantage to the other, as each has given the same amount of labour, and the material made use of by each were of equal value. But if the hatter should obtain *two* pairs of shoes for *one* hat—time and value of material being as before—the exchange would clearly be an unjust one. The hatter would defraud the shoemaker of one day's labour; and were the former to act thus in all his exchanges, he would receive, for the labour of *half a year,* the product of some other person's *whole year;* therefore the gain of the first would necessarily be a loss to the last.

We have heretofore acted upon no other than this most unjust system of exchanges—the workmen have given the capitalist the labour of a whole year in exchange for the value of only half a year—and from this, and not from the assumed inequality of bodily and mental powers in individuals, has arisen the inequality of wealth and power which at present exists around us. It is an inevitable condition of inequality of exchanges—of buying at one price and selling at another—that capitalists shall continue to be capitalists and working men be working men—the one a class of tyrants and the other a class of slaves—to eternity. By equality of exchanges, however, no able-bodied individual can exist, as thousands now do, unless he fulfil that condition of the economist, "that there shall be labour"; nor can one class appropriate the produce of the labour of another class, as the capitalists now appropriate and enjoy the wealth which the powers of the working man daily call into existence. It is inequality of exchanges which enables one class to live in luxury and idleness, and dooms another to incessant toil.

By the present unjust and iniquitous system exchanges are not only *not* mutually beneficial to all parties, as the political economists have asserted, but it is plain, from the very nature of an exchange, that there is, in most transactions between the capitalist and the producer, *after the first remove,* no *exchange* whatever. An exchange implies the giving of one thing for another. But what is it that the capitalist, whether he be manufacturer or landed proprietor, gives in exchange for the labour of the working man? The capitalist gives no labour, for he does not work—he gives no capital, for his store of wealth is being perpetually augmented. It is certain that the capitalist can have only his labour or his capital to exchange against the labour of the working man; and if, as we daily see, the capitalist gives no labour, and his original stock of capital does not decrease, he cannot in the nature of things make an exchange with anything that belongs to himself. The whole transaction, therefore, plainly shews that the the capitalists and proprietors do no more than give the working man, for his labour of one week, a part of the wealth which they obtained from him the week before!—which just amounts to giving him *nothing* for *something*—and is a method of doing business which, however consonant with the established usages of the present system, is by no means compatible with a working man's ideas of justice. The wealth which the capitalist appears to give in exchange for the workman's labour was generated neither by the labour nor the riches of the capitalist, but it was originally obtained by the labour of the workman; and it is still daily taken from him, by a fraudulent system of unequal exchanges. The whole transaction, therefore, between the producer and the capitalist is a palpable deception, a mere farce: it is, in fact, in thousands of instances no other than a barefaced though legalised robbery, by means of which the capitalists and proprietors contrive to fasten themselves upon the productive classes, and suck from them their whole substance.

Those who assist not in production can never justly be exchangers, for they have nothing on which to draw, and therefore nothing which they can exchange. No man possesses any natural and inherent wealth within himself—he has merely *a capability of labouring;* therefore, if a man possess any created wealth—any capital—and have never made use of this capability, and have never laboured, the wealth which he holds in possession cannot rightly belong to him. It must belong to some persons who have created it by labour; for capital is not self-existent. The vast accumulations now in Great Britain therefore—as they are neither the production of the labour of the present race of capitalists nor their predecessors, and were never given to them in exchange for any such labour—do not belong to the capitalists either on the principle of creation or the principle of exchange. Nor are they theirs by right of heirship; for having been produced nationally, they can only justly be inherited by the nation as a whole. Thus, view the matter as we will, there is to be seen no towering pile of wealth that has not been scraped together by rapacity—no transaction between the man of labour and the man of money, that is not characterised by fraud and injustice. (*pp.* 48–50)

4

EARLY TRADE UNION SOCIALISM

Trade unions developed rapidly after the repeal of the Combination Laws in 1824, and their struggles naturally gave rise to the concept of class conflict and the belief that the working class could use its industrial power to achieve social aims. In 1832 one William Benbow wrote a pamphlet advocating united strike action by " the productive classes ", who would declare a " national holiday " in order to establish a co-operative system of society (a).

Owen did not approve of these ideas, which threatened a syndicalist revolt against the capitalist class. At this time the hopes of his followers centred on his scheme for the establishment of labour exchanges, where goods might exchange at their labour value. Owen's own London labour exchange was publicised in his journal the *Crisis* (b). But neither this exchange nor any of the others later founded in the provinces was successful; and Owen was embarrassed by the growth of the idea of class conflict among his working-class supporters, such as " Senex ", a contributor to the *Pioneer,* the organ of the Operative Builders (c). " Senex " has been identified with J. E. Smith, who was editor of the *Crisis.* The Union to which the article refers is the Grand National Consolidated Trades Union, which had been founded to cover all trades, and which Smith and James Morrison, editor of the *Pioneer,* tried to win over to their syndicalist point of view. Owen's opposition to their plans resulted in the closing down of both papers in 1834; and these differences, combined with the inexperience of the unionists and the legal obstacles that they met with, led to the early collapse of the Union.

(a) WILLIAM BENBOW. *Grand National Holiday and Congress of the Productive Classes*

1832

It is almost superfluous to say, that the horrid and merciless tyrants, whom we have allowed to lord it over us, have no feeling in common with us. The whole study of their lives is to keep us in a state of ignorance, that we may not be sensible of our own degradation and of their weakness. To expect good at their hands, to hope that they will break one link of the chain with which they bind us, to dream that they will ever look with pity upon us, is the vainest of all dreams. But enough; they have fattened upon the sweat of our body; they are determined to continue to do so; it is our business to prevent it, to put a stop to it. We are the people, our business is with the people, and to transact it properly, we must take it into our own hands. The people are called upon to work for themselves! We lay down the plan of operation; we despair of all safety, we despair of liberty, we despair of equality, we despair of seeing ease, gaiety, pleasure, and happiness becoming the possessions of the people, unless they co-operate with us. We chalk down to them a plan; woe to them if they do not follow in its traces!

A holiday signifies a *holy* day, and ours is to be of holy days the most holy. It is to be most holy, most sacred, for it is to be consecrated to promote—to create rather—the happiness and liberty of mankind. Our holy day is established to establish plenty, to abolish want, to render all men equal! In our holy day we shall legislate for all mankind; the constitution drawn up during our holiday, shall place every human being on the same footing. Equal rights, equal liberties, equal enjoyments, equal toil, equal respect, equal share of production. This is the object of our holy day—of our sacred day—of our festival. (*p.* 8)

(b) *United Trades Association of London* Address to the Trades Unions of Dublin 16 May 1833

Friends and Fellow-workmen—The members of the United Trades Association of London offers to you their heartfelt sympathy for the oppressions which you have endured too long. Suffering and misery have accumulated with you, and with us also, to an extent at length unbearable. *Our* suffering is great—but what is ours compared with that of unhappy Ireland, inflicted by one continuation of ignorant and vicious mis-government? . . . .

The earth teems with abundance of everything which can make existence happy, yet the labourers are destitute. Those of mankind who prepare everything for the ease and happiness of all are those who are in the greatest want. How strange is this anomaly! How are we to account for it? The same ignorance and division which are concomitant with political despotism have established among us a social despotism equally grievous. This social despotism developes itself in the system of competition. The whole system of trade and commerce is conducted on this false, baleful, destroying system. Political despotism makes us dependent on the few for government; social despotism makes us dependent on the few for employment. The former it is not for us to discuss on this occasion. The engine of social despotism is the money capital in the hands of the few. As it is with money that all the necessary exchanges in our productions are effected, there is a general struggle for it, and those who want it are placed at the mercy of those who have it. Production and producers are alike at the mercy of the money holder. To get money the merchants and tradesmen undersell each other—the labourers underwork each other, and what are the consequences? They are before our eyes. Political despotism is execrable—social despotism is still more execrable. The former is open, the latter insidious. Social despotism feeds the ever-burning fire of political misrule. Let us do away with the former, and extinguish the latter.

The instrument is in our hands—we are moving it; but to use it effectually the strength of numbers is required. This instrument is Labour Exchange.

In their dealings with each other, the members of the traders' societies absolve themselves from the money of social despots; they use the labour note, a time-standard, the only equitable standard of value. It is easy to see that by following this system consumption must keep pace with production—that there will always be an ever-open market for industry—always sufficient employment and commensurate remuneration;—in fine an exchange of labour, or, as labour is the source of wealth, of wealth for wealth. It is by this system of commerce alone that the axiom we adopt as our motto can be wholesomely proved.

There are obstacles in our progress: monopoly and prejudice are the chief. Prejudice will be removed by time and the exercise of common sense. Monopoly, the monopoly of the few, can be opposed only by the union of the many. The land is monopolised, and all raw material comes from it. We can get it only with the capitalists' money at present, though it must be otherwise when the value of our own money comes to be generally acknowledged. We propose then, that part of the funds of a society, or a fund raised for the purpose by weekly advances of a small amount, be laid out in the purchase of raw material, and that those members of the society who are out of work be employed upon it. The produce, then, put into the Exchange Bazaar to be disposed of to the members of other trades who do business in the same manner, and also to the public. The money advanced for the purchase of material can then be returned into the hands of those who advanced it, in the form of labour notes; and with them they can get anything they may want, which is produced by the other trades united. This is the plan we have followed. We thus not only relieve ourselves from the burthen of supporting our more unfortunate fellow workmen, but furnish them with honourable employment and at the same time, by diminishing the competition for labour in the outer market, raise the price of labour there. A few of the trades of London united some time ago to work for each other in this manner; and within the last three months they have done business to the amount of 1,200*l*. Our fellow-workmen of Birmingham, and many other places in the north and west of England, have also united in the same manner. We, therefore hope in a short time that a general union of this kind may be effected throughout the country, and that that system may be carried into the freest operation. We have also invited our fellow-workmen of New York to join us; which we expect they will do, as soon as the necessary arrangements can be effected.

We have thus given you a slight outline of our views. Robert Owen, the philanthropist, the originator of Equitable Labour Exchange, will shortly be among you. He has spent nearly the whole of his life and fortune in endeavouring to emancipate mankind from the slavery, mental and physical, in which they have ever been. He has for many years addressed himself to the governments of, what is called, the civilized world; but in vain. He now comes forward among the industrious classes to point out the way by which they may emancipate themselves, and acquire the means of happiness. He will explain at lectures and public meetings the entire subject in all its bearings to you. We earnestly entreat you to give your deep attention to him, confident that though you may possibly differ from him upon some speculative points, you will find the practical subjects he will bring before you of the highest importance and most vital interest. (*Crisis*, 1 June 1833)

(c) "SENEX." *The Real Object of United Labour* 1834

WAS the Union of which you, brethren, have lain the foundation, perfectly understood, its success would be secure, and the happiness which is its object would very speedily be attainable. Its strength, however, is necessarily dependant upon its extent, and it can be perfect only when it shall have become universal. Its basis is Christianity, pure Christianity; and he that does not "love his neighbour as himself",—he who prefers in the slightest degree his own individual gain to the general welfare, is at most a *Unionist in name*: he is far, very far, from being a *Unionist in heart*.

In my present letter, brethren, I am about to follow up the design which I commenced in my earlier addresses to you; in which I endeavoured to show you that *labour* is at the present period in its transition state between *hireling labour*—in which the life of a man is sold piecemeal, by the day or the week, at or below the market price, and *associated labour*—in which men will, and must, act together for the mutual benefit of the whole body of the association. I showed you that this transition was the inevitable consequence of the plenty which man, by the exercise of his talents and industry, is found capable of producing. Plenty is perpetually passing the limit of profit, by what the wise men of McCulloch's school call over-production, and is checked by what we have a right to call the *masters' strike;* but which they themselves, with a shake of their empty noddles, and a stroke or two on their full bellies, call a *glut*.

Their remedy, my worthy brethren, for this, to their *profit-mongering* system, ruinous influx of plenty, is the turning you off for a time, to starve in winter with your families, by the side of a fireless grate; and then, as the *surplus produce* (what a term the political economists have dared to make use of, amidst a half-naked people who can read!)—as this *surplus produce* begins to find vent in the market, they gradually recall you to your toil, at the lowest wages, which your long period of suffering amidst your famishing children has induced you to be glad to accept. Oh! these dreadful *strikes of the capitalists*! I have been a witness of them in various places. In the large manufacturing towns of the north they are truly horrible. The recent slaughter at Lyons presents to the agonized sensibilities of the human heart something more suddenly and instantaneously atrocious. But conceive for a moment the silent yet certain ravages which disease and famine make among thousands who are told that the market for their labour is closed, and that they can no longer sell the weeks and days of their lives for the coarsest food or for the humblest rags for themselves and their children. Some of the master-manufacturers used to advise you to raise funds for your support during these stagnations of your labour; and there were among them a few conscientious persons who were humane enough to subscribe to such funds; but you soon became aware that after every one of these *glut-strikes* of the capitalists, your wages were reduced lower and lower, while the capitalists themselves, with the cry that the profits would not rise to what they had previously been, insisted upon having you (enslaved by day or week purchase) at a less and less price.

Under such circumstances, the *profit-mongering* system is continued only by forcing down, by every possible means, the wages of labour; and in effecting this it is again met by an increase of pauperism and the poor's-rate. Your numbers, brethren, are very great; the majority of you exist upon the extreme brink of want; your sufferings are often severe, and too many of you are ignorant and imprudent; hence it happens that, notwithstanding your murmurs and your partial strikes, your wages are easily kept down; and if, in your present important struggle, you had no other object but to get a higher payment by the day or week for your labour, your success would only be in certain trades where the profits of your employers were extraordinarily high, and it would be of very short duration. You may possibly obtain, here and there, a greater share of such profits; but profits of every sort are declining, and the poor's-rate is everywhere increasing, and those among you (I hope there are few such) who are actuated by a selfish desire of sharing with their masters in the luxuries which their present profits obtain for them, must also expect to share in their fate.

The question for the liberal-minded producers of plenty, now, for the first time since Adam, in UNION with one another, is not whether such and such a set of producers shall participate more largely with the capitalists in their profits; but whether, since it is now easily demonstrable, and has been repeatedly demonstrated, that more commodities, conducive to the sustenance, the comfort and luxury of man, can be produced with facility in this country, or brought into it by commerce, than all its inhabitants can consume; the question is, I say, whether there are not means to modify the existing system, so as to approximate at least to that by which the abundance produced shall be more generally and more equally enjoyed? (*Pioneer,* 24 May 1834)

5

THE CHARTIST LEFT

Chartism was not essentially a Socialist movement. Although it derived most of its support from the widespread economic distress among the lower classes, its original aims as expressed in the Charter were entirely political and were limited to proposals for democratising the constitution. Feargus O'Connor, the most popular of the Chartist leaders, endeavoured to find a solution for economic distress by means of a scheme to buy land and to establish labourers' allotments; but this was from the Socialist point of view no more than a palliative, and a poor one at that.

There were, however, a few Chartist leaders who from the study of the great French Revolution and of subsequent Socialist experiments developed a theory of social revolution by means of winning political power and collectivizing property. The pioneer of this group was James Bronterre O'Brien, a graduate of Trinity College, Dublin, who was prominent in Chartist journalism and became known as "the Chartist schoolmaster" (a). He translated into English Buonarotti's account of the Babeuf conspiracy, and published it with numerous comments of his own. He was largely responsible for the formation of the National Reform League in 1850, with a strongly Socialistic programme (c).

The most notable among those influenced by O'Brien was George Julian Harney, an active working-class journalist who sought to develop international labour solidarity through the Society of Fraternal Democrats (founded in 1845), and who came into close contact with Marx and Engels in this cause (b). The climax of Harney's Socialist activity was his publication of the weekly *Red Republican* for some months in 1850 (d). But the gradual weakening of his militant attitude that took place in the 1850's disappointed the Marxist exiles, who came to rely more and more on Ernest Jones as their link with the Chartists. Ernest Jones, a barrister, was not only a fine speaker but also a poet of some merit. He held a Chartist rump together until 1858. The passage here quoted (e) is from a debate of his with the co-operative propagandist Lloyd Jones.

(a) BRONTERRE O'BRIEN. Letter to R. G. (Gammage) 1841

. . . And what, after all, my dear friend, were Cartwright and Cobbett, but a brace of *Quacks*? Take, for example, Cobbett's far-famed "Norfolk Petition", and his "Fourteen Manchester Propositions", which contain the whole of his scheme—the whole of his plan for settling the affairs of the nation—and, after comparing the Reforms therein demanded with the actual state of society, tell me who but a quack could think such paltry remedies adequate to cure the evils we groan under? For what do they amount to? Why, just to this—make sale of the bulk of our public property (tithes, corporate property, crown lands, etc.) and with the proceeds pay off the National Debt (after reducing it by equitable adjustment), disband the bulk of the army, abolish pensions, etc.; and, in short, go on retrenching our establishments, and cutting down our expenses, till we have got our taxation back to the standard of 1792; and then, by an improved mode of raising the taxes that will still be required, that is, about *sixteen million a year*—and making the Parliament shift its sittings to York and Dublin—every thing will be renovated, and all will ever after run smooth!!! I defy the devil, or the devil's grandmother, to match this for quackery. Yet, if all this were done, we should be once more, according to Cobbett's disciples, the most flourishing people in the world!!! Ah, my friend, I would almost give up one half of my remaining days to have a large weekly paper established in Manchester, with about £1,000 to carry it on. Were it only to demolish all such rubbish as this, with Cartwright, Paine, and Volney into the bargain—not forgetting our old friend, Robert Owen, who, with all his hallucinations, is the only one of the lot that is worth the name of Reformer. Owen is right, at any rate, as to the end, but his means are delusive. The others seem to me to have completely mistaken both the *end* and the *means*. Were all the practical reforms proposed by Paine, Cartwright, and Co. to be carried into complete effect to-morrow, they would not realise any of the results anticipated by their authors. They would leave the *radix* or root of this evil where they found it, and consequently cause no substantial change in the condition of the bulk of society.

The *radix*, or root of the evil, lies in allowing the *riches of nature* to be *private* property, and in a false system of exchanges throughout every department of society. In other words, the root of the evil lies in allowing land to be the exclusive property of individuals, and in allowing other particular individuals to have the making, issuing, and regulation of the circulating medium, or currency, through the intervention of which all *valuables* are interchanged. So long as this double evil endures, there can be no real reform in society. Any attempts at "practical reforms" (so called) which shall not rectify this two-fold source of evil, will prove utter abortives. They will mend one hole by making another—they will but transfer power and pelf from one set of schemers to another.

By the *riches of nature,* I mean of course the land and sea, and all that they contain. These, which comprise within them all the raw materials of wealth, are the gift of Almighty God to all men alike, and, therefore, were never intended to be private property; and, indeed, cannot be made the *exclusive* property of any individual, or set of individuals, without violating the private property and rights of all the individuals excluded, and consequently destroying *private property itself* as an institution of society. Whatever God has made belongs equally to all; it is the common property of all God's creatures. It is only what man has made that can be the subject of *private property*, without sapping the very foundation of the institution, and opening hell under the feet of society. It is for want of making this distinction *in practice*, that society continues to be what it is—a chaos of antagonism, and crime, and folly. The two errors combined have made a riddle of human nature, and a pandemonium of the world. It belongs to enlightened reason to remove both sources of evil, without pulling society to pieces in the attempt. But that is a task which nature, or nature's god, never intended for such minds as those of Paine, Cartwright, Cobbett, or even the boasted Volney, whom certain shallow Chartists almost worship as a divinity.

The taxes and the monopoly accruing from them are not what Paine and Cobbett represented them. They are not the staple of our burthens; they are not the main source of the plunder we complain of. They are but a small slice of the plunder *set apart* or *put in a corner* by the plunderers to *protect the rest*, which rest contributes nearly the whole. Remove the whole of the taxes to-morrow, and in a few years, or perhaps months, the great majority of us would find ourselves no better off than we are now. The landlord and moneymonger, with their standing armies of lawyers, priestly soldiers, constabulary, literary prostitutes, bailiffs, brokers, gaolers, hired satellites, etc., etc., would almost immediately swallow up the proportion of the saving that ought to fall to our share. That result would be inevitable under the present constitution of society. *Alas*, while the land continues to be *private property*, and until the universality of the nation shall be sole maker, issuer, and regulator of the currency, as well as the sole landlord, there is no hope for the millions. . . . (*Northern Star*, 27 March 1841)

(b) *Society of Fraternal Democrats.* Message to the Democratic Association of Brussels

1847

BROTHER Democrats.—Your address of date the 26th of November, 1847, was received at a public meeting of the members and friends of this society, held on the 29th ultimo, in commemoration of the glorious, though ill-fated, Polish Insurrection of 1830. . . .

Our society has existed for more than two years. Taking for our motto " All Men are Brethren ", we have laboured to unite the friends of veritable liberty belonging to all countries. In England our efforts have created a brotherly feeling on the part of that great body of the British people, the Chartists, towards the real reformers of all other lands. Our manifestoes have circulated in France and Germany, with the happiest results. We have laid bare the atrocities of the tyrannical governments of Europe towards Poland and Portugal. At a moment when war between England and the United States appeared to be imminent, we appealed to the people of both nations against the madness or wickedness of their government, and exhibited the folly and crime of national wars for territory, or that phantom folly of the hideous past called " glory ". We spoke not in vain. We *know* that our words largely contributed towards the creation of a brotherly feeling between the two great branches of the Anglo-Saxon family.

On the occasion of our late anniversary (the 22nd of September) we recommend the calling of a Democratic Congress of all nations, and we rejoice to learn that you have published a similar proposition. The conspiracy of kings should be met by the counter-combination of the peoples. Whenever the Democratic Congress may assemble, you may rely upon the English Democracy being represented thereat. It must be the work of your society in connexion with ours to assemble the representatives of our brethren throughout Europe.

Your delegate, Dr. Marx, will inform you of the arrangements we have entered into with him to render effective the union of the two associations.

The oppressed people of the several European countries may propose to themselves various modes of accomplishing their emancipation; they may differ as to the peculiar forms of the free political systems they seek to establish, and they may not agree on the social reforms necessary to render liberty a reality; on these points, unity of sentiment and action may be neither possible nor necessary. But there are two points of agreement for the Democrats of all countries, namely, THE SOVEREIGNTY OF THE PEOPLE, and THE FRATERNITY OF NATIONS. That the actual power of the state—the power to make and amend the political and social institutions of society, shall be vested in the entire people, is demanded by Democrats of all lands. All Democrats, too, worthy of the name, acknowledge that the interests of the PEOPLE of all countries are the same, and that all nations should aid each other in their struggles for justice. These two principles—*Popular Sovereignty* and *Universal Fraternity*, may, therefore, bind the veritable Reformers of all countries in one invincible phalanx.

Earnestly hoping the success of your association, and the welfare of its members, we tender to you our fraternal salutation, and pledge to you our aid in promoting the triumph of the glorious principles our respective societies are established to propagate.

We are aware that it is to the *veritable* people, the Proletarians, the men whose sweat and blood are poured out daily under the slavery imposed upon them by the present system of society, we are aware that it is to these we must look for the establishment of universal brotherhood. It is the interest of landlords and money-lords to keep the nations divided; but it is the interest of the Proletarians, everywhere oppressed by the same kind of taskmasters, and defrauded of the fruits of their industry by the same description of plunderers, it is their interest to unite. And they will unite. From the loom, the anvil, and the plough, from the hut, the garret, and the cellar, will come forth, are even *now* coming forth, the apostles of fraternity, and the destined saviours of humanity.

HURRAH FOR DEMOCRACY! HURRAH FOR THE FRATERNITY OF NATIONS!

(*Northern Star,* 11 December 1847)

(c) *National Reform League. Propositions for the Peaceful Regeneration of Society*

1850

Liberty in Right; Equality in Law; Fraternity in Interest.

The following resolutions, on behalf of the League, were unanimously passed at a crowded meeting of the National Regeneration Society, held on the 16th March, 1850, in the large theatre of the Literary Institution, Leicester Square, London, on the motion of J. Bronterre O'Brien, seconded by Richard Hart. They have also received the assent of the National Charter Association, and the Fraternal Democrats, and have been carried at various public meetings:—

"This meeting is of opinion that in addition to a full, fair, and free representation of the whole people in the Commons House of Parliament, upon principles the same or similar to those laid down in the People's Charter—the following measures,—some of a provisional, the others of a permanent nature, are necessary to ensure real political and social justice to the oppressed and suffering population of the United Kingdom, and to protect society from violent revolutionary changes:—

"1. A repeal of our present wasteful and degrading system of poor-laws, and the substitution of a just and efficient poor-law (based upon the original Act of Elizabeth) which should centralise the rates, and dispense them equitably and economically for the beneficial employment and relief of the destitute poor. The rates to be levied only upon the owners of every description of realised property. The employment to be of a healthy, useful, and reproductive kind, so as to render the poor self-sustaining and self-respecting. Till such employment be procured, the relief of the poor to be, in all cases, promptly and liberally administered, as a right, and not grudgingly doled out, as a boon. The relief not to be accompanied with obduracy, insult, imprisonment to the workhouses, separation of married couples, breaking up of families, or any such other harsh and degrading conditions as, under the present systems, convert relief into punishment, and treat the unhappy applicant rather as a convicted criminal than as (what he really is) the victim of an unjust and vitiated state of society.

"2. In order to lighten the pressure of rates, and at the same time gradually to diminish, and finally to absorb, the growing mass of pauperism and surplus population, it is the duty of the Government to appropriate its present surplus revenue, and the proceeds of national or public property, to the purchasing of lands, and the location thereon of the unemployed poor. The rents accruing from those lands to be applied to further purchases of land, till all who desired to occupy land, either as individual holders or industrial communities, might be enabled to do so. A general law empowering parishes to raise loans upon the security of their rates, would greatly facilitate and expedite the operation of Government towards this desirable end.

"3. Pending the operation of these measures, it is desirable to mitigate the burdens of taxation and of public and private indebtedness upon all classes who suffer thereby,—the more especially as these burdens have been vastly aggravated by the recent monetary and free trade measures of Sir Robert Peel. To this end, the Public Debt and all private indebtedness affected by the fall of prices should be equitably adjusted in favour of the debtor and productive classes, and the charges of Government should be reduced upon a scale corresponding with the general fall of prices and wages. And, as what is improperly called the National Debt has been admitted, in both Houses of Parliament, to be in the nature of a *bona fide* mortgage upon the realized property of this country, it is but strict justice that the owners of this property, and they only, should be henceforward held responsible for both capital and interest. At all events, the industrious classes should not be held answerable for it, seeing the debt was not borrowed by them, nor for them, nor with their consent; and that, even if it had been so, they have had no assets left them for the payment of it. Moreover, the realized property of the country, being estimated at eight times the amount of the debt, the owners or mortgagers have no valid excuse or plea to offer on the score of inability, for refusing to meet the claims of their mortgagees.

"4. The gradual resumption by the State (on the acknowledged principle of equitable compensation to existing holders, or their heirs) of its ancient, undoubted, inalienable dominion, and sole proprietorship, over all the lands, mines, turbaries, fisheries, &c., of the United Kingdom and our colonies; the same to be held by the State, as trustees in perpetuity, for the entire people, and rented to them in such quantities, and on such terms, as the law and local circumstances shall determine; because the land, being the gift of the Creator to ALL, can never become the exclusive property of individuals—because the monopoly of the land, in private hands, is a palpable invasion of the rights of the excluded parties, rendering them, more or less, the slaves of landlords and capitalists, and tending to circumscribe, or annul, their other rights and liberties—because the monopoly of the earth by a portion of mankind is no more justifiable than would be the monopoly of air, light, heat, or water—and because the rental of the land (which justly belongs to the whole people) would form a national fund adequate to defray all charges of the public service, execute all needful public works, and educate the population, without the necessity for any taxation.

"5. That, as it is the recognised duty of the State to support all those of its subjects who, from incapacity or misfortune, are unable to procure their own subsistence; and as the nationalisation of landed property would open up new sources of occupation for the now surplus industry of the people (a surplus which is daily augmented by the accumulation of machinery in the hands of the capitalists), the same principle which now sanctions a public provision for the destitute poor should be extended to the providing a sound system of National Credit, through which any man might (under certain conditions) procure an advance from the national funds arising out of the proceeds of public property, and thereby be enabled to rent and cultivate land on his own account, instead of being subjected, as now, to the injustice and tyranny of wage-slavery (through which capitalists and profitists are enabled to defraud him of his fair recompense) or induced to become a hired slaughterer of his fellow-creatures at the bidding of godless diplomatists; enabling them to foment and prosecute international wars, and trample on popular rights, for the exclusive advantage of aristocrats and 'vested interests'. The same privilege of obtaining a share in the national credit to be applicable to the requirements of individuals, companies, and communities in all other branches of useful industry, as well as in agriculture.

"6. That the National Currency should be based on real, consumable wealth, or on the *bona fide* credit of the State, and not upon the variable and uncertain amount of scarce metals; because a currency depending on such a basis, however suitable in past times, or as a measure of value in present international commerce, has now become, by the increase of population and wealth, wholly inadequate to perform the functions of equitably representing and distributing that wealth: thereby rendering all commodities liable to perpetual fluctuation in price, as those metals happen to be more or less plentiful in any country; increasing to an enormous extent the evils inherent in usury, and in the banking and funding systems (in support of which a legitimate function of the law—the *protection* of property—is distorted into an instrument for the *creation* of property to a large amount for the benefit of a small portion of society, belonging to what are called vested interests); because, from its liability to become locally or nationally scarce, or in excess, that equilibrium which should be maintained between the production and consumption of wealth is destroyed; because, being of intrinsic value in itself, it fosters a vicious trade in money, and a ruinous practice of commercial gambling and speculation; and finally, because under the present system of society, it has become confessedly the 'root of all evil', and the main support of that unholy worship of Mammon which now so extensively prevails, to the supplanting of all true religion—natural and revealed.

"7. That in order to facilitate the transfer of property or service, and the mutual interchange of wealth among the people; to equalise the demand and supply of commodities; to encourage consumption, as well as production, and to render it as easy to sell as to buy, it is an important duty of the State to institute, in every town and city, public marts or stores, for the reception of all kinds of exchangeable goods, to be valued by disinterested officers appointed for the purpose, either upon a corn or labour standard; the depositors to receive symbolic notes representing the value of their deposits; such notes to be made legal currency throughout the country, enabling their owners to draw from the public stores to an equivalent amount, thereby gradually displacing the present reckless system of competitive trading and shop-keeping—a system which, however necessary or unavoidable in the past, now produces a monstrous amount of evil, by maintaining a large class living on the profits made by the mere sale of goods, on the demoralising principle of buying cheap and selling dear, totally regardless of the ulterior effects of that policy upon society at large, and the true interests of humanity."

It is not assumed that the foregoing Propositions comprise all the reforms needed in society. Doubtless, there are many other reforms required beside those alluded to; doubtless, we want a sound system of national education for youth, made compulsory upon all parents and guardians; doubtless, we require a far less expensive system of military and naval defence than now obtains; doubtless, we require the expropriation of railways, canals, bridges, docks, gas-works, &c; and doubtless, we require a juster and more humane code of civil and penal law than we now possess. But these and all other needful reforms will be easy of accomplishment when those comprised in the foregoing propositions shall have been effected. Without these, indeed, justice cannot be done to humanity; society cannot be placed in the true path of improvement, never again to be turned aside or thrown back; nor can those natural checks and counter-checks be instituted without which the conflicting passions and propensities of man fail to produce a harmonious whole; but with which, as in the material world, all things are made to work together for good, reconciling man to his position in the universe, and exalting his hopes of future destiny. (*Red Republican,* 13 July–31 August 1850)

(d) G. J. HARNEY. Editorial in the *Red Republican* 14 September 1850

ALARMED at the threat of a general strike on the railways, the [*Daily*] *News,* throwing off all reserve, demands the subjection of the railway workers to a system of military discipline. . . .

We answer, let the railways be declared a national property, and we shall have no objection to the workers thereon being subjected to national regulations. Let the directors and superintendents be appointed by the public *at large,* or at least by a government elected by Universal Suffrage, and we still agree to accept their management. But against the monstrous system of managing railways by public officers and military discipline for the benefit of private companies, we protest; and we cry to the working classes to arouse themselves, and oppose with energy the despotic designs of the money mongers, and the damnable doctrines of their advocates.

Acknowledging that strikes are often unavoidable, and admitting that "associations" may do something towards rescuing a few of the sons of toil from the slough of misery, we must add the expression of our conviction that by no such means can the working classes as a body be redeemed from their present state of slavery. For one strike that succeeds there are at least two that fail. And as regards "associations", is it possible for the weavers of Hyde to command the requisite capital to enable them to manufacture on their own account? Can the agricultural labourers with eight shillings or less per week, accumulate capital with which to purchase and cultivate the land? Can the coal-miners become (under the present system) *possessors* of coal-mines to work for their own benefit? Can the railway-workers find the necessary capital with which to supersede the present owners of railways? If not, how can "associations" under existing circumstances secure the salvation of the wealth producers?

For the proletarians in the mass there is but one mode of escape from their present state of thraldom and misery, namely by transforming the entire country into one association, of which they—the workers—shall be the sole lords. To command that means of salvation they must become the masters of the State. To secure that mastery, they must obtain Universal Suffrage.

We will plead the cause of every trade, or section of a trade, driven to a strike to resist an increase, or to obtain an abatement of suffering. We will wish good speed to every "association", and commend the same to popular support, though but a few units should be thereby saved from the general mass of misery. But we must and will warn the proletarians against the fatal delusion of trusting to any such means for their elevation as a class. The question of their deliverance lies in the compass of a nutshell. They are miserable because they are robbed. They are robbed because they are destitute of power. They must acquire political power—the sovereignty of the state to be enabled to put an end to the reign of the robbers. If they cannot, or will not, pursue the course hereby indicated there is no hope for them; they will remain wretched and down-trodden while their race shall endure.

(e) ERNEST JONES. *Speech in a Debate on Co-operation* 1852

. . . REPORT of a discussion which took place in the Odd Fellows' Hall, St. James's Road, Halifax, on Monday and Wednesday evenings, the 26th and 28th of January, 1852, between Mr Ernest Jones and Mr Lloyd Jones; when Mr Ernest Jones undertook to vindicate the following propositions:

1st—"That Co-operation cannot be successfully carried out without first obtaining the Political Rights of the People."

2—"The errors of the present Movement, showing that it carries within it the germs of dissolution; would inflict a renewed evil on the masses of the people, and is essentially destructive of the real principles of Co-operation: instead of abrogating profit-mongering, it recreates it; instead of counteracting competition, it re-establishes it; instead of preventing centralization, it renews it, merely transferring the *role* from one set of actors to another."

. . . . . . [After Mr Lloyd Jones had spoken] Mr Ernest Jones then rose and addressed the meeting. He said he wished expressly to explain to the audience that in rising to take part in the present discussion he was not one of those who thought co-operation a wrong thing. He was one of those, on the contrary, who believed that their social regeneration could not be established unless it was established upon a system of co-operation; but he was one, at the same time, who believed that that system of co-operation could not be carried out, unless they first did away with the obstacles that lay in its way. He was one of those, moreover, who thought that the present system of co-operation was one that even if those obstacles were removed would lead them back into a greater gulph of misery than that from which they were trying to emancipate themselves. In the first place he believed that co-operation even on a good basis, could not be carried into effect as a national remedy without political power to precede it. In the second place he was one of those who believed that the present system of co-operation was merely a recreation of the present system of profit-mongering, competition and monopoly. At the same time he hoped that there would be no misapprehension established as to the estimation in which he held the present members of the co-operative movement. He believed that they were an honest, well-meaning, reflecting and good body of men; but he believed that they were being misled; as the well-meaning, aye, the intelligent, the intellectual and the honest of all ages had so often been, by leaders who did not understand the evils and vices inherent in the system which they no doubt honestly recommended; and by not being able to perceive the downward slope of misery that they were tending towards while fancying they were ascending the heights of social happiness. Now he did anticipate that since the first part of this discussion appeared to have been allotted to this point "That Co-operation cannot be carried out successfully without first obtaining the Political Rights of the People"; he did anticipate that his honourable opponent would have shown that it could. Therefore he (Mr Ernest Jones) humbly conceived that he had failed to assail that part of his position—that he had scarcely touched upon it. . . . . He (Mr Ernest Jones) would draw their attention to the first part of the subject and touch upon a few points that had been brought forward by his worthy opponent; who had told them that the fundamental part of the co-operative principle was its productive element—to produce, to manufacture, to grow corn, to manufacture cotton clothes, and to make machinery. The next point he described was the distributive principle, the shop-keeping portion of the business. Now, let them see how far they could carry their productive system out (and this was the most important branch of the co-operative principle) without having political power. They combine—they associate—for the purpose of production; they must have money to do so. In a co-operative store a few of them might club their pence together and might buy the articles they required, and sell to themselves, and to the public also, making profits, with a comparatively small amount of capital to begin with. But the capital they required for the productive portion was infinitely greater than that required for the distributive branch—they had to buy land, to build or to buy a factory and purchase machinery and raw materials required for their manufactures, and they would need a large amount of capital. They clubbed their pence for this purpose, but how was it to be carried on, on a large scale?

. . . As long as there were men starving and men wanting work, the capitalist would have wages-slaves. As long as he had wages-slaves, he could undersell the co-operative, and thus prevent him from reproducing his capital; and prevent the low-paid multitude to spare from their daily bread enough to compete with him by co-operation. . . . By trying co-operation before they got political power they were putting the cart before the horse. The co-operative cart was very good when laden not with profit-mongering, but with Christian co-operation. It was very good for piling their sugar, tea, and coffee in. But they would stick in the mud of competition and misrule—theirs was the cart—but political power was the horse that must pull them out of the mire. (*Notes to the People*, vol. 2, *pp*. 793–796)

6

THE CHRISTIAN SOCIALISTS

Christian Socialism was the product of a group of Anglican clergymen and laymen who were roused to the study of social questions by the unrest of the late 1840's. They were little influenced, however, by earlier British Socialism. Their leading theorist was J. M. Ludlow, a barrister who derived his knowledge of socialist experiments from Paris, where he was educated. He and two clergymen, the theologian F. D. Maurice and the well-known novelist Charles Kingsley, at that time a country parson, started the Christian Socialist movement in 1848 with the publication of a journal called *Politics for the People* (a) in which they announced their sympathy with the poor in their distress. The paper was not a financial success, and soon died; but they later produced another paper, the *Christian Socialist*, and also published two series of tracts. In the first of these tracts Maurice explained that the object of Christian Socialist propaganda was to "Christianize Socialism" (b). In particular, as is clear from Kingsley's powerful *Cheap Clothes and Nasty* (c), they sought to encourage co-operative societies, and founded an association for this purpose. Their success was limited, but they played an important part in the passing of the Act of Parliament which gave a legal status to co-operative societies (1852).

Although some of the Christian Socialists, notably Maurice, were opposed to democratic reform, the group provided a valuable example of positive sympathy with working-class distress, and the tradition of Christian Socialism was taken up again in the eighteen-eighties by Stewart Headlam's Guild of St. Matthew and (in a less controversial fashion) by the Christian Social Union. An undenominational association with similar objects also existed at the end of the century—the Christian Socialist League.

(a) J. M. LUDLOW. *The Great Partnership*

1848

THE word Society, in the languages from which it is derived, means the same thing as Partnership. And I really think that many misconceptions on the subject would be cleared away, if we could accustom ourselves to think of Society simply as the Great Partnership, either of one nation in itself, or of mankind at large, according as we look upon it from a special or a general point of view. One thing is clear, that the modern idea and word of "Socialism" could never have sprung up, but from the forgetfulness of this great fact of human partnership. Socialism is but the recoil of Individualism, of that splitting up of society under a thousand of influences of sceptical and vicious selfishness in the last century, through which indeed nations seemed to have become mere aggregations of units, heaped together without cohesion, like the shingle on the sea-beach, instead of being built up into glorious palaces and temples of brotherhood and worship. If men really felt themselves to be partners in the great business of life, they would not need to be reminded that they should be so. And thus the mere word of Socialism,—which means nothing of itself but the science of making men partners, the science of partnership, —conveys to us a great lesson and a great warning.

But the Socialists should not fancy, as they are too prone to do, that in the use of this word they are setting forth any new truth of their own discovery. That truth, such as it is, is a very old one; only it has lain slumbering more or less for centuries beneath the surface of our common speech. If they can show it to the world with more distinctness and energy than it has hitherto been exhibited, we at least shall be most grateful to them. We do need to be told anew, and unceasingly, that we are all partners; we do need to be made better partners than we are. Socialism as a science can but afford us the means of carrying out that partnership into new fields of material or intellectual exertion, of better husbanding the common stock, of more simply and successfully carrying on the common business, of assigning more judiciously to every partner such duties as he is best able to fulfil. But the germ of all these things lay in the simple word society, from the first hour when God put into some man's head to apply the same term to the common life of a whole nation, which had till then been confined to the fellowship of two or three traders. And from that hour to this, centuries and centuries before Robert Owen or Charles Fourier were born, all good men have been tending, consciously or unconsciously, to the accomplishment of some or all of these ends,—to the making society a more thriving and a better partnership. True Socialism is not a new, but a very old thing,—and all the better for that.

A partnership always has an object in view; some benefit, to be common to all the members. That object, and not chance or fancy, is the sole foundation from which it springs; there can be no partners but for a purpose. And the purpose again can be but one of common benefit;—a benefit which can only be attained by joining the efforts of several in one. No man enters into a partnership, but for the sake of bettering himself, of adding in some shape or other to his wealth, or his influence, or his pleasure, or his sense of duty fulfilled; and no man remains in a partnership but as a means of so bettering himself. And thus society must be felt to be a blessing, for men to enter into it, and for men to remain in it. It is not, as has been shown elsewhere in this paper, the giving up of a part of one's liberty as the price of certain advantages. For, indeed, Louis Blanc has added something to the truth of our conception of the word "liberty", when he has shown us that it includes the idea of power. It is increase of power to do that which man seeks to do, and to obtain that which he seeks to obtain; that is the real end of Society, as of every partnership. There may be fetters and burdens connected with the relation which were not felt before, and yet those fetters and burdens arise not out of the relation itself, but from a cause, the very opposite to it,—from the spirit of individual selfishness jarring still against the higher spirit of fellowship and community of purpose. It is because the partners are not partners enough,—because they are not sufficiently impressed with the need of co-operation, not sufficiently willing to merge individual interests in the pursuit of the common object, that they quarrel and fall out with one another, and feel their union as a galling chain. The more harmoniously they do act together, the more they will feel their power, their true freedom, increased and multiplied. Then, the confidence which they have in one another, allows each to devote himself the more entirely to his own branch of the business, to the purchases or to the sales, to the books or to the works.

And thus it is with society. So long as we look upon it only as a system of mutual checks and chains, hemming in on all sides I know not what so-called natural rights (which, if closely inquired into, would very likely be found nothing more than depraved and unnatural rights,) still more when we openly rail at the tyranny of society, and speak of it as a mere mass of corruption and injustice,—we can never be really free within its bosom, we can never work successfully towards its ends. True, all the partners may not fill such places as they ought to fill, enjoy such share of the common profit as they ought to enjoy; the deed of settlement may contain useless and ill-devised clauses, which clog and hamper the partnership business instead of promoting its success. But still, it is a partnership; it is the union of men bent together for a common purpose, and whose true interest is not to quarrel and break up the concern, but to learn to manage it better,—nay, to work each man the more wisely and zealously, the more the common business appears likely to lose by the folly or indolence of another partner,—though not without endeavouring by all possible means, by open reproof if necessary, to bring him round to a sense of duty, nor without remembering that the party in fault may have to be turned out wholly, sooner than that the whole concern should go to ruin.

Let us all try to love the society in which we live, and we shall soon make it easy for us to live in. Let us learn to look not for difference, but for agreement, seeking to reconcile divisions and not to make them, and we shall at last understand and feel what a blessing and privilege it is to be members of the Great English Partnership, and we shall be able to exert the combined and harmonious efforts of that partnership to such great and good purposes as never nation achieved before. (*Politics for the People*, July 1848)

(b) F. D. MAURICE. *Dialogue between Somebody (a person of respectability) and Nobody (the writer).* 1850

N. I wish to assure you as strongly as I can, that it is not in the machinery which these men have invented that I find the causes of my dissent from them.

S. Where then? For you have given in your adhesion to the principle. You have intimated that you consider their anti-competitive doctrine a godly doctrine.

N. I have arrived at that conviction, and I mean to maintain it.

S. The end being good and the means innocent, I see not through what loophole or crevice evil can have crept in.

N. I should wish, for many reasons, that you might perceive it. The lesson may be good for other cases besides this one. I will, therefore, try to point out the crevice.

S. I will strain my eyes and see what I can see.

N. The authors of these social systems felt that there was something wrong in the present condition of the world. They found that rivalship or competition was recognised very generally indeed by almost all classes of persons in all the concerns of life as the law which was to govern it. They found that a society which seemed to be built upon this principle, assumed Christianity as a faith sent from Heaven, that the institutions of this society implied this faith and were more or less leavened by it. The old scheme of the world, they said, must be done away with. But Christianity was part of this old scheme, what was to be done with *it*?

S. There can be no doubt about the conclusion from such premises.

N. But there was a doubt about the conclusion. Only a few could bring themselves at once and decidedly to adopt it. The rest were content to say " Christianity is, at all events, not that which we want now. It may be true or it may be false. But the social problem which we are considering must be solved without its help."

S. Was it possible to rest in this negative opinion?

N. I think not. The next step in the process made retreat or advance inevitable. If this was not the method of improving the condition of the world, another must be tried. Then co-operative systems were elaborated; some with much greater skill, experience, knowledge of the human faculties than others all with a certain amount of sagacity—all with some insight into existing evils. One or other of these systems was to be the cure for the miseries of the world. Upon one or other it was to be re-organized.

S. To be sure. Who could expect any other issue when

once men entered upon the career which you seem to think so hopeful a one?

N. A further consequence soon followed. A great machinery was to be the means of reforming society. Can a machinery, it was asked, reform society? The practical course must be defended by a theory. A broad maxim must be put forth, or there seems to be no defence for the particular project. What was that maxim? Not a very new one. A maxim upon which people had acted for a long time, which moralists had often sanctioned along with many assertions quite inconsistent with it, a maxim which seemed to have the very strongest justification from experience, which might be made the foundation of the greatest tolerance and compassion for human infirmities. "We have a right," said they, "to believe that men can be made blessed by a certain set of circumstances, for man is the creature of circumstances."

S. Your Socialist friends will not have a very high notion of your orthodoxy, if you repudiate that fundamental article of their creed.

N. I fear not. But then they do not want my alliance here. They have three-fourths of the world on their side. All the stoutest asserters of competition agree with them in their worship of circumstances. There is nothing in any of the maxims of the most corrupt system the world has ever seen to make this tenet unpalatable. But it is just here that they find the breach with Christianity, which had been continually widening, has become irreconcilable. Christianity evidently contemplates men as something else than the creatures of circumstances. If divines do not perceive that fact, our Owenites, with a much clearer and juster instinct, do perceive it. Therefore they say, "Christianity and our system must be for ever at war till one has either banished the other, or reduced it into a tributary."

S. By what charms do you hope to persuade Socialists to

cast aside their favourite dogma and to embrace one the most directly opposed to it?

N. I have no charms for the purpose. Possibly experience may have some. One and another scheme of co-operation has been tried—

S. There, at last, I am at one with you—has been tried and has come to nothing. Tried, too, on what a scale! The revolution of a whole nation, undertaken for the sake of organizing labour, of establishing co-operation. And what is the result? Why, we with our competitive principle laugh you to scorn! You have tried to set aside the laws of the universe, and they have been found too strong for you. The old doctrine of gravitation was not refined enough for your tastes. You must have a new universe constructed without gravitation, upon some sublimer method. Alas! alas! poor Phaeton, Louis Blanc! he had the chariot of the sun for a single day. What a drive he made of it, Ovid and the French *ouvriers* can tell. But I do not see why the poor doctrine of circumstances is to be charged with this calamity. Your own beautiful maxim must surely bear its moiety—more than its moiety—of the blame.

N. You cannot be more anxious than I am that all the experiments and all the failures of honest and dishonest men who have tried to embody that maxim in practice should be fairly reported, carefully examined, earnestly reflected upon. But you must permit me to say that your triumph is a little premature. There may be other Phaetons besides M. Louis Blanc. There may be a principal which sets up a hundred different coaches to run along that same road and commits each to a driver, sometimes not much more experienced, always with much less benevolent intentions than the derided member of the Paris provisional government. People may have their own tastes. I would rather be driven in that chariot or any other by Louis Blanc than by Moses and Son. In plain language, if the year of revolutions produced poor fruits, I cannot yet perceive that the year of reactions has produced any better. If the supporters of co-operation made some strange plunges and some tremendous downfalls, I believe the progress to perdition under your competitive system is sufficiently steady and rapid to gratify the most fervent wishes of those who seek for the destruction of order, and above all, of those who would make England a by-word among the nations. Thousands and tens of thousands of tailors, needlewomen, bootmakers, dock-workers, Spitalfields weavers, are saying to us, "Hold your tongues, gentlemen, about Louis Blanc and French revolutionists. Be silent in the name of common sense, if not of common modesty, till you have settled your accounts with us, till you have proved that your everlasting law of society does not mean a law of mutual destruction." (*Tracts on Christian Socialism*, No. 1, *pp.* 2*f.*)

(c) CHARLES KINGSLEY. *Cheap Clothes and Nasty*

1850

AND now comes the question—What is to be done with these poor tailors, to the number of between fifteen and twenty thousand? Their condition, as it stands, is simply one of ever-increasing darkness and despair. The system which is ruining them is daily spreading, deepening. While we write, fresh victims are being driven by penury into the slopworking trade, fresh depreciations of labour are taking place. Like Ulysses's companions in the cave of Polyphemus, the only question among them is, to scramble so far back as to have a chance of being eaten at last. Before them is ever-nearing slavery, disease, and starvation. What can be done?

First—this can be done. That no man who calls himself a Christian—no man who calls himself a man—shall ever disgrace himself by dealing at any showshop or slop-shop. It is easy enough to know them. The ticketed garments, the impudent puffs, the trumpery decorations, proclaim them, —every one knows them at first sight. He who pretends not to do so is simply either a fool or a liar. Let no man enter them—They are the temples of Moloch—their thresholds are rank with human blood. God's curse is on them, and on those who, by supporting them, are partakers of their sins. Above all, let no clergyman deal at them. Poverty—and many clergymen are poor—doubly poor, because society often requires them to keep up the dress of gentlemen on the income of an artisan; because, too, the demands on their charity are quadruple those of any other class—yet poverty is no excuse. The thing is damnable—not Christianity only, but common humanity cries out against it. Woe to those who dare to outrage in private the principles which they preach in public. God is not mocked; and His curse will find out the priest at the altar, as well as the nobleman in his castle.

But it is so hard to deprive the public of the luxury of cheap clothes. Then let the public look out for some other means of procuring that priceless blessing. If that, on experiment, be found impossible—if the comfort of the few be for ever to be bought by the misery of the many—if civilisation is to benefit every one except the producing class —then this world is truly the devil's world, and the sooner so ill-constructed and infernal a machine is destroyed by that personage, the better.

But let, secondly, a dozen, or fifty, or a hundred journeymen say to one another; "It is competition that is ruining us, and competition is division, disunion, every man for himself, every man against his brother. The remedy must be in association, co-operation, self-sacrifice for the sake of one another. We can work together at the honourable tailor's workshop—we can work and live together in the sweater's den for the profit of our employers; why should we not work and live together in our own workshops, or our own homes, for our own profit? The journeymen of the honourable trade are just as much interested as the slopworkers in putting down sweaters and slopsellers, since their numbers are constantly decreasing, so that their turn must come some day. Let them, if no one else does, lend money to allow us to set up a workshop of our own, a shop of our own. If the money be not lent, still let us stint and strain ourselves to the very bone, if it were only to raise one sweater's security-money, which one of us should pay into the slopseller's hands, in his own name, but on behalf of all: that will at least save one sweater's profit out of our labour, and bestow it upon ourselves; and we will not spend that profit, but hoard it, till we have squeezed out all the sweaters one by one. Then we will open our common shop, and sell at as low a price as the cheapest of the show-shops. We can do this,—by the abolition of sweaters' profits,—by the using, as far as possible, of one set of fires, lights, rooms, kitchens, and washhouses,—above all, by being true and faithful to one another, as all partners should be. And then, all that the master slopsellers had better do, will be simply to vanish and become extinct."

And again, let one man, or half a dozen men arise, who believe that the world is not the devil's world at all, but God's: that the multitude of the people is not, as Malthusians aver, the ruin, but as Solomon believed, "the strength of the rulers"; that men are not meant to be beasts of prey, eating one another up by competition, as in some confined pike pond, where the great pike, having despatched the little ones, begin to devour each other, till one overgrown monster is left alone to die of starvation. Let a few men, who have money, and believe that, arise to play the man.

Let them help and foster the growth of association by all means. Let them advise the honourable tailors, while it is time, to save themselves from being degraded into slop-sellers by admitting their journeymen to a share in profits. Let them encourage the journeymen to compete with Nebuchadnezzer and Co. at their own game. Let them tell those journeymen that the experiment is even now being tried, and, in many instances successfully, by no less than one hundred and four associations of journeymen in Paris. Let them remind them of that Great Name which the Parisian "ouvrier" so often forgets—of Him whose everlasting Fatherhood is the sole ground of all human brotherhood, whose wise and loving will is the sole source of all perfect order and government. Let them, as soon as an association is formed, provide for them a properly ventilated workshop, and let it out to the associate tailors at a low, fair rent. I believe that they will not lose by it—because it is right. God will take care of their money. The world, it comes out now, is so well ordered by Him, that model lodginghouses, public baths, wash-houses, insurance offices, all pay a reasonable profit to those who invest money in them—perhaps associate workshops may do the same. At all events, the owners of these show-shops realise a far higher profit than need be, while the buildings required for a tailoring establishment are surely not more costly than those absurd plate-glass fronts, and brass scroll-work chandeliers, and puffs, and paid poets. A large house might thus be taken, in some central situation, the upper floors of which might be fitted up as model lodging-rooms for the tailor's trade alone. The drawing-room floor might be the work-room; on the ground floor the shop; and, if possible, a room of call or registration office for unemployed journeymen, and a reading-room. Why should not this succeed, if the owners of the house and the workers who rent it are only true to one another? Every tyro in political economy knows that association involves a saving both of labour and of capital. Why should it not succeed, when every one connected with the establishment, landlords and workmen, will have an interest in increasing its prosperity, and none whatever in lowering the wages of any party employed?

But above all, so soon as these men are found working together for common profit, in the spirit of mutual self-sacrifice, let every gentleman and every Christian, who has ever dealt with, or could ever have dealt with, Nebuchadnezzar and Co., or their fellows, make it a point of honour and conscience to deal with the associated workmen, and get others to do the like. It is by securing custom, far more than by gifts or loans of money, that we can help the operatives. We should but hang a useless burthen of debt round their necks by advancing capital, without affording them the means of disposing of their produce.

Be assured, that the finding of a tailors' model lodging-house, work-rooms, and shop, and the letting out of the two latter to an association, would be a righteous act to do. If the plan does not pay, what then? only a part of the money can be lost; and to have given that to an hospital or an almshouse would have been called praiseworthy and Christian charity; how much more to have spent it not in the cure, but in the prevention of evil—in making almshouses less needful, and lessening the number of candidates for the hospital.

Regulations as to police order, and temperance, the workmen must, and, if they are worthy of the name of free men they can organise for themselves. Let them remember that an association of labour is very different from an association of capital. The capitalist only embarks his money on the venture; the workman embarks his time—that is, much at least of his life. Still more different is the operatives' association from the single capitalist, seeking only to realise a rapid fortune, and then withdraw. The association knows no withdrawal from business; it must grow in length and in breadth, outlasting rival slopsellers, swallowing up all associations similar to itself, and which might end by competing with it. "Monopoly" cries a free-trader, with hair on end. Not so, good friend; there will be no real free trade without association. Who tells you that tailors' associations are to be the only ones?

Some such thing, as I have hinted, might surely be done. Where there is a will there is a way. No doubt there are difficulties—Howard and Elizabeth Fry, too, had their difficulties. Brindley and Brunel did not succeed at the first trial. It is the sluggard only who is always crying, "There is a lion in the streets." Be daring—trust in God, and He will fight for you; man of money, whom these words have touched, godliness has the promise of this life, as well as of that to come. The thing must be done, and speedily; for if it be not done by fair means, it will surely do itself by foul. The continual struggle of competition, not only in the tailors' trade, but in every one which is not like the navigators' or engineers', at a premium from its novel and extraordinary demand, will weaken and undermine more and more the masters, who are already many of them speculating on borrowed capital, while it will depress the workmen to a point at which life will become utterly intolerable; increasing education will serve only to make them the more conscious of their own misery; the boiler will be strained to bursting pitch, till some jar, some slight crisis, suddenly directs the imprisoned forces to one point, and then—

What then?

Look at France, and see. (*Works of Charles Kingsley*, vol. 3, 1887, *pp*. lxxxii–lxxxvii)

7

MARX, ENGELS, AND THE BRITISH WORKING CLASS

During the generation after Chartism Socialist activity in Britain was virtually confined to a tiny group of exiles in London, headed by Marx and Engels. Marx was preparing his great work *Capital* in the British Museum, but no English translation of the first volume appeared until twenty years after its publication in German in 1867. Nevertheless, Marx and Engels exerted themselves to influence British politics whenever there was opportunity. Thus in 1850 Engels contributed to Harney's *Democratic Review* (a), and Marx sent a letter to Ernest Jones's Labour Parliament in 1854. When the First International was founded in 1864, the address was written by Marx, and was designed to appeal to a British audience (b). After the Paris commune of 1871, there was a brief revival of interest in Socialism in England, as is indicated by the appearance of the *International Herald* edited by William Harrison Riley. Among its contributors was John Hales, a member of the British Federal Council of the International, who though clearly a Socialist at this time (c), was from 1872 a rebel against Marx's authority.

At the beginning of the following decade Engels wrote a series of articles for the *Labour Standard*, a paper run by the then secretary of the London Trades Council (d). These articles had some influence in paving the way for the more permanent revival of Socialism that took place thereafter. It will be seen that both Marx and Engels had acquired some skill in the use of contemporary reform issues to point the moral of the comprehensive revolutionary cause that they were urging.

(a) FRIEDRICH ENGELS. *The Ten Hours' Question*

1850

But if the Ten Hours' Bill be lost, yet the working classes will be the gainers in this case. Let them allow the factory-lords a few moments of exultation, in the end it will be they who will exult, and the factory-lords who will lament. For—

Firstly. The time and exertions spent in agitating so many years for the Ten Hours' Bill is not lost, although its immediate end be defeated. The working classes, in this agitation, found a mighty means to get acquainted with each other, to come to a knowledge of their social position and interests, to organise themselves and to know their strength. The working man, who has passed through such an agitation, is no longer the same he was before, and the whole working class, after passing through it, is a hundred times stronger, more enlightened, and better organised than it was at the outset. It *was* an agglomeration of mere units, without any knowledge of each other, without any common tie; and now it is a powerful body, conscious of its strength, recognised as the " Fourth Estate ", and which will soon be the FIRST.

Secondly. The working classes will have learned by experience that *no lasting benefit whatever can be obtained for them by others, but that they must obtain it for themselves by conquering, first of all, political power.* They must see now that *under no circumstances have they any guarantee for bettering their social position unless by Universal Suffrage,* which would enable them to seat a *Majority of Working Men* in the House of Commons. And thus the destruction of the Ten Hours' Bill will be an enormous benefit for the Democratic movement.

Thirdly. The virtual repeal of the act of 1847 will force the manufacturers into such a rush at overtrading that revulsions after revulsions will follow, so that very soon all the expedients and resources of the present system will be exhausted, and a REVOLUTION made inevitable, which, uprooting society far deeper than 1793 or 1848 ever did, will speedily lead to the social and political ascendancy of the proletarians. We have already seen how the present social system is dependent upon the ascendancy of the manufacturing capitalists, and how this ascendancy is dependent upon the possibility of always extending production and, at the same time, reducing its cost. But this extended production has a certain limit: it cannot outdo the existing markets. If it does, a revulsion follows, with its consequent ruin, bankruptcy, and misery. We have had many of these revulsions, happily overcome hitherto by the opening of new markets (China in 1842), or the better exploring of old ones, by reducing the cost of production (as by free trade in corn). But there is a limit to this, too. There are no new markets to be opened now; and there is only one means left to reduce wages, namely, radical financial reform and reduction of the taxes by *repudiation of the national debt.* And if the free-trading mill-lords have not the courage to go the length of that, or if this temporary expedient be once exploded, too, why they will die of repletion. It is evident that, with no chance of further extending markets, under a system which is obliged to extend production every day, there is *an end to mill-lord ascendancy.* And WHAT NEXT? "Universal ruin and chaos", say the free-traders. SOCIAL REVOLUTION AND PROLETARIAN ASCENDANCY, SAY WE.

Working men of England! If you, your wives, and children are again to be locked up in the "rattle-boxes" for thirteen hours a-day, do not despair. This is a cup which, though bitter, must be drunk. The sooner you get over it the better. Your proud masters, be assured, have dug their own graves in obtaining what they call a victory over you.

The virtual repeal of the Ten Hours' Bill is an event which will materially hasten the approaching hour of your delivery. Your brethren, the French and German working men, never were satisfied with Ten Hours' Bills. They wanted to be *entirely freed from the tyranny of Capital.* And you—who have, in machinery, in skill, and in comparative numbers, far more materials at hand to work out your own salvation, and to produce enough for all of you—*surely you will not be satisfied to be paid off with a small instalment.* Ask, then, no longer for "Protection for Labour", but boldly and at once struggle for THAT POLITICAL AND SOCIAL ASCENDANCY OF THE PROLETARIAN CLASS WHICH WILL ENABLE YOU TO PROTECT YOUR LABOUR YOURSELVES. (*Democratic Review*, March 1850)

(b) *International Workingmen's Association.* Address 1864

. . . THE period passed since the revolutions of 1848 has not been without its compensating features. We shall here only point to two great facts.

After a thirty years' struggle, fought with most admirable perseverance, the English working classes, improving a momentous split between the landlords and the money-lords, succeeded in carrying the Ten Hours' Bill. The immense physical, moral, and intellectual benefits hence accruing to the factory operatives, half-yearly chronicled in the reports of the inspectors of factories, are now acknowledged on all sides. Most of the Continental Governments had to accept the English Factory Act in more or less modified forms, and the English Parliament itself is every year compelled to enlarge its sphere of action. But besides its practical import, there was something else to exalt the marvellous success of this working men's measure. Through their most notorious organs of science, such as Dr. Ure, Professor Senior, and other sages of that stamp, the middle classes had predicted, and to their hearts' content proved, that any legal restriction of the hours of labour must sound the death knell of British industry, which, vampire like, could but live by sucking blood, and children's blood, too. In olden times, child murder was a mysterious rite of the religion of Moloch, but it was practised on some very solemn occasions only, once a year perhaps, and then Moloch had no exclusive bias for the children of the poor. This struggle about the legal restrictions of the hours of labour raged the more fiercely since, apart from frightened avarice, it told indeed upon the great contest between the blind rule of the supply and demand laws which form the political economy of the middle class, and social production controlled by social foresight, which forms the political economy of the working class. Hence the Ten Hours' Bill was not only a great practical success, it was the victory of a principle; it was the first time that in broad daylight the political economy of the middle class succumbed to the political economy of the working class.

But there was in store a still greater victory of the political economy of labour over the political economy of property. We speak of the co-operative movement, especially the co-operative factories raised by the unassisted efforts of a few bold "hands". The value of these great social experiments cannot be overrated. By deed, instead of by argument, they have shown that production on a large scale, and in accord with the behests of modern science, may be carried on without the assistance of a class of masters employing a class of hands; that to bear fruit the means of labour need not be monopolised as a means of dominion over, and of extortion against, the labouring man himself;

and that, like slave labour, like serf labour, hired labour is but a transitory and inferior form, destined to disappear before associated labour plying its toil with a willing hand, a ready mind, and a joyous heart. In England, the seeds of the co-operative system were sown by Robert Owen; the working man's experiments, tried on the Continent, were, in fact, the practical upshot of the theories, not invented, but loudly proclaimed, in 1848.

At the same time, the experience of the period from 1848 to 1864, has proved beyond doubt that, however excellent in principle, and however useful in practice, co-operative labour if kept within the narrow circle of the casual efforts of private workmen, will never be able to arrest the growth in geometrical progression of monopoly, to free the masses, nor even to perceptibly lighten the burden of their miseries. It is perhaps for this very reason that plausible noblemen, philanthropic middle-class spouters, and even keen political economists, have all at once turned nauseously complimentary to the very co-operative labour system they had vainly tried to nip in the bud by deriding it as the Utopia of the dreamer, or stigmatising it as the sacrilege of the socialist. To save the industrious masses, co-operative labour ought to be developed to national dimensions, and, consequently, to be fostered by national means. Yet, the lords of the land and the lords of capital will always use their political privileges for the defence and perpetuation of their economical monopolies. So far from promoting, they will continue to lay every possible impediment in the way of the emancipation of labour. Remember the sneer with which, last session, Lord Palmerston put down the advocates of the Irish Tenants' Right Bill. "The House of Commons," said he, "is a house of landed proprietors." To conquer political power has therefore become the great duty of the working classes. They seem to have comprehended this, for in England, Germany, Italy, and France there have taken place simultaneous revivals, and simultaneous efforts are being made at the political reorganisation of the working man's party.

One element of success they possess—numbers; but numbers weigh only in the balance if united by combinations and led by knowledge. Past experience has shown how disregard of that bond of brotherhood which ought to exist between the workmen of different countries, and invite them to stand firmly by each other in all their struggles for emancipation, will be chastised by the common discomfiture of their incoherent efforts. This thought prompted the working men of different countries assembled on September 28, 1864, in public meeting at St. Martin's Hall, to found the International Association. (G. M. Stekloff, *History of the First International*, 1928, *pp*. 443–5)

(c) JOHN HALES. *The Reconstruction of Society*

1872

ALL political changes are transitory and valueless unless they are made by the people, and used by them to work out their social emancipation. The fullest political liberty can avail nothing so long as the greatest part of the human race is steeped in ignorance, want, and destitution. Under the present system our portion of Society is doomed to slave and suffer in order that the other portion may revel in luxury and idleness, and so it will ever continue, until the people see that the interest of the individual must be merged in the interest of the community, and that it is the duty of each not only to *let* others live, but to *help* them to do so. That they can do by recognising *that each is included in all.*

The principle upon which Society is based must be changed; until that is done no permanent improvement can take place in the condition of the wealth producers. Tinkering amendments to the present order of things can only palliate, not remedy. So long as it is considered honest for some to live upon the labour of others without producing something in return, so long will selfishness be the ruling spirit of Society. Man is said to be naturally selfish, he is ever likely to be when Society practically teaches that selfishness and honesty are synonymous terms, as witness the proverb "*Honesty is the best policy*".

At present competition is the basis of Society, and that simply means the rule of the Strong at the expense of the Weak—the rule of force, as opposed to the rule of justice; for the result is the same whether money-force, brain-force or physical force be the test. The weak must slave to keep the strong. In proof of this it need only be pointed out that breech-loaders and bayonets are used as civilizing agents, and have quite as much to do with deciding the affairs of nations as ever reason has, if not more. Physical force revolutions, which it is so much the fashion to condemn, are always put down by physical force, as it was in France by the massacre of June 1848, the Coup d'Etat, and the wholesale slaughter of the workmen of Paris by the Marquis Galifet upon the suppression of the Commune; but woe betide anyone who would dare to attempt to subvert a Government by physical force unless the attempt should happen to be successful.

The people of one nation slaughter the people of another, when bid to do so by their self appointed rulers, without knowing why and wherefore, and thank God for giving them the victory. Can blasphemous impious mockery go further? Yet it is only the logical application of the competition system. Men and women, like beasts, kill each other in the struggle for existence.

Competition is the cause of the preventible evils which exist in Society; prostitution, theft, and violence are its natural concomitants and must continue until Society is reconstructed upon a different principle. That principle is Communism. The antidote to a poison is its opposite, and Communism is the opposite of Competition. (*International Herald*, 22 June 1872)

(d) FRIEDRICH ENGELS. *A Fair Day's Wage for a Fair Day's Work*

1881

THIS has now been the motto of the English working-class movement for the last fifty years. It did good service in the time of the rising Trade Unions after the repeal of the infamous Combination Laws in 1824; it did still better service in the time of the glorious Chartist movement, when the English workmen marched at the head of the European working class. But times are moving on, and a good many things which were desirable and necessary fifty, and even thirty years ago, are now antiquated and would be completely out of place. Does the old, time-honoured watchword too belong to them?

A fair day's wage for a fair day's work? But what is a fair day's wage, and what is a fair day's work? How are they determined by the laws under which modern society exists and develops itself? For an answer to this we must not apply to the science of morals or of law and equity, nor to any sentimental feeling of humanity, justice, or even charity. What is morally fair, what is even fair in law, may be far from being socially fair. Social fairness or unfairness is decided by one science alone—the science which deals with the material facts of production and exchange, the science of political economy.

Now what does political economy call a fair day's wages

and a fair day's work? Simply the rate of wages and the length and intensity of a day's work which are determined by competition of employer and employed in the open market. And what are they, when thus determined?

A fair day's wage, under normal conditions, is the sum required to procure to the labourer the means of existence necessary, according to the standard of life of his station and country, to keep himself in working order and to propagate his race. The actual rate of wages, with the fluctuations of trade, may be sometimes above, sometimes below this rate; but, under fair conditions, that rate ought to be the average of all oscillations.

A fair day's work is that length of working day and that intensity of actual work which expends one day's full working power of the workman without encroaching upon his capacity for the same amount of work for the next and following days.

The transaction, then, may be thus described—the workman gives to the Capitalist his full day's working power; that is, so much of it as he can give without rendering impossible the continuous repetition of the transaction. In exchange he receives just as much, and no more, of the necessaries of life as is required to keep up the repetition of the same bargain every day. The workman gives as much, the Capitalist gives as little, as the nature of the bargain will admit. This is a very peculiar sort of fairness.

But let us look a little deeper into the matter. As, according to political economists, wages and working days are fixed by competition, fairness seems to require that both sides should have the same fair start on equal terms. But that is not the case. The Capitalist, if he cannot agree with the Labourer, can afford to wait, and live upon his capital. The workman cannot. He has but wages to live upon, and must therefore take work when, where, and at what terms he can get it. The workman has no fair start. He is fearfully handicapped by hunger. Yet, according to the political economy of the Capitalist class, that is the very pink of fairness.

But this is a mere trifle. The application of mechanical power and machinery to new trades, and the extension and improvements of machinery in trades already subjected to it, keep turning out of work more and more " hands "; and they do so at a far quicker rate than that at which these superseded " hands " can be absorbed by, and find employment in, the manufactures of the country. These superseded " hands " form a real industrial army of reserve for the use of Capital. If trade is bad they may starve, beg, steal, or go to the workhouse; if trade is good they are ready at hand to expand production; and until the very last man, woman or child of this army of reserve shall have found work—which happens in times of frantic over-production alone—until then will its competition keep down wages, and by its existence alone strengthen the power of Capital in its struggle with Labour. In the race with Capital, Labour is not only handicapped, it has to drag a cannon-ball riveted to its foot. Yet this is fair according to Capitalist political economy.

But let us inquire out of what fund does Capital pay these very fair wages? Out of capital, of course. But capital produces no value. Labour is, besides the earth, the only source of wealth; capital itself is nothing but the stored-up produce of labour. So that the wages of Labour are paid out of labour, and the working man is paid out of his own produce. According to what we may call common fairness, the wages of the labourer ought to consist in the produce of his labour. But that would not be fair according to political economy. On the contrary, the produce of the workman's labour goes to the Capitalist, and the workman gets out of it no more than the bare necessaries of life. And thus the end of this uncommonly " fair " race of competition is that the produce of the labour of those who do work, gets unavoidably accumulated in the hands of those who do not work, and becomes in their hands the most powerful means to enslave the very men who produced it.

A fair day's wage for a fair day's work! A good deal might be said about the fair day's work too, the fairness of which is perfectly on a par with that of the wages. But that we must leave for another occasion. From what has been stated it is pretty clear that the old watchword has lived its day, and will hardly hold water nowadays. The fairness of political economy, such as it truly lays down the laws which rule actual society, that fairness is all on one side—on that of Capital. Let, then, the old motto be buried for ever and replaced by another:

POSSESSION OF THE MEANS OF WORK—RAW MATERIAL, FACTORIES, MACHINERY—BY THE WORKING PEOPLE THEMSELVES. (*Labour Standard,* 7 May 1881)

8

CRITICS OF VICTORIAN SOCIETY

Only one of the four writers under this heading can be called a Socialist, but all of them had considerable influence on the development of the movement, especially in the period of revival in the last quarter of the century. Both Carlyle and Ruskin assailed the orthodox political economics and sought a more humane definition of wealth and value. Carlyle, a merciless critic of the industrial society that took shape in his time, preferred the closer ties of feudal society to the simple 'cash nexus' of the capitalist (a). His concept of a 'chivalry of labour' was paralleled by Ruskin's demand for the re-establishment of trade gilds (b and d)—a suggestion later taken up by the Guild Socialists.

Frederic Harrison, barrister and author, was an adherent of the Positivist philosophy of Auguste Comte. The lecture here quoted (c), which was delivered under the auspices of the London Trades Council, illustrates the Positivist influence on British Socialism, and especially on Fabianism. Harrison expounds the concept of a peaceful political revolution involving the abandonment of *laissez faire* and the extension of state control.

Finally, Edward Carpenter conveniently falls into this section because his contribution was an individual one, and because he avoided close association with any particular socialist group. Socialism for him was only part of a complete rejection of contemporary society in all its aspects. Following the example of Thoreau, he sought the simple life, and gave up a clerical fellowship at Trinity Hall, Cambridge, in order to work as a sandal-maker in a cottage some miles from Sheffield. His influence on many members of the Socialist groups of the end of the century, and especially of the I.L.P., was considerable. His best known work was a 'prose-poem' in the style of Walt Whitman, *Towards Democracy*, published in 1883.

(a) THOMAS CARLYLE. *Past and Present*

1843

STANDING on the threshold, nay as yet outside the threshold, of a 'Chivalry of Labour', and an immeasurable Future which it is to fill with fruitfulness and verdant shade; where so much has not yet come even to the rudimental state, and all speech of positive enactments were hazardous in those who know this business only by the eye,—let us here hint at simply one widest universal principle as the basis from which all organization hitherto has grown up among men, and all henceforth will have to grow: The principle of Permanent Contract instead of Temporary. . . .

The very horse that is permanent, how much kindlier do his rider and he work, than the temporary one, hired on any hack principle yet known! I am for permanence in all things, at the earliest possible moment, and to the latest possible. Blessed is he that continueth where he is. Here let us rest, and lay out seedfields; here let us learn to dwell. Here, even here, the orchards that we plant will yield us fruit; the acorns will be wood and pleasant umbrage, if we wait. How much grows everywhere, if we do but wait! Through the swamps we will shape causeways, force purifying drains; we will learn to thread the rocky inaccessibilities; and beaten tracks, worn smooth by mere travelling of human feet, will form themselves. Not a difficulty but can transfigure itself into a triumph; not even a deformity but, if our own soul have imprinted worth on it, will grow dear to us. The sunny plains and deep indigo transparent skies of Italy are all indifferent to the great sick heart of a Sir Walter Scott: on the back of the Appennines, in wild spring weather, the sight of bleak Scotch firs, and snow-spotted heath and desolation, brings tears into his eyes.

O unwise mortals that for ever change and shift, and say, Yonder, not Here! Wealth richer than both the Indies lies everywhere for man, if he will endure. Not his oaks only and his fruit-trees, his very heart roots itself wherever he will abide;—roots itself, draws nourishment from the deep fountains of Universal Being! Vagrant Sam-Slicks, who rove over the Earth doing 'strokes of trade', what wealth have they? Horseloads, shiploads of white or yellow metal; in very sooth, what *are* these? Slick rests nowhere, he is homeless. He can build stone or marble houses; but to continue in them is denied him. The wealth of a man is the number of things which he loves and blesses, which he is loved and blessed by! The herdsman in his poor clay shealing, where his very cow and dog are friends to him, and not a cataract but carries memories for him, and not a mountain-top but nods old recognition: his life, all encircled as in blessed mother's-arms, is it poorer than Slick's with the ass-loads of yellow metal on his back? Unhappy Slick! Alas, there has so much grown nomadic, apelike, with us: so much will have, with whatever pain, repugnance and 'impossibility', to alter itself, to fix itself again,—in some wise way, in any not delirious way!

A question arises here: Whether, in some ulterior, perhaps some not far-distant stage of this 'Chivalry of Labour', your Master-Worker may not find it possible, and needful, to grant his workers permanent *interest* in his enterprise and theirs. So that it become, in practical result, what in essential fact and justice it ever is, a joint enterprise; all men, from the Chief Master down to the lowest Overseer and Operative, economically as well as loyally concerned for it? —Which question I do not answer. The answer, near or else far, is perhaps, Yes;—and yet one knows the difficulties. Despotism is essential in most enterprises; I am told, they do not tolerate 'freedom of debate' on board a Seventy-four! Republican senate and *plebiscita* would not answer well in Cotton-Mills. And yet observe there too: Freedom, not nomad's or ape's Freedom, but man's Freedom; this is indispensable. We must have it and will have it! To reconcile Despotism with Freedom:—well, is that such a mystery? Do you not already know the way? It is to make your Despotism *just*. Rigorous as Destiny; but just too as Destiny and its laws. The Laws of God: all men obey these, and have no 'Freedom' at all but in obeying them. The way is already known, part of the way;—and courage and some qualities are needed for walking on it! (*Works*, 1857, *pp*. 286, 288–90)

(b) JOHN RUSKIN. *Political Economy of Art*

1857

SUPPOSING half a dozen or a dozen men were cast ashore from a wreck on an uninhabited island, and left to their own resources, one of course, according to his capacity, would be set to one business and one to another; the strongest to dig and cut wood, and to build huts for the rest; the most dexterous to make shoes out of bark and coats out of skins; the best educated to look for iron or lead in the rocks, and to plan the channels for the irrigation of the fields. But though their labours were thus naturally severed, that small group of shipwrecked men would understand well enough that the speediest progress was to be made by helping each other,—not by opposing each other: and they would know that this help could only be properly given so long as they were frank and open in their relations, and the difficulties which each lay under properly explained to the rest. So that any appearance of secrecy or separateness in the actions of any of them would instantly, and justly, be looked upon with suspicion by the rest, as the sign of some selfish or foolish proceeding on the part of the individual. If, for instance, the scientific man were found to have gone out at night, unknown to the rest, to alter the sluices, the others would think, and in all probability rightly think, that he wanted to get the best supply of water to his own field; and if the shoemaker refused to show them where the bark grew which he made the sandals of, they would naturally think, and in all probability rightly think, that he didn't want them to see how much there was of it, and that he meant to ask from them more corn and potatoes in exchange for his sandals than the trouble of making them deserved. And thus, although each man would have a portion of time to himself in which he was allowed to do what he chose without let or inquiry so long as he was working in that particular business which he had undertaken for the common benefit, any secrecy on his part would be immediately supposed to mean mischief; and would require to be accounted for, or put an end to: and this all the more because, whatever the work might be, certainly there would be difficulties about it which, when once they were well explained, might be more or less done away with by the help of the rest; so that assuredly everyone of them would advance with his labour not only more happily, but more profitably and quickly, by having no secrets, and by frankly bestowing, and frankly receiving, such help as lay in his way to get or to give.

And, just as the best and richest result of wealth and happiness to the whole of them would follow on their perseverance in such a system of frank communication and of helpful labour;—so precisely the worst and poorest result would be obtained by a system of secrecy and of enmity; and each man's happiness and wealth would assuredly be diminished in proportion to the degree in which jealousy and concealment became their social and economical principles. It would not, in the long run, bring good, but only evil, to the man of science, if, instead of telling openly where he had found good iron, he carefully concealed every new bed of it, that he might ask, in exchange for the rare ploughshare, more corn from the farmer, or in exchange for the rude needle, more labour from the sempstress: and it would not ultimately bring good, but only evil, to the farmers, if they sought to burn each other's cornstacks, that they might raise the value of their grain, or if the sempstresses tried to break each other's needles, that each might get all the stitching to herself.

Now, these laws of human action are precisely as authoritative in their application to the conduct of a million of men, as to that of six or twelve. All enmity, jealousy, opposition, and secrecy are wholly, and in all circumstances, destructive in their nature—not productive; and all kindness, fellowship, and communicativeness are invariably productive in their operation,—not destructive; and the evil principles of opposition and exclusiveness are not rendered less fatal, but more fatal, by their acceptance among large masses of men; more fatal, I say, exactly in proportion as their influence is more secret. For though the opposition does always its own simple, necessary, direct quantity of harm, and withdraws always its own simple, necessary, measurable quantity of wealth from the sum possessed by the community, yet, in proportion to the size of the community, it does another and more refined mischief than this, by concealing its own fatality under aspects of mercantile complication and expediency, and giving rise to multitudes of false theories based on a mean belief in narrow and immediate appearances of good done here and there by things which have the universal and everlasting nature of evil. So that the time and powers of the nation are wasted, not only in wretched struggling against each other, but in vain complaints, and groundless discouragements, and empty investigations, and useless experiments in laws, and elections, and inventions; with hope always to pull wisdom through some new-shaped slit in a ballot-box, and to drag prosperity down out of the clouds along some new knot of electric wire; while all the while Wisdom stands calling at the corners of the streets, and the blessing of Heaven waits ready to rain down upon us, deeper than the rivers and broader than the dew, if only we will obey the first plain principles of humanity, and the first plain precepts of the skies: "Execute true judgment, and show mercy and compassion, every man to his brother; and let none of you imagine evil against his brother in your heart".

Therefore, I believe most firmly, that as the laws of national prosperity get familiar to us, we shall more and more cast our toil into social and communicative systems; and that one of the first means of our doing so, will be the re-establishing guilds of every important trade in a vital, not formal, condition;—that there will be a great council or government house for the members of every trade, built in whatever town of the kingdom occupies itself principally in such trade, with minor council-halls in other cities; and to each council-hall, officers attached, whose first business may be to examine into the circumstances of every operative, in that trade, who chooses to report himself to them when out of work, and to set him to work, if he is indeed able and willing, at a fixed rate of wages, determined at regular periods in the council-meetings; and whose next duty may be to bring reports before the council of all improvements made in the business, and means of its extension: not allowing private patents of any kind, but making all improvements available to every member of the guild, only allotting, after successful trial of them, a certain reward to the inventors. (*Works*, vol. XI, 1880, *pp.* 115–21)

(c) FREDERIC HARRISON. *The Political Function of the Working Classes*

1868

I WOULD sum up in a word, the element which it is your part to bring into English politics—it is the Revolutionary element. Now I use this word in its true sense, not as meaning violence or anarchy, or disorder of any kind, but the vigorous adaptation of old social elements to new conditions. I say it deliberately, be in the true sense of the word Revolutionists. It is the want of our time. The materials of our whole social and political fabric have long been growing more and more disorganised. They are unworthy of their tasks. Let it be yours not to destroy them, or to ignore them—but to recast them. Question after question has been gathering up and waiting for its answer in vain. Church establishments, the work of education, the condition of the poor, the tenure of the land, the state of the rural labourer, the growth and incidence of taxation, the standing army, the whole framework and administration of law, the sanitary administration, the management of public works—these are all matters in which the whole machinery is used up. These great matters of public necessity are accumulating a burden of duties and of tasks to be performed. They cannot be touched but by a hand that cannot be resisted, and that will not be turned. They need swift, energetic, uncompromising efforts. There is not here any old-fashioned grievance to be rid of, it is not a chartered monopoly, or a bit of class privilege to be abolished. These were the tasks of the old times, and these were the triumphs, and the legitimate triumphs, of the parliaments of the past: our difficulties are those of construction, not of destruction. We have no mere nuisance to extinguish, but new and appropriate conditions to be found for deep and complicated diseases of the State. To deal with such is needed broad, comprehensive, deep-searching, yet rapid and potent remedies. Such changes in State policy are called revolutions—revolutions it may be most orderly, most beneficent, most moderate, but revolutions because effecting vast complex and permanent changes. And from whom can come such changes, if not from you? . . . .

You who have had practical experience of its results are not likely to be caught by the cant which is so dear to the commercial and a portion of the literary class, the cant about self-government and non-legislation. . . . Local self-government, as at present practised, is but too often local oppression and local fraud. From the nature of the thing it must fall into the hands of pushing men of capital and business. You have enough to do in dealing with them in your private relations with them. Beware of entrusting them with the absolute control over the building of your cities, the protection of your health, with the maintenance of your poor and your infirm, with the management of your public works. For real and efficient control over this, look to the State. Fear not over-legislation. The name of local self-government stands but too often for local mis-government and local no-government. Far better to have one incapable ruler, than fifty incapable rulers. From the State at least you can expect a higher experience and skill, national publicity, greater concentration of power, a more Imperial aim and spirit, and far more responsibility.

Still less is it likely that you will be deluded by the strange paradox of some minds, the grand principle of no-government. Keep order they say, and leave everything else to unrestricted competition and self-management. Leave the weak at the mercy of the strong, leave the ignorant to teach themselves, leave the pauper to feed himself, leave the holders of privileges the free enjoyment of their rights, leave the administration of justice in its time-honoured confusion, leave Ireland to starve and rebel, rebel and starve, leave the peasant in his misery, leave every one who profits by a corrupt system to make the most of it for himself. It is not true that everything which has to be removed by legislation is already destroyed. Our system is most artificial, every side of it is the creation of old class-law. We live in a perfect network of legislative trammels which the past has imposed upon the present; trammels the most obvious parts of which have been thrown off by the middle class themselves; whilst the parts which reach down to the depths of society have still to be examined and recast. (*pp.* 12–15)

(d) JOHN RUSKIN. *To the Trades Unions of England*

1880

Now I write to you, observe, without knowing, except in the vaguest way, who you *are*!—what trades you belong to, what arts or crafts you practise—or what ranks of workmen you include, and what manner of idlers you exclude. I have no time to make out the different sets into which you fall, or the different interests by which you are guided. But I know perfectly well what sets you *should* fall into, and by what interests you *should* be guided. And you will find your profit in listening while I explain these to you somewhat more clearly than your penny-a-paragraph liberal papers will.

In the first place, what business have you to call yourselves only *Trade* Guilds, as if 'trade', and not production, were your main concern? Are you by profession nothing more than pedlars and mongers of things, or are you also makers of things?

It is true that in our City wards our chapmen have become the only dignitaries—and we have the Merchant-

Tailors' Company, but not the plain Tailors'; and the Fishmongers' Company, but not the Fishermen's; and the Vintners' Company, but not the Vinedressers'; and the Ironmongers' Company, but not the Blacksmiths'; while, though, for one apparent exception, the Goldsmiths' Company proclaims itself for masters of a craft, what proportion, think you, does its honour bear compared with that of the Calf-worshipful Guild of the Gold Mongers?

Be it far from me to speak scornfully of trade. My Father—whose Charter of Freedom of London Town I keep in my Brantwood treasury beside missal and cross—sold good wine, and had, over his modest door in Billiter Street, no bush. But he grew his wine, before he sold it; and could answer for it with his head, that no rotten grapes fermented in his vats, and no chemist's salt effervesced in his bottles. Be you also Tradesmen—in your place—and in your right; but be you, primarily, Growers, Makers, Artificers, Inventors, of things good and precious. What talk you of Wages? Whose is the Wealth of the World but yours? Whose is the Virtue? Do you mean to go on for ever, leaving your wealth to be consumed by the idle, and your virtue to be mocked by the vile?

The wealth of the world is yours; even your common rant and rabble of economists tell you that—"no wealth without industry." Who robs you of it, then, or beguiles you? Whose fault is it, you clothmakers, that any English child is in rags? Whose fault is it, you shoemakers, that the street harlots mince in high-heeled shoes, and your own babes paddle barefoot in the street slime? Whose fault is it, you bronzed husbandmen, that through all your furrowed England, children are dying of famine? Primarily, of course, it is your clergymen's and masters' fault: but also in this your own, that you never educate any of your children with the earnest object of enabling them to see their way out of this, not by rising above their father's business, but by setting in order what was amiss in it: also is this your own, that none of you who do rise above your business, ever seem to keep the memory of what wrong they have known, or suffered; nor, as masters, set a better example than others.

Your own fault, at all events, it will be now, seeing that you have got Parliamentary power in your hands, if you cannot use it better than the moribund Parliamentary body has done hitherto.

To which end, I beg you first to take these following truths into your good consideration.

First. Men don't and can't live by exchanging articles, but by producing them. They don't live by trade, but by work. Give up that foolish and vain title of Trades Unions; and take that of Labourers' Unions.

And, whatever divisions chance or special need may have thrown you into at present, remember there are essential and eternal divisions of the Labour of man, into which you *must* practically fall, whether you like it or not; and these eternal classifications it would be infinitely better if you at once acknowledged in thought, name, and harmonious action. Several of the classes may take finer divisions in their own body, but you will find the massive general structure of working humanity range itself under these following heads, the first eighteen assuredly essential; the three last making twenty-one altogether, I shall be able, I think, to prove to you are not superfluous:—suffer their association with the rest in the meantime.

1. Shepherds.
2. Fishermen.
3. Ploughmen.
4. Gardeners.
5. Carpenters and Woodmen.
6. Builders and Quarrymen.
7. Shipwrights.

8. Smiths and Miners.
9. Bakers and Millers.
10. Vintners.
11. Graziers and Butchers.
12. Spinners.
13. Linen and Cotton-workers.
14. Silk-workers.
15. Woollen-workers.
16. Tanners and Furriers.
17. Tailors and Milliners.
18. Shoemakers.
19. Musicians.
20. Painters.
21. Goldsmiths.

Get these eighteen, or twenty-one, as you like to take them, each thoroughly organised, proud of their work, and doing it under masters, if any, of their own rank, chosen for their sagacity and vigour, and the world is yours, and all the pleasures of it, that are true; while all false pleasures in such a life fall transparent, and the hooks are seen through the baits of them. (Ruskin, *Fors Clavigera*, vol. 8, *pp*. 138–42)

(e) EDWARD CARPENTER. *Desirable Mansions*

1883

... THERE was a time when the rich man had duties attending his wealth. The lord or baron was a petty king and had kingly responsibilities as well as power. The Sir Roger, of Addison's time, was the succeeding type of landlord. And even to the present day there lingers here and there a country squire who fulfils that now antiquated ideal of kindly condescension and patronage. But the modern rush of steam engines, and the creation of an enormous class of wealthy folk living on stocks, have completely subverted the old order. It has let loose on society a horde of wolves! — a horde of people who have no duties attaching to their mode of life, no responsibility. They roam hither and thither, seeking whom and what they may devour. Personally I have no objection to criminals, and think them quite as good as myself. But, Talk of criminal classes—can there be a doubt that the criminal classes in our modern society are this horde of stock and share-mongers? If to be a criminal is to be an enemy of society, then they are such. For their mode of life is founded on the principle of taking without giving, of claiming without earning—as much as that of any common thief. It is in vain to try and make amends for this by charity organisations and unpaid magistracies. The cure must go deeper. It it no good trying to set straight the roof and chimneys, when the whole foundation is aslant. These good people are not boarded and lodged at Her Majesty's pleasure, but the Eternal Justice, unslumbering, causes them to build prisons (as I have said) for themselves—plagues them with ill-health and divers unseen evils—and will and must plague them, till such time as they shall abandon the impossible task they have set themselves, and return to the paths of reason.

The whole foundation is aslant—and aslip, as anyone may see who looks. In short, it is an age of transition. No mortal power could make durable a society founded on Usury—universal and boundless Usury. The very words scream at each other. The baron has passed away; and the landlord is passing. They each had their duties, and while they fulfilled them served their time well enough. The shareholder has no duties, and is an excrescence on the world, a public pest; and will remain so until the final landslip, when, the foundations having given completely away, he will crawl forth out of the ruins of his desirable mansion into the life and light of a new day.

Less oracular than this one may not be! As I have said before, there is no conceivable condition of life in which the human soul may not find the materials of its surpassing deliverance from evil and mortality. And I for one would not, if I had the power, cramp human life into the exhibition of one universal routine. If anyone desires to be rich, if anyone desires to gradually shut himself off from the world, to build walls and fences, to live in a house where it is impossible to get a breath of fresh air without going through half a dozen doors, and to be the prisoner of his own servants; if he desires it so that when he walks down the street he cannot whistle or sing, or shout across the road to a friend, or sit upon a doorstep when tired, or take off his coat if it be hot, but must wear certain particular clothes in a certain particular way, and be on such pins and needles as to what he may or may not do, that he is right glad when he gets back again to his own prison walls; if he loves trusteeships and Egyptian bonds, and visits from the lawyer, and feels glad when he finds a letter from the High Court of Chancery on his breakfast table, and experiences in attending to all these things that satisfaction which comes of all solid work; if he feels renovated and braced by lying in bed of a morning, and by eating feast dinners every day, and by carefully abstaining from any bodily labour; if dyspepsia and gout and biliousness are not otherwise than grateful to him; and if he can obtain all these things without doing grievous wrong to others, by all means let him have them.

Only for those who do not know what they desire I would lift up the red flag of warning. Only of that vast and ever vaster horde which to-day (chiefly, I cannot but think, in ignorance) rushes to Stocks, would I ask a moment's pause, and to look at the bare facts. If these words should come to the eye of such an one I would pray to him to think for a moment—to glance at this great enthroned Wrong in its dungeon palace (not the less a wrong because the laws countenance and encourage it)—to listen for the cry of the homeless many, trodden under foot, a yearly sacrifice to it—to watch the self-inflicted sufferings of its worshippers, the ennui, the depression, the unlovely faces of ill-health—to observe the falsehood, on which it is founded, and therefore the falsehood, the futility, the unbelief in God or man which spring out of it—and to turn away, determined, as far as in him lies, to worship in that Dagon-house no longer. (Carpenter, *England's Ideal*, 1906, *pp.* 91–4)

9

SOCIAL-DEMOCRATIC FEDERATION

In 1881 the Democratic Federation was founded in London to unite working-class Radicalism in opposition to the Liberal Government's policy of coercion in Ireland, and to counter-balance the National Liberal Federation controlled by Chamberlain. It was 'captured' for Socialism by H. M. Hyndman, a London city man who had travelled widely in America and the East and had read Marx's *Capital* in the French edition. Hyndman's *England for All* (a), was his first Socialist work: he distributed it to those who attended the foundation conference of the Democratic Federation in 1881. His failure openly to acknowledge his debt to Marx in this work caused a rift between him and his master; and he was regarded by both Marx and Engels as a chauvinist with an imperfect knowledge of the true doctrine.

Nevertheless, it was Hyndman's tireless propaganda which really introduced Marxism to the British people. In 1883 he succeeded in making the Democratic Federation adopt a Socialist programme (b), and in the following year he had the body renamed the Social-Democratic Federation. Among his supporters at this time was an ex-army officer, H. H. Champion, who became the Federation's secretary and one of its ablest propagandists (c). Champion's exposition of Surplus Value, though based directly on Marx, bears a striking resemblance to the passage in Charles Hall already quoted, written eighty years before (Id, above). Hyndman's public debates with prominent Radicals such as Charles Bradlaugh and the American land reformer Henry George (d) were also effective in publicising the new doctrine.

However, the tactics of the S.D.F. under Hyndman's leadership lacked the flexibility of Marx and Engels, who were for co-operating with the trade unions and other working-class bodies without imposing any shibboleth of theory upon them, at least in the early stages of Socialist propaganda. Consequently Engels, who lived on in London for twelve years after Marx's death in 1883, did not support Hyndman's group but preferred to work through rival organisations—first the Socialist League, and then the I.L.P.

One of the few British Socialists to have some understanding of Dialectical Materialism was Belfort Bax (e), who had picked up a good knowledge of German philosophy while in Berlin as a journalist and who, though friendly with Engels and for a time a member of the Socialist League, returned to the S.D.F. after the failure of the League.

The last extract in this section illustrates the attitude of the S.D.F. to the problems of foreign policy (f). Harry Quelch, one of Hyndman's most loyal supporters, was a self-educated labourer who was for a long time employed in running the S.D.F.'s journal, *Justice*. He died in 1913, almost a year before the outbreak of war, but would no doubt have supported the allied cause, as Hyndman did.

(a) H. M. HYNDMAN. *England for All: the Textbook of Democracy*

1881

MEN who are now deprived of the fruits of their labour, who live under bad social conditions, who are forced to resort to scamped work and adulterated manufacture in order that their employers may make a profit, would feel very differently if for their honest labour embodied in sound goods they could obtain a rightful return themselves. The magic of property would then be felt in the general as well as the individual improvement. That industry will always have the better of laziness, that thrift must be more beneficial than extravagance, are truths which no political or social changes can shake. But as we stand, our laws and customs are directly calculated to foster excessive wealth on the one side and miserable poverty on the other. What wonder that the people should begin to ask themselves the why and the wherefore of all this disparity between the men who work and those who use them? None are more ready to pay for mental toil than those who work with their hands, none more ready to give up a portion of their labour for the benefit of their fellows. Now, however, the perpetual conflict of wages, the strife with capital, where the possibility of final success is pushed farther and farther into the distance, necessarily blunts that feeling of national greatness in the best sense which does so much to sweep away, even as it is, the meanness engendered by mere narrowness and greed. Those who are never certain of continuous employment, and have little time left for education, might well be pardoned if they thought only of their own selfish interests. That in the mass they do not do so, is the best hope for the future.

But in coming changes it behoves us to be careful, lest, in getting rid of the excessive influence of one dominant class, we do but strengthen the power of a meaner and a worse one in its place. If possession of land—as all reformers agree—should be regulated in the interests of the country in time to come, so also must capital, machinery, and the national highways. Conservatism has come to mean the dominance of landowners: Liberalism has been degraded to the service of capitalists. There is little perhaps to choose; but for the people it is to the full as important in the future that capital should be controlled as the land. Mere destruction for its own sake is not in accordance with the views of Englishmen. To pull down a system, however bad, they must see that something is ready to take its place. The infinite mischiefs of capitalism must be removed as a better method of production grows up from below. We have sad experience that our so-called individual liberty means too often only the development of monopoly and the tyranny of wealth. But that faculty of organization, that ingenuity in turning science and invention to account, may as well be used in the service of the many as to the selfish gratification of personal desires. There is room enough for the use of the highest powers, without the perpetual money-getting now in the ascendant. No man can live out of the current of his age; but it is time that a higher ideal were placed before the nation, and that the common sense of the community at large should save the next generation from the power of oppression now accorded to a system which develops in those who handle it neither foresight, patriotism, nor honesty. The very tendency of capital itself renders this essential. Each year sees it rolling up into larger and larger masses. The great joint-stock enterprises, where enormous capital is obtained from many contributors, gradually crush out smaller houses; large emporiums undersell small; large factories dwarf smaller. With this increase too, the personal relation between employers and employed ceases, and powerful corporations begin to assert themselves as a political influence solely for selfish ends, and with the cold persistence and disregard for human interests which such associations invariably display. England, the greatest capitalist country, may well show the world how to take order with this dangerous growth which threatens to overshadow human progress, and regulate without injustice those purely selfish motives which hitherto have been looked to as the sole hope of advance in civilization. (*pp.* 85–7)

(b) *Democratic Federation. Socialism Made Plain*

1883

Fellow Citizens, we of the Democratic Federation demand complete adult suffrage for every man and woman in these islands, because in this way alone can the whole people give free expression to their will; we are in favour of paid delegates and annual Conventions because by this means alone can the people control their representatives; we stand up for the direct reference of all grave issues to the country at large, and for the punishment as felony of every species of corruption, because thus only can tyranny be checked and bribery uprooted; we call for the abolition of all hereditary authority, because such authority is necessarily independent of the mass of the people. But all these reforms when secured mean only that the men and women of these islands will at length be masters in their own house. Mere political machinery is worthless unless used to produce good social conditions.

All wealth is due to labour; therefore to the labourers all wealth is due.

But we are strangers in our own country. Thirty thousand persons own the land of Great Britain against the 30,000,000 who are suffered to exist therein. A long series of robberies and confiscations has deprived us of the soil which should be ours. The organised brute force of the few has for generations robbed and tyrannised over the unorganised brute force of the many. We now call for Nationalisation of the Land. We claim that Land in country and land in towns, mines, parks, mountains, moors should be owned by the people, for the people, to be held, used, built over and cultivated upon such terms as the people themselves see fit to ordain. The handful of marauders who now hold possession have and can have no right save brute force against the tens of millions whom they wrong.

But private ownership of Land in our present society is only one and not the worst form of monopoly which enables the wealthy classes to use the means of production against the labourers whom they enslave. Of the £1,000,000,000 taken by the classes who live without labour out of a total yearly production of £1,300,000,000, the landlords who have seized our soil, and shut us from its enjoyment, absorb little more than £60,000,000 as their direct share. The few thousand persons who own the National Debt, saddled upon the community by a landlord Parliament, exact £28,000,000 yearly from the labour of their countrymen for nothing; the shareholders who have been allowed to lay hands upon our great railway communications take a still larger sum. Above all, the active capitalist class, the loan-mongers, the farmers, the mine-exploiters, the contractors, the middlemen, the factory-lords—these, the modern slave-drivers, these are they who, through their money, machinery, capital, and credit turn every advance in human knowledge, every further improvement in human dexterity, into an engine for accumulating wealth out of other men's labour, and for exacting more and yet more surplus value out of the wage-slaves whom they employ. So long as the means of production, either of raw materials or of manufactured goods are the monopoly of a class, so long must the labourers on the farm, in the mine or in the factory sell themselves for a bare subsistence wage. As land must in future be a national possession, so must the other means of producing and distributing wealth. The creation of wealth is already a social business, where each is forced to co-operate with his neighbour; it is high time that exchange of the produce should be social too, and removed from the control of individual greed and individual profit.

As stepping-stones to a happier period, we urge for immediate adoption:—

The COMPULSORY CONSTRUCTION of healthy artisans' and agricultural labourers' dwellings in proportion to the population, such dwellings to be let at rents to cover the cost of construction and maintenance alone.

FREE COMPULSORY EDUCATION for all classes, together with the provision of at least one wholesome meal a day in each school.

EIGHT HOURS or less to be the normal WORKING DAY in all trades.

CUMULATIVE TAXATION upon all incomes above a fixed minimum not exceeding £300 a year.

STATE APPROPRIATION OF RAILWAYS, with or without compensation.

The establishment of NATIONAL BANKS, which shall absorb all private institutions that derive a profit from operations in money or credit.

RAPID EXTINCTION of the NATIONAL DEBT.

NATIONALISATION OF THE LAND, and organisation of agricultural and industrial armies under State control on co-operative principles.

By these measures a healthy, independent, and thoroughly educated people will steadily grow up around us, ready to abandon that baneful competition for starvation wages which ruins our present workers, ready to organise the labour of each for the benefit of all, determined, too, to take control finally of the entire social and political machinery of a State in which class distinctions and class privileges shall cease to be. (*pp.* 3*f.*)

(c) H. H. CHAMPION. *Surplus Value: for Workers who are not Socialists*

1884

How is it that idle, rich people ever get hold of this money at all? Why do they, instead of someone else, have the spending or investing of it? They get it in one of two ways. As a return for money invested either in land—that is, rent—or in some undertaking in which labour is employed—that is, interest on capital. Just think if there is any other way in which a man who does not work gets an income—a rich man, I mean. We all know that a poor man who gets a living without work must be either a pauper or a thief.

. . . You can easily see who pays the rent, because you yourself have to pay it every week out of your earnings. It is not quite so easy to see who pays the interest. The landlords take part of your wage and live on it. The capitalists don't take their share out of your earnings after they have been paid to you; they keep it back before your wages are paid. So to what you pay for nothing in the shape of rent you must add the amount of wealth you create by your work over and above the amount you get in wages: and the total will show you how much work you do for nothing, how much unpaid labour you have performed—in fact, how much "surplus value" you have created.

How do I know that there is any "surplus value", any unpaid wages? Look at it this way. You all work at different trades, either in producing raw materials, such as iron, corn, or leather, or else in working them up, making hammers, loaves, or boots. Now the cost of the corn is the labour of the labourer who ploughs, sows, or reaps. The cost of the loaf is the cost of the corn added to the labour of the workmen who grind, knead, and bake it. So with hammers and boots. Their cost is the labour of the men who raise and smelt the ore, and forge the hammer, and of those who raise the cattle, tan and dress the leather, and make it into boots. This is the cost of production, and the amount the working class gets is the wages of these workmen. But when you want to buy loaf, hammer, boots, anything, in fact, what have you to pay? You know very well. You pay the cost of the labour which goes to others of the working class, and on top of that you have to pay all that goes to form the income of everyone who is not a producer. If you don't thus provide the income of the landlords and capitalists, where does it come from? Their income is not so many pieces of metal; those are only symbols, it is the food, clothing, and other things they use up. If they do not make these things they consume, somebody does. If they do not make anything in return for these things, clearly the somebody who does make them does not get any return for doing so. In fact, for that amount of work they do not get any wages, and this is the unpaid labour, the "surplus value" which the idle get.

What is the amount? If you could find out exactly how much wealth is produced every year in this country, and take from that the amount of wealth consumed by the working class, you could find out how much wealth you as a class produce every year for nothing. This is not easy to do: but you can see for yourselves, by looking round you, that it is not only the amount consumed by the Royal Family, or the aristocracy, or the perpetual pensioners, or the landowners, but the total absorbed by the whole of the leisure classes, and by those who work only for them. The whole of the inhabitants of the wealthy districts and the big squares live on your unpaid labour, not the rich man only, but his family, his servants, his wife's maids, his children's governess, his son's schoolmaster, the parson of his church, his dentist. Every man in this kingdom who is rich enough to give away money in charity is only giving as a favour what he has got because you were not paid for so many hours' work. Every man who wears a clean shirt every day and calls you the great unwashed pays his laundress with your wages.

If you don't think the total amount worth talking about, take a walk through West London on the next Bank Holiday. Look and see if the amount of labour you do without pay is not so great that if you only did half of it, and were paid for it, you as a class would have plenty of leisure, and no longer suffer from under-feeding and over-crowding. Then you will see that so far from it being an advantage to you that the idle rich should employ you to provide them with all that you so much want yourselves, all that they do is to live on your unpaid labour, and that as long as this system of "surplus value" goes on, there must be disease and poverty, vice and crime, amongst your own class, and in your own families. (*Christian Socialist*, March 1884)

(d) H. M. HYNDMAN. Debate with Henry George, St. James's Hall

2nd July, 1889

. . . Mr. George agrees with us that capital is rolling up into larger and larger masses, and if he would only look at home in his own country he would find that this is one of the principal reasons of the number of the unemployed whom he himself has seen around in the streets of San Francisco, as I did myself in 1870 on the Sand Lots. The great factory farms are directed and worked it may be by 500 men in the summer and ten in the winter. Where do the 490 go? They are a body of men discharged to find labour where they can. A new machine is introduced into any department of industry which ought to be useful and beneficial to the whole community. The result under present conditions is that men are thrown out on the streets as unskilled labourers, while greater wealth is produced with fewer hands, and the capitalist alone benefits by that monopoly which the machinery gives him. (Applause.) Mr. George says in some parts of his works that he is in favour of taking over all the monoplies by the State. Very well, then. The State, if controlled by the people, is not therefore, such a hideous enemy after all. (Hear, hear.) The State to-day controlled by the landlords and capitalists is an enemy to the whole people, and I maintain that even the middle-class themselves and the well-to-do are stunted in their faculties and their power of enjoying life by the miserable system we have to labour under. (Cheers.) If, then, this concentration of the means of production in fewer and fewer hands, if the rolling up of capital into larger and larger masses, renders it more and more impossible for an individual man to come to the front as Mr. George says in *Social Problems* it does, then, as a matter of fact, you have to deal with these larger and larger growths of capital even before you touch the land. We Social Democrats do not claim to be filled with any divine afflatus. We do not believe in any utopia come down from above. But we build up our ideas from the facts we see under our eyes every day. (Applause.) What do we see at the present time? We see that in this very capitalist system which, based on the devil-take-the-hindmost for the many and economic harmonies for the few, the capitalists themselves are eating up one another, and that the present system means monopoly in every direction. You have the salt "ring" you have the copper "ring" this "ring" and that; and especially on Mr. George's side of the Atlantic. Such "rings" are being organised every day, not "rings" in relation to the land only, but "rings" in relation to every department of manufacture. (Hear, hear.) These rings crush the worker far more than the initial monopoly of the land. (Applause.) Further than this, we see that it is impossible under present conditions speedily to nationalise or communalise that which has not already passed into the company form. I do not say that in countries where you have the communal system still surviving, as for instance in Russia, it may not be possible to pass direct into a higher and more elevated form of it. But here, in this country, circumstances are altogether different, and the industries must pass through the company form. The present system need not have been accompanied by the horrors it has been, but being historically inevitable it is working out its complete evolution. At the present moment the capitalist class has proclaimed its own bankruptcy. The landlord after all, in this country, and even in America, is but a sleeping partner in the process of expropriation which is carried on at the expense of the workers. (Cheers.) If you kill the sleeping partner and leave the active one at work what the better are you? (Hear, hear.) We say look at the facts around you. Look at the great railway organisations. This is not a question of the wages of superintendence. The manager of a railway is paid at the outside £3,000 or £4,000 a year; the manager of the London and Westminster Bank is paid at the outside £3,000 or £4,000 a year; the managers of the coal companies, as of other rings, are paid at the outside a few thousands a year. But those who never superintend anything, those who can roam about the Mediterranean superintending nothing, but consume an enormous deal, take the lion's share. Then I ask you this, Mr. Chairman and fellow-citizens, even from the ethical point of view, if you are going, as a matter of fact, to tax income from land, why not tax income from all robbery of labour? Why not put a stop to that confiscation of labour which makes the mass of the people mere slaves in the hands of the few? Social Democrats assert that the poverty and misery to-day are the necessary result of the capitalist system, and if Mr. George's Single Tax were applied our principles would have to be taken into consideration before one human being who works for his living would be in any way benefited. These principles which I advocate are spreading throughout the length and breadth of our land, not merely as the result of our agitation, not merely owing to the misery and poverty that exists, but in accordance with the natural evolution of society, and when they triumph, as they most assuredly will, the establishment of Social Democracy will give the fullest outlet to every man and woman. I say that Mr. George as he stands on this platform is a reactionary and not a revolutionist. (Cheers.) I say that we should combine together in order to work for the co-operative organisation of society in which the railways, the mines, the machines which at present dominate the worker, shall be the handmaid of labour, and where labour shall have its full reward and the mental capacity, the physical power and the health of the people their full development—a condition of things now easily within our reach, but such as the world has never yet seen. (Loud applause.) (Report entitled *Single Tax versus Social Democracy*, 1889, *pp.* 10–12)

(e) E. BELFORT BAX. *Men versus Classes*

1889

How, then, it may be said, if we admit class-feeling to be that element in the modern character in which its worst and anti-social features are embodied, can we make the accentuation and exacerbation of class-feeling the starting point for a social reconstruction in which classes shall be abolished? Is not the attitude of the benevolent old gentleman who says, let us ignore classes, let us regard each other as human beings, more consonant with what we have been saying? We answer no, if we are to deal with facts and not with phrases. Classes exist; you may ignore them, but they will exist still with the respective characters they engender. Though you ignore them they will not ignore you. The difference between the Socialist and the benevolent bourgeois Radical in their respective crusades against classes is, that while the one would affirm the form of class-distinction, knowing that thereby the reality of class-distinction will be negated, the other, though ostentatiously denying the form of class-distinction, would affirm the content or reality of class-distinction, inasmuch as he would leave it untouched. He thinks to get rid of class-instincts while maintaining classes. To be rid of classes, the possessing and expropriating class must be itself expropriated of its power of expropriating—in other words, of that control of the instruments of production by which its class-character is maintained, when it will disappear together with its correlate, the possessed and expropriated class.

It is not true, as might at first sight be supposed, that the political class-feeling of the Socialist workman is the mere anti-social class-feeling of the ordinary proletarian (*lumpen proletarier*) or of the mere blood-thirsty Anarchist. The class-feeling of the former is a class-feeling with a difference. It is a class-feeling that has already negated itself; otherwise expressed it is human feeling in a class guise. The Socialist workman's conscious end and aspiration is the annihilation of classes, with the class-element in character. He knows well enough that his classhood places him at a disadvantage. He knows that the fact of his belonging to an oppressed class is an insuperable obstacle to the development of the best within him; just as the middle class Socialist knows that the fact of his belonging to an oppressing class is equally an obstacle to the development of his nobler qualities. Mere class-instinct which *per se* is necessarily anti-social, can never give us Socialism. That is why the most degraded section of the proletariat are, to a large extent, useless for the Cause of Socialism. Their lower class-instincts are incapable of being purified of their grosser elements, and transformed into that higher instinct which, though on its face it has the impress of a class, is in its essence above and beyond class; which sees in the immediate triumph of class merely a means to the ultimate realisation of a purely human Society, in which class has disappeared. With those who have attained to this instinct, classhood or class-interest has become identical with humanity or human interests. In the Socialist workman the class-instinct has become transformed into the conviction that, in the words of Lassalle, " he is called to raise the principle of his class into the principle of the age ". He knows that in the moment of victory—of the realisation of the dominion of his class—the ugly head of class itself must fall, and Society emerge. Militant, his cause is identified with class; triumphant, with Humanity.

Meanwhile, we who live to-day, who are the off-spring of a class-society, and who breathe the atmosphere of a class-society, bear ineradically the mark of the class-demon upon us. It is engrained in our characters. Even among Socialists, where its grosser features are toned down or obliterated, it shows itself ever and anon. It is only a question of more or less. In no human being born in a class Society can the class-element be altogether absent from his character. In the best working-class Socialist there is a strain of possible brutality. In the best middle-class Socialist there is a strain of possible snobbishness. Meanwhile, we know that these things endure but for a day. We may, therefore, take heart of grace. After one more decisive affirmation of class-interest, we may expect to see the end of *Classes* (with their hypocritical vulgarity on the one side and their servile brutality on the other) and the beginning of *Men*. (Bax, *Ethics of Socialism*, 1889, *pp*. 103–5)

(f) HARRY QUELCH. *Socialism and Foreign Affairs*

1912

CONVINCED internationalists as we are, recognizing that, theoretically, there is no cause of quarrel between the workers of the world; that the proletarian has no country to fight for, and therefore no occasion to fight—we must recognize that as a matter of fact humanity is at present divided into different nationalities with conflicting interests. To us, with our deep conviction that the only thing that matters is the class war, and our eagerness to fight that war to a finish, these other divisions and conflicting interests may appear absurd and puerile. They are certainly irritating; but nevertheless they are there as facts to be reckoned with. However true, theoretically, it may be to say that the proletarian has no part nor lot in these national concerns, he finds that in spite of himself he is bound up with them; and, frequently, more closely bound up with them than are his masters. It is true that they may have property in the State—" a stake in the country "—while he has none. But that very fact ties him to a particular country, and gives him a keener interest in the conditions of existence there—economic, political, and social—than is felt by his masters, who, by the possession of property, are able to make their home where they please and to remove themselves from any country or district, which for any reason may not be to their liking. He, poor devil, has frequently no choice.

In the same way we say that the interests of the capitalist class and those of the working class are diametrically opposed to each other. That is perfectly true, and yet how often it happens that the interests, the vital interests, the very existence, of a number of workpeople may be entirely bound up with the interests of a single employer. This fact, indeed, is one of the very worst features of the capitalist system, or of any other system of slavery in which the well-being or otherwise of the great mass of the people does not depend upon their own industry or idleness, their own capacity or lack of it, but upon the honesty, ability, enterprise, judgment or caprice of others.

In present circumstances, therefore, however objectionable it may be to us, the fact is that proletarian interests in the different countries are, in many relations, bound up with the national interests. The proletarian of every country has not less but more interest than the plutocrat in the maintenance and development of democratic institutions, in the maintenance of personal liberty, of national autonomy, of civic rights, and of a high minimum standard of comfort. These are of small moment to the master class, because they are the master class; to the proletariat they are of vital moment, because it is only by these means that they can peaceably achieve their emancipation. Without carrying further, at present, the academic controversy between Bax and myself as to what constitutes a nation, I submit here that, in the main, we have, for practical purposes, to take the present grouping of peoples in Europe as a working basis, and to recognize that willy-nilly there is, as a rule, in each national group, in spite of all differences, certain principles which bind together as a nation those within that group, and that, with certain exceptions, all those in each group, notwithstanding personal, class, and other antagonisms, are bound together by a common interest to defend the national autonomy and the right of each nationality to be free to work out its own salvation.

These facts, it appears to me, are self-evident. Assuming that to be the case, and reasoning from these facts we come to this : that each national group must have a foreign policy; that is, a policy by which its relations with other groups are guided and determined. In this foreign policy all classes in a given nation are interested; but it depends upon the extent to which that policy is influenced by one class or another whether capitalist or proletarian interests have the greater weight and influence in that policy. So far the former, of course, in all European countries have been paramount. That fact has had mischievous consequences, but that result only proves, once more, that we, as Socialists, and on behalf of the working class, are, after all, vitally concerned with the question of foreign policy. (Quelch, *Literary Remains*, 1914, *pp.* 250–2)

10

SOCIALIST LEAGUE

William Morris, the founder of the Socialist League, accepted Marxian Socialism in its entirety, and grappled bravely with its economic theory, which he nevertheless found "dreary". He found it impossible to continue in the Democratic Federation with the domineering personality of Hyndman: and at the end of 1884 a crisis, partly personal, partly political, led to the secession of Morris and a mixed band of supporters to found the Socialist League. These supporters consisted of the Marx-Engels family group; a working-class group of East London who veered towards Anarchism; and a few personal friends and admirers of Morris himself. Morris's Socialism shows the influence of his experience as an artist and craftsman. He took from Ruskin the idea that the medieval gild gave the craftsman a better opportunity to express his skill and to enjoy his work. He believed that educational work for Socialism was more important than immediate political action, and his ideal was a community in which the State has truly withered away—as is apparent from his utopian romance *News from Nowhere* (1889) which he wrote as an answer to the rather mechanical nationalisation schemes of the American Edward Bellamy. Morris's hostility to the Hyndmanite conception of State Socialism is clear in the opening manifesto of the League, which he drafted (a); but he was not an outright Anarchist, and he was much worried by the conflict which developed inside the League between the Marxists and the Anarchists, the latter being under the lead of Joseph Lane, a working man who had run a "Labour Emancipation League" in East London for some years (b). Morris's attitude to Anarchism is indicated clearly in the second of his four letters to the Rev. George Bainton (c), in which he explained his political standpoint most fully. When finally the Anarchists won control, Morris retired from the League (1890) which rapidly disintegrated after the withdrawal of his prestige and financial support. He continued Socialist propaganda work in the Hammersmith Socialist Society, which consisted of those in London who remained loyal to his personal leadership. The lecture on Communism which is here quoted (d) was delivered during this last phase of his life: he died in 1896.

(a) *Socialist League.* Manifesto issued by the Provisional Council

1885

WHAT remedy, then, do we propose for this failure of our civilisation, which is now admitted by all thoughtful people?

We have already shown that the workers, although they produce all the wealth of society, have no control over its production or distribution: the *people,* who are the only really organic part of society, are treated as a mere appendage to capital—as a part of its machinery. This must be altered from the foundation: the land, the capital, the machinery, factories, workshops, stores, means of transit, mines, banking, all means of production and distribution of wealth, must be declared and treated as the common property of all. Every man will then receive the full value of his labour, without deduction for the profit of a master, and as all will have to work, and the waste now incurred by the pursuit of profit will be at an end, the amount of labour necessary for every individual to perform in order to carry on the essential work of the world will be reduced to something like two or three hours daily; so that everyone will have abundant leisure for following intellectual or other pursuits congenial to his nature.

This change in the method of production and distribution would enable everyone to live decently, and free from the sordid anxieties for daily livelihood which at present weigh so heavily on the greatest part of mankind.

But, moreover, men's social and moral relations would be seriously modified by this gain of economical freedom, and by the collapse of the superstitions, moral and other, which necessarily accompany a state of economical slavery: the test of duty would now rest on the fulfilment of clear and well-defined obligations to the community rather than on the moulding of the individual character and actions to some preconceived standard outside social responsibilities. . . .

As to mere politics, Absolutism, Constitutionalism, Republicanism, have all been tried in our day and under our present social system, and all have alike failed in dealing with the real evils of life.

Nor, on the other hand, will certain incomplete schemes of social reform now before the public solve the question.

Co-operation so-called—that is, competitive co-operation for profit—would merely increase the number of small joint-stock capitalists, under the mask of creating an aristocracy of labour, while it would intensify the severity of labour by its temptations to overwork.

Nationalisation of the land alone, which many earnest and sincere persons are now preaching, would be useless so long as labour was subject to the fleecing of surplus value inevitable under the Capitalist system.

No better solution would be that State Socialism, by whatsoever name it may be called, whose aim it would be to make concessions to the working class while leaving the present system of capital and wages still in operation: no number of purely administrative changes, until the workers are in possession of all political power, would make any real approach to Socialism.

The Socialist League therefore aims at the realisation of complete Revolutionary Socialism, and well knows that this can never happen in any one country without the help of the workers of all civilisation. For us neither geographical boundaries, political history, race, nor creed makes rivals or enemies; for us there are no nations but only varied masses of workers and friends, whose mutual sympathies are checked or perverted by groups of masters and fleecers whose interest it is to stir up rivalries and hatreds between the dwellers in different lands.

It is clear that for all these oppressed and cheated masses of workers and their masters a great change is preparing: the dominant classes are uneasy, anxious, touched in conscience even, as to the condition of those they govern; the markets of the world are being competed for with an eagerness never before known; everything points to the fact that the great commercial system is becoming unmanageable, and is slipping from the grasp of its present rulers.

The one change possible out of all this is Socialism. As chattel-slavery passed into serfdom, and serfdom into the so-called free-labour system, so most surely will this latter pass into social order.

To the realisation of this change the Socialist League addresses itself with all earnestness. As a means thereto it will do all in its power towards the education of the people in the principles of this great cause, and will strive to organise those who will accept this education, so that when the crisis comes, which the march of events is preparing, there may be a body of men ready to step into their due places and deal with and direct the irresistible movement.

Close fellowship with each other, and steady purpose for the advancement of the Cause, will naturally bring about the organisation and discipline amongst ourselves absolutely necessary to success; but we shall look to it that there shall be no distinctions of rank or dignity amongst us to give opportunities for the selfish ambition of leadership which has so often injured the cause of the workers. We are working *for* equality and brotherhood for all the world, and it is only *through* equality and brotherhood that we can make our work effective.

Let us all strive, then, towards this end of realising the change towards social order, the only cause worthy the attention of the workers of all that are proposed to them: let us work in that cause patiently, yet hopefully, and not shrink from making sacrifices to it. Industry in learning its principles, industry in teaching them, are most necessary to our progress; but to these we must add, if we wish to avoid speedy failure, frankness and fraternal trust in each other, and single-hearted devotion to the religion of Socialism, the only religion which the Socialist League professes. (*Commonweal*, February 1885)

(b) JOSEPH LANE. *An Anti-Statist, Communist Manifesto*

1887

POLITICS properly so-called, that is the science of government or the art of directing men gathered in social community, is entirely based upon the principle of authority, and, it being so, we oppose with all our might the reactionary notion which consists in the pretence that the revolutionary socialists must seek to seize on the political machine, and to acquire power for themselves. We decline to recognise a divine absolutism because it can only give rise to the enslavery of reason and intelligence. Why, then, should we recognise a human absolutism, that can only engender the material exploitation of the ruled by the rulers? In this argument we are not specially concerned with any particular form of government, for all without distinction had their rise from the same source: Autocratic, Oligarchic systems, constitutional monarchy, plutocracy, the republic, as governmental forms, are all antagonistic to human freedom, and it is because of this that we are opposed to every form of government. If it be admitted that individual man has no right to govern, we cannot admit that a number of men should have this right, be they a minority or a majority. It is claimed that the theory of government is the outcome of a tacit agreement between all the citizens for the acceptance of some form of government, but this theory is inadmissible, for such tacit agreement cannot exist since men have never been consulted anywhere upon the abdication of their own freedom.

A certain school of socialists, while sharing our ideas upon the majority of forms of government, seeks nevertheless to defend what they call the democratic state, ruling nations by means of a parliamentary system, but we argue just precisely that freedom does not exist any more in this system than in any of the others, and it is for this reason that we oppose it. Act as it will, this popular state will nevertheless require for its maintenance to appeal to the reactionary forces, which are the natural allies of authority—the army, diplomacy, war, centralisation of all the powers which operate in restraint of freedom, and the initiative of individuals and social groups. Once launched upon this arbitrary career, it is an inevitable necessity to mount up round after round of the ladder, there being no resting place. On the contrary they must be ever trenching more and more upon the freedom and autonomy of the individual until these undergo a process of complete absorption and annihilation. In opposition therefore to those who desire by means of parliamentaryism to achieve a conquest of political power, we say for ourselves that we wish to forgo power and monopoly alike, which means that we seek to bring out from the very bosom of the people, from the depths of labour a factor more potent, that we shall deal with capital and the state and subdue them. This powerful factor will be realised by the organisation of Industrial and

Agricultural groups, having studied and being able to apply the laws of exchange, possessing the key and secret of the contradictions and antagonism of the Bourgeois political economy, standing possessed in a word of social science. And what does social science teach to those who consult it? It teaches that political reforms, as a preliminary to social reforms, are a Utopia or a mere trick and an eternal mystification, by which the radicals of every shade, including parliamentary socialists, have up till now deceived the workers. Social science protests against these subterfuges and palliatives; it repudiates every alliance with the policy of parliaments. Far from expecting any succour from them, it begins its work of exclusion by eliminating politics and parliamentaryism. We revolutionary socialists desire to organise ourselves in such a manner as to render politics useless and the powers that be superfluous, i.e., that we aim at the abolition of the State in every form and variety. We are waging a battle of labour against capital, i.e., against the State proprietary, financial and industrial. We pursue a warfare of freedom against authority, i.e., against the State, the respecter of religion and the master of all systems of teaching. We champion the cause of the producers as arrayed against that of the non-producers, i.e., we combat the State in its military and civil functionaries. We fight the battle of equality against privilege, i.e., we oppose the State, having all monopolies industrial, bankocratic, agricultural, etc. Now in order to subdue capital, to subjugate the powers that be, and destroy them, we in no way need to win by means of a parliamentary system that political power which as a matter of fact we seek to destroy, we do not wish, by acquiring power, to increase the number of non-producers that our socialistic organisation is meant to reduce more and more until none are left, i.e., until the complete annihilation of power, until the abolition of the State whatever be its form, monarchical or democratic.

We need not waste time over those Socialists who while condemning the political action of the proletariate, at the same time wish to avail themselves of parliamentary action as a means of propaganda; such Socialists are wanting in logic. If the participation of Socialists in the policy of governments be condemned as fatal to the interests of the proletariate, then a propaganda in favour of parliamentary action on behalf of the proletariate can be neither good in itself nor serviceable in the development of Socialism. On the other hand, as regards socialistic propaganda in times of election, all the good achieved by a candidate for parliamentary honors would be counterbalanced by the evil which he would otherwise cause, by filling the minds of the workers with notions false and reactionary, thus creating complete confusion among those who are struggling for the emancipation of mankind. The only means in our view of making the most of a period of political excitement, such as may be an electoral contest, would be to take advantage of it to disseminate among the masses revolutionary papers, pamphlets, leaflets, etc., got up specially for the occasion, and showing the people that it is not by Parliamentary means but by social revolution, that their lot will be ameliorated materially, morally and socially. Summing up we may, therefore, say that as far as politics are concerned we are Anti-statists, and as such we abstain from taking any part whatsoever in parliamentary action, whatever be the end assigned to such action. (*pp.* 6–9)

(c) WILLIAM MORRIS. Letter to the Rev. George Bainton

4 April, 1888

Allow me to suggest to you that if you do not agree with the abolition of monopoly which we Socialists all think is a *necessary* step to take, it is because you do not see the bearing of it; because, I think you confuse the Community with the State or the Government as it exists at present.

You see you must either have a Community master of itself, or a government master of the Community as at present. It is true that some persons, like my friend Auberon Herbert, for instance, try to conceive a condition of things in which every man is independent of every other, but that is not only impossible to be, but impossible even to conceive of.

If the means of production were "nationalised" the following changes would result.

(1) Everyone would be obliged to render some service to the Community in return for livelihood; thus getting rid of the class which lives by *owning* property.

(2) Everyone could claim useful employment, and the duly resulting livelihood.

(3) The waste of labour power now caused by (*a*) the watching over the individual interests of the plundering classes (competition we call it) and (*b*) by the rich classes *forcing* the workers to work uselessly, would come to an end.

In fact artificial compulsion would come to an end, for the Community cannot compel the Community.

Even the crudest form of State Socialism (which I do not agree to) would have this advantage over the individual ownership of the means of production, that whereas the State *might* abuse its ownership, the individual owners *must* do so.

You see as long as there is individual ownership of capital (to put it short) there must be a superior and an inferior class; and between these classes there must be antagonism, each can only thrive at the others' expense.

Class antagonism is really the key to the solution of the social question.

You must not forget also that the Socialism of to-day being like every vital movement a political one, that is to say one that embraces the daily life of the *whole* people, is forced to look to the transitional period as a practical business. Doubtless there will be much trouble and blundering over the carrying of society into this stage; and that is why I think we may expect democracy which has no longer any principles, nothing but a vague instinct pushing it on, to do something for us. We want the dying old system to make the experimental blunders for us so that the new order may set them right, which it can do because its action is based on principles.

With thanks for the kind words of your letter . . .
(P. Henderson, *Letters of William Morris*, 1950, *pp.* 284–6.)

(d) WILLIAM MORRIS. *Communism*

1893

. . . . . . SINCE, as you have just heard, it seems to me necessary that, in order to make any due use of socialist machinery one should have some sort of idea as to the life which is to be the result of it, let me now take up the often told tale of what we mean by communism and socialism; for between complete Socialism and Communism there is no difference whatever in my mind. Communism is in fact the completion of Socialism; when that ceases to be militant and becomes triumphant, it will be communism.

The Communist asserts in the first place that the resources of nature, mainly the land and those other things which can only be used for the reproduction of wealth and which are the effect of social work, should not be owned in severalty, but by the whole community for the benefit of the whole. That where this is not the case the owners of these means of production must of necessity be the masters of those who do not own a sufficiency of them to free them from the need of paying with a portion of their labour for the use of the said means of production; and that the masters or owners of the means of production do practically own the workers; very practically, since they really dictate to them the kind of life they shall lead, and the workers cannot escape from it unless by themselves becoming owners of the means of production, i.e., of other men. The resources of nature therefore, and the wealth used for the production of further wealth, the plant and stock in short, should be communized. Now if that were done, it would at once check the accumulation of riches. No man can become immensely rich by the storing up of wealth which is the result of the labour of his own brain and hands: to become very rich he must by cajolery or force deprive others of what their brains or hands have earned for them: the utmost that the most acquisitive man could do would be to induce his fellow citizens to pay him extra for his special talents, if they specially longed for his productions. But since no one could be very rich, and since talent for special work is never so very rare, and would tend to become less rare as men were freer to choose the occupations most suitable for them, producers of specialities could not exact very exorbitant payment, so that the aristocracy of talent, even if it appeared, would tend to disappear even in this first state of incomplete Communism. In short, there would be no very rich men: and all would be well off: all would be far above the condition of satisfaction of their material necessities. You may say how do I know that? The answer is that there could not be so much waste as there is now. Waste would tend to disappear. For what is waste? First, the causeless destruction of raw material; and secondly the diverting of labour from useful production. You may ask me what is the standard of usefulness in wares? It has been said, and I suppose the common view of that point is, that the price in the market gives us the standard; but is a loaf of bread or a saw less useful than a Mechlin lace veil or a diamond necklace? The truth is that in a society of inequality, a society in which there are very rich people and very poor ones, the standard of usefulness is utterly confused; in such a society the market price of an article is given us by the necessities of the poor and the inordinate cravings of the rich; or rather indeed *their* necessity for spending their wealth, or rather their riches, somehow: by no means necessarily in pleasures. But in a society of equality the demand for an article *would* be a standard of its usefulness in one way or another. And it would be a matter of course that until everybody had his absolute necessities and his reasonable comforts satisfied, there would be no place for the production of luxuries; and always labour would be employed in producing things that people (all the people, since classes would have disappeared) really want.

Remember what the waste of a society of inequality is: 1st: The production of sordid makeshifts for the supply of poor folk who cannot afford the real article. 2nd: the production of luxuries for rich folk, the greater part of which even their personal folly does not make them want. And 3rdly: the wealth wasted by the salesmanship of competitive commerce, to which the production of wares is but a secondary object, its first object being the production of a profit for the individual manufacturer. You understand that the necessary distribution of goods is not included in this waste; but the endeavour of each manufacturer to get as near as he can to a monopoly of the market which he supplies.

The minimization of waste therefore, which would take place in the incomplete 1st stages of a society of equality—a society only *tending* to equality—would make us wealthy: labour would not be wasted: workmen would not be employed in producing either slave wares, or toys for rich men: their genuine well made wares would be made for other workmen who would know what they wanted. When the wares were of such a kind as required very exquisite skill and long training to produce, or when the material used was far fetched and dear bought, they would not cease to be produced, even though private citizens could not acquire them: they would be produced for the public use, and their real value be enormously increased thereby, and the natural and honest pride of the workman duly satisfied. For surely wealthy people will not put up with sordid surroundings or stinginess in public institutions: they will assuredly have schools, libraries, museums, parks and all the rest of it real & genuine, not makeshifts for such things: especially as being no longer oppressed by fears for their livelihood, and all the dismal incidents of the battle for mere existence, they will be able to enjoy these things thoroughly: they will be able in fact to use them, which they cannot do now. But in all I have been saying about this new society hitherto I have been thinking I must remind you of its inchoate and incomplete stages. The means of production communized but the resulting wealth still private property. Truth to tell, I think that such a state of things could only embrace a very short period of transition to complete communism: a period which would only last while people were shaking down into the new Society; for if there were no poor people I don't see how there could be any rich. There would indeed be a natural compulsion, which would prevent any man from doing what he was not fitted for, because he could not do it usefully; and I need not say that in order to arrive at the wealth I have been speaking of we must all work usefully. But if a man does work usefully you can't do without him; and if you can't do without him you can only put him into an inferior position to another useful citizen by means of compulsion; and if you compel him to it, you at once have your privileged classes again. Again, when all people are living comfortably or even handsomely, the keenness of the strife for the better positions, which will then no longer involve a life of idleness or power over ones neighbours, will surely tend to abate : men get rich now in their struggles not to be poor, and because their riches shield them from suffering from the horrors which are a necessary accompaniment of the existence of rich men, e.g., the sight of slums, the squalor of a factory country, the yells and evil language of drunken and brutalized poor people & so forth. But when all private life was decent and, apart from natural accident, happy; and when public institutions satisfied your craving for splendour and completeness; and when no one was allowed to injure the public by defiling the natural beauty of the earth, or by forbidding men's craving for making it more beautiful to have full sway, what advantage would there be in having more nominal wealth than your neighbour? Therefore, as on the one hand men whose work was acknowledged as useful would scarcely subject themselves to a new system of caste; and on the other, people living happily with all their reasonable needs easily satisfied would hardly worry themselves with worrying others into giving them extra wealth which they could not use, so I think the communization of the means of industry would speedily be followed by the communization of its product : that is that there would be complete equality of condition amongst all men. Which again does not mean that people would (all round) use their neighbours' coats, or houses or tooth brushes, but that everyone, whatever work he did, would have the opportunity of satisfying all his reasonable needs according to the admitted standard of the society in which he lived : i.e., without robbing any other citizen. And I must say it is in the belief that this is possible of realisation that I continue to be a socialist. Prove to me that it is not; and I will not trouble myself to do my share towards altering the present state of society, but will try to live on, as little a pain to myself and a nuisance to my neighbour as I may. But yet I must tell that I shall be more or less both a pain to myself (or at least a disgrace) and a nuisance to my neighbour. For I do declare that any other state of society but communism is grievous & disgraceful to all belonging to it.

Some of you may expect me to say something about the machinery by which a communistic society is to be carried on. Well, I can say very little that is not merely negative. Most antisocialists and even some socialists are apt to confuse, as I hinted before, the co-operative machinery towards which modern life is tending with the essence of socialism itself; and its enemies to attack it, and sometimes its friends defend it on those lines; both to my mind committing a grievous error, especially the latter. E.G. An anti-socialist will say How will you sail a ship in a socialist condition? How? Why with a captain and mates & sailing master and engineer (if it be a steamer) and ABs and stokers & so on and so on. *Only* there will be no 1st 2nd and 3rd class among the passengers; the sailors and stokers will be as well fed & lodged as the captain or passengers; and the Captain and the stoker will have the same pay.

There are plenty of enterprises which will be carried on then, as they are now (and, to be successful, must probably remain) under the guidance of one man. The only difference between then and now will be, that he will be chosen because he is fit for the work, & not because he must have a job found for him; and that he will do his work for the benefit of each and all, and not for the sake of making a profit. For the rest, time will teach us what new machinery may be necessary to the new life; reasonable men will submit to it without demur; and unreasonable ones will find themselves compelled to by the nature of things, and can only, I fear, console themselves, as the philosopher did when he knocked his head against the door post, by damning the Nature of things.

Well, since our aim is so great and so much to be longed for, the substituting throughout all society of peace for war, pleasure and self-respect for grief and disgrace, we may well seek about strenuously for some means for starting our enterprise; and since it is just these means in which the difficulty lies, I appeal to all socialists, while they express their thoughts & feelings about them honestly and fearlessly, not to make a quarrel of it with those whose aim is one with theirs, because there is a difference of opinion between them about the usefulness of the details of the means. It is difficult or even impossible not to make mistakes about these, driven as we are by the swift lapse of time and the necessity for doing something amidst it all. So let us forgive the mistakes that others make, even if we make none ourselves, and be at peace amongst ourselves, that we may the better make War upon the monopolist. (*pp.* 11–15)

11

FABIAN SOCIETY

The Fabian Society, founded in 1884, was the offshoot of a utopian "Fellowship of the New Life" which contemplated founding a colony in South America. The Fabians decided to concentrate on the transformation of society at home, and at first their political attitude did not differ widely from that of the S.D.F. and the Socialist League, except that they were a middle-class group who preferred drawing-room discussion to street-corner agitation. Bernard Shaw, who joined the society in its first year, is to be found at first expressing the orthodox Marxist attitude to society, though in an unusually witty fashion (a). He had read *Capital* in the French translation, but was soon convinced by P. H. Wicksteed, the economist, that the Jevonian theory of Marginal Utility was superior to Marx's Labour Theory of Value. Shaw and his friend Sidney Webb, a disciple of John Stuart Mill, developed an eclectic attitude to Marxist doctrine which is evident in Shaw's review of the first English translation of *Capital* (b). As may be seen from their most important work, *Fabian Essays* (1889), the majority of the leading Fabians rejected the Marxian prophecy of deepening capitalist crisis, and believed rather in the possibility of peaceful progress towards Socialism. Webb, identifying Socialism with state control in any form, regarded this process as already far advanced in the eighteen-eighties (c).

One of the ablest Fabian propagandists at that time was Annie Besant (d), the former Secularist and Neo-Malthusian agitator who soon left the Society to become a Theosophist. She imparted a degree of enthusiasm to her politics that went far beyond the boundaries later prescribed by the *Report on Fabian Policy,* which was prepared for the London International Socialist Congress of 1896 (e). The last two quotations illustrate, first, the society's attitude to the South African War, in a report drafted by Bernard Shaw (f); and secondly, the

Webb concept of national efficiency based on a national minimum of welfare—a concept that was later to find expression in Beatrice Webb's Minority Report of the Poor Law Commission in 1909, and in the policy of the Labour Party in the following forty years (g).

(a) BERNARD SHAW. Speech at the Industrial Remuneration Conference

30 January 1885

MR. George Bernard Shaw (Fabian Society) said: . . . On the general question of the welfare of the community no reasonable defence could be advanced of the existence of any class that consumed the product of the national industry without rendering any service to the nation in return. It was the desire of the President that nothing should be said that might give pain to particular classes. He was about to refer to a modern class—the burglars; but if there was a burglar present, he begged him to believe that he cast no reflection upon his profession (laughter), and that he was not unmindful of his great skill and enterprise; his risks—so much greater than those of the most speculative capitalist, extending as they did to risk of liberty and life (laughter); his abstinence; or, finally, of the great number of people to whom he gave employment, including criminal attorneys, policemen, turnkeys, gaolers, builders of gaols, and, it might be, the hangman. He did not wish to hurt the feelings of shareholders, who drew interest year after year, and, if they sold out, expected to get the original investment back again, or of landlords, who did nothing for the rents they received, any more than he wished to pain the burglars. He would merely point out that all three inflicted on the community an injury of precisely the same nature (laughter). We must stop this state of things before we could reform our present condition. It would be said that to expropriate the landlord and capitalist would be unjust, immoral, confiscation, and so forth; but the truth was that it was absolutely immoral to allow them any longer to confiscate daily the labour of others for whom they did nothing. Political economists, who were supposed to understand these things, would render a service if they would state the laws of rent and interest in their true light, as relations between one man and another, instead of obscuring the matter by stating the law of rent as a relation between one piece of land which pays rent and another piece which does not pay rent, and the law of wages as a relation between the normal rate of wages in one trade and the normal rate in another, thereby producing a law which is true, but which obscures the ethical aspect of the case by concealing the immoral relation between the worker and the employer who exploits his labour. (*Report of the Industrial Remuneration Conference*, 1885, *pp.* 400*f.*)

(b) BERNARD SHAW. Review of the English translation of Marx's *Capital*, vol. I

1887

. . . Compare Mr. William Morris after Oxford, or Mr. H. M. Hyndman after Cambridge, with the same gentlemen after Marx. In the first stage they are conscious of having been incommoded by a useless dose of the " dismal science ". In the second they are crying out with a burning conviction that the old order is one of fraud and murder; that its basis is neither kingcraft nor priestcraft, but the divorce of the laborer from the material without which his labor is barren; and that it is changing and giving place to the new by an inexorable law of development. It is easy to show that Mill and Cairnes and Sidgwick knew this and said it; but the fact is that the average pupil of Marx never forgets it, whilst the average pupil of Mill and the rest never learns it. But it must immediately be added, as a considerable set-off, that the average Marxite never understands rent, and confuses employers with capitalists and profits with interest in a way which the modest disciples of General Walker despise. For Marx, in this first book of his, treats of labor without reference to variations of skill between its parts; of raw material without reference to variations of fertility; and of the difference between the product of labor and the price (wage) of labor power, as "surplus value" without reference to its subdivision into rent, interest, and profits. This will explain to any student how it is that those who know nothing of economics except what they have learnt from this Marxian fragment, and who innocently believe that it covers the whole subject, are repeatedly betrayed into taking up absurd positions in economic discussions. Also how some economists, too confident in their own skill to do more with any new treatise than slip into it here and there, have supposed that Marx himself was ignorant of the considerations he purposely omitted, and have dismissed him with a contempuously adverse decision, which they will some day, possibly, be glad to forget.

Whatever may be the ultimate verdict as to Marx, it must be borne in mind that the extraordinary impression he makes does not depend on the soundness of his views, but on their magnificent scope and on his own imperturbable conviction of their validity. It is impossible to be sure that further historical research will confirm his interpretation of the past, or experience verify his anticipations; but whilst capitalism lasts he will still make his mark upon his readers, and, through them, on the world; for whether he was right or wrong, great synthetic philosopher or finder of marc's nests, be believed in his theory of society, and had the power of making others believe in it. You can no more get rid of such a man by a quip or two at his use of the word value, than you can of Mahomet by explaining that the dove which whispered to him really came to pick a pea out of his ear, or of Comte by burlesquing the ritual of the Religion of Humanity.

But it is one thing to give an extraordinary man his due, and quite another to encourage or acquiesce in the setting up of his book as a Holy Scripture. (*National Reformer*, 7 August 1887)

(c) SIDNEY WEBB. *The Progress of Socialism*

1888

THREE hundred years ago, for fear of the horde of "sturdy beggars," which even hanging had failed to extirpate, the wise Cecil was led to institute the general system of poor relief, a deduction from rent and interest for the benefit of those who were excluded from directly sharing in them. But the industrial evolution has not yet made this condition universal; and little further progress was made in Socialism until the beginning of our century. Then, indeed, the acme of individualism was reached. No sentimental regulations hindered the free employment of land and capital to the highest possible personal advantage, however many lives of men, women, and children were used up in the process. Capitalists still speak of that time with exultation. "It was not five per cent or ten per cent," says one, "but thousands per cent that made the fortune of Lancashire." But opinion turned against *laisser faire* fifty years ago. Mainly by the heroic efforts of a young nobleman, who lately passed away from us as Lord Shaftesbury, a really effective Factory Act was won; and the insatiate greed of the manufacturers was restrained by political power, in the teeth of their most determined opposition. Since then the progress has been rapid. Slice after slice has, in the public interest, been cut off the profits of land and capital, and therefore off their value, by Mines Regulations Acts, Truck Acts, Factory Acts, Adulteration Acts, Land Acts. Slice after slice has been cut off the already diminishing incomes of the classes enjoying rent and interest, by the gradual shifting of taxation from the whole nation as consumers of taxed commodities to the holders of incomes above £150, the average family income of the Kingdom. Step by step political power and political organisation have been used for industrial ends, until a Minister of the Crown is the largest employer of labour in the country, and at least 200,000 men not counting the army and navy, are directly in the service of the community, without the intervention of the profit of any middleman. All the public needs supplied by the labour of these public servants, were at one time left to private enterprise, and were a source of legitimate individual investment of capital. Step by step the community has absorbed them, wholly or partially; and the area of private exploitation has been lessened. Parallel with this progressive nationalisation or municipalisation of industry a steady elimination of the purely personal element in business management has gone on. The older economists doubted whether any thing but banking could be carried on by joint-stock enterprise; now every conceivable industry, down to baking and milk-selling, is successfully managed by the salaried officers of large corporations of idle share-holders. More than one-third of the whole business of England measured by the capital employed, is now done by joint-stock companies, whose shareholders could be expropriated by the community with little more dislocation of industry than is caused by the daily purchase of shares on the Stock Exchange.

Besides its direct supersession of private enterprise, the State now registers, inspects, and controls nearly all the industrial functions which it has not yet absorbed. The inspection is often detailed and rigidly enforced. The State in most of the larger industrial operations prescribes the age of the worker, the hours of work, the amount of air, light, cubic space, heat, lavatory accommodation, holidays, and meal times; where, when, and how wages shall be paid; how machinery, staircases, lift-holes, mines and quarries are to be fenced and guarded; how and when the plant shall be cleaned, repaired and worked. Even the kind of package in which some articles shall be sold is duly prescribed, so that the individual capitalist shall take no advantage of his position. On every side he is being registered, inspected, controlled; eventually he will be superseded by the community, and he is compelled in the meantime to cede for public purposes an ever increasing share of his rent and interest.

This is the rapid progress of "Collectivism" which is so noticeable in our generation. England is already the most Socialist of all European communities, though the young Emperor of Germany is now compelled by the uneasy ground swell of German politics to emulate us very closely. English Collectivism will, however, inevitably be Democratic —a real "Social Democracy" instead of the mere Political Democracy with which Liberals coquet. As the oldest industrial country, we are likely to keep the lead, in spite of those old-fashioned politicians who innocently continue to regard Socialism as a dangerous and absolutely untried innovation. Are there not still, in obscure nooks, disbelievers and despisers of all science? The schoolmaster never penetrates into all the corners in the same generation.

But some will be inclined to say, "This is not what we thought Socialism meant. We imagined that Socialists wanted to bring about a sanguinary conflict in the streets, and then the next day to compel all delicately nurtured people to work in the factories at a fixed rate of wages."

It is not only in the nursery that bogey-making continues to be a very general though quite unnecessary source of anxiety. Socialists do but foretell the probable direction of English social evolution; and it needs nothing but a general recognition of that development, and a clear determination not to allow the selfish interests of any class to hinder it or hamper it, for Socialism to secure universal assent. All other changes will easily flow from this acquiescent state of mind, and they need not be foreshadowed in words. (*pp.* 13–15)

(d) ANNIE BESANT. Speech on Socialism versus Individualism, in a Debate with Mr. Frederick Millar of the Liberty and Property Defence League, Nottingham

25 October 1890

Mrs. Besant, in her second address, said she would at once clear away all difficulty as to limitation introduced by Mr. Millar into his original statement of living and doing as he liked. She would take the case of two hungry men and one loaf of bread. Each man would like to have the loaf and satisfy his hunger. Each grabbed it, and the strongest man got it. He did as he liked, and ate the loaf, and the other had to starve. (Loud applause.) Mr. Millar had reiterated his statement as to state employment. She had no notion of advocating centralised State control, to which so many Socialists were adverse, or State employ as they had it now. But even so, to-day, the State employment was more sought after than private employment. And why? Because it was more thought of, more secure, and on the whole, more considerate. . . .

Mr. Millar says Mrs. Besant would admit that there was once a fair start in the scramble for property. Indeed, Mrs. Besant would admit nothing so foolish. (Applause.) There had never been a fair start; they could not have a fair start in a scramble. (Hear, hear.) In a scramble the strongest and most brutal, those with the least conscience and sense of duty were the people who succeeded—the most unfit for society and not the most fit. Superior cunning and strength were not the qualities she desired to see develop. Superior cunning was very good for a beast of prey but it was no good for human brotherhood. (Applause.) Superior strength used to trample on the weaker, might be very well in a mass of pigs fighting over a trough, but that was not her ideal of rational human society. (Hear, hear.) Then they were told by Mr. Millar, with a most extraordinary use of language, that any class legislation was Socialistic legislation. She had never before even heard an Individualist call class legislation Socialist legislation. However, Mr. Millar was very consistent. Mr. Millar was strong. What chance would she have with him in a scramble? Beyond question those who were strong and muscular would like a scramble, while the weak and feeble would shrink from it. But they were not always sure that the result of the scramble would be in favour of the highest mental development. Take a British Grenadier, six feet high and proportionately broad—was he necessarily the wisest man with the strongest brain? She thought less muscle and more brain would be more to the advantage of society; but, certainly a British Grenadier would get the better of a Professor Clifford in a free scramble. They were told that the strong, fit, and able should be triumphant; that that was the natural law. It was the natural law of the vegetable and the brute; it was not the natural law of the human being; and to set up such a law crushed out everything that differentiated man from the brute. To make man nothing but a mere brute of a superior kind, with superior cunning and intelligence, was that to be the ideal of society in an Individualistic state? On the contrary, the qualities which made men fit to be men were qualities of sympathy, of brotherhood, of respect for others, of love and of justice. They had heard something about Greece and Rome, and their failure in days of old. Why did they fail? They failed because they had a privileged class and a helot class, and because their patricians claimed a position not based on justice, but on tyranny. And they failed as England would fail, and other empires would finish, if they used their strength to trample on the weaker, and their superior brain ability to crush those less able than themselves. (Applause.) Did they in any society let any man have the benefit of his strength? If a strong man garotted a weaker man in the street he was locked up. And why? For the protection of the weaker. But the thief was only doing as he liked, just as the fraudulent director was doing as he liked, when he, by his superior cunning, took advantage of a man of inferior business ability. These were qualities they wished to grow out of and not to nourish; and as they grew further and further from the brute they rose nearer and nearer to true humanity. (Applause.) Mr. Millar said that Mrs. Besant once preached against over-population. Mrs. Besant had not changed her opinion on the subject. It was true that she somewhat exaggerated the consequences which would accrue from adherence to Malthusianism, and had since had occasion to modify her view as regarded national poverty, but she had not changed her teaching; and she had told her friends over and over again that no Socialist state could permanently obtain unless the great law of nature was recognized and acted upon. So she found in the struggle before them they were going to break down the ideal of true human life, and that Mr. Millar was going to maintain what she called the ideal of selfishness, while she stood up for the ideal of brotherhood and mutual help. She would not care for any society that trampled on its weakest for the sake of its strongest; and if she asked that all materials necessary for life might be communalised, it was because it was only thus that it was possible that all should have a fair chance. She was not foolish enough to think that all human beings could be made equal; she was not foolish enough to imagine that all men would be alike because every one had a chance; but she did say: give them all access to means of production and the material out of which all wealth must come, for only by such control could they prevent the destruction of society. (Loud applause.) (*Socialism versus Individualism,* 1890, *pp.* 21-4)

(e) *Fabian Society.* Report on Fabian Policy

1896

I.

The Mission of the Fabians

THE object of the Fabian Society is to persuade the English people to make their political constitution thoroughly democratic and so to socialize their industries as to make the livelihood of the people entirely independent of private Capitalism.

The Fabian Society endeavours to pursue its Socialist and Democratic objects with complete singleness of aim. For example:

It has no distinctive opinions on the Marriage Question, Religion, Art, abstract Economics, historic Evolution, Currency, or any other subject than its own special business of practical Democracy and Socialism.

It brings all the pressure and persuasion in its power to bear on existing forces, caring nothing by what name any party calls itself, or what principles, Socialist or other, it professes, but having regard solely to the tendency of its actions, supporting those which make for Socialism and Democracy, and opposing those which are reactionary.

It does not propose that the practical steps towards Social-Democracy should be carried out by itself, or by any other specially organised society or party.

It does not ask the English people to join the Fabian Society.

II.

Fabian Electoral Tactics

The Fabian Society does not claim to be the people of England, or even the Socialist party, and therefore does not seek direct political representation by putting forward Fabian candidates at elections. But it loses no opportunity of influencing elections and inducing constituencies to select Socialists as their candidates. No person, however, can obtain the support of the Fabian Society, or escape its opposition, by merely repeating a few shibboleths and calling himself a Socialist or Social-Democrat. As there is no Second Ballot in England, frivolous candidatures give great offence, and discredit the party in whose name they are undertaken, because any third candidate who is not well supported will not only be beaten himself, but may also involve in his defeat the better of the two candidates competing with him. Under such circumstances the Fabian Society throws its weight against the third candidate whether he calls himself a Socialist or not, in order to secure the victory to the better of the two candidates between whom the contest really lies. But when the third candidate is not only a serious representative of Socialism, but can organise his party well, and is likely to poll sufficient votes to make even his defeat a respectable demonstration of the strength and growth of Socialism in the constituency, the Fabian Society supports him resolutely under all circumstances and against all other parties.

III.

Fabian Toleration

The Fabian Society, far from holding aloof from other bodies, urges its members to lose no opportunity of joining them and permeating them with Fabian ideas as far as possible. Almost all organizations and movements contain elements making for Socialism, no matter how remote the sympathies and intentions of their founders may be from those of the Socialists. On the other hand, unintentionally reactionary proposals are constantly being brought forward in Socialist bodies. Fabians are therefore encouraged to join all other organizations, Socialist or non-Socialist, in which Fabian work can be done.

IV.

Fabian Constitutionalism

The Fabian Society is perfectly constitutional in its attitude; and its methods are those usual in political life in England.

The Fabian Society accepts the conditions imposed on it by human nature and by the national character and political circumstances of the English people. It sympathises with the ordinary citizen's desire for gradual, peaceful changes, as against revolutionary, conflict with the army and police, and martyrdom. It recognises the fact that Social-Democracy is not the whole of the working-class program, and that every separate measure towards the socialization of industry will have to compete for precedence with numbers of other reforms. It therefore does not believe that the moment will ever come when the whole of Socialism will be staked on the issue of a single General Election or a single Bill in the House of Commons as between the proletariat on one side and the proprietariat on the other. Each instalment of Social-Democracy will only be a measure among other measures, and will have to be kept to the front by an energetic socialist section. The Fabian Society therefore begs those Socialists who are looking forward to a sensational historical crisis, to join some other Society.

V.

Fabian Democracy

Democracy, as understood by the Fabian Society, means simply the control of the administration by freely elected representatives of the people. The Fabian Society energetically repudiates all conceptions of Democracy as a system by which the technical work of government administration and the appointment of public officials, shall be carried on by referendum or any other form of direct popular decision. Such arrangements may be practical in a village community, but not in the complicated industrial civilizations which are ripening for Social Democracy. When the House of Commons is freed from the veto of the House of Lords and thrown open to candidates from all classes by an effective system of Payment of Representatives and a more rational method of election, the British parliamentary system will be, in the opinion of the Fabian Society, a first-rate practical instrument of democratic government.

Democracy, as understood by the Fabian Society, makes no political distinction between men and women.

VI.

Fabian Compromise

The Fabian Society, having learnt from experience that Socialists cannot have their own way in everything any more than other people, recognises that in a Democratic community Compromise is a necessary condition of political progress.

VII.

Fabian Socialism

Socialism, as understood by the Fabian Society means the organization and conduct of the necessary industries of the country and the appropriation of all forms of economic rent of land and capital by the nation as a whole, through the most suitable public authorities, parochial, municipal, provincial, or central.

The Socialism advocated by the Fabian Society is State Socialism exclusively. The foreign friends of the Fabian Society must interpret this declaration in view of the fact that since England now possesses an elaborate democratic State machinery, graduated from the Parish Council or Vestry up to the central Parliament, and elected under a franchise which enables the working class vote to overwhelm all others, the opposition which exists in the continental monarchies between the State and the people does not hamper English Socialists. For example, the distinction made between State Socialism and Social-Democracy in Germany, where the municipalities and other local bodies are closed against the working classes, has no meaning in England. The difficulty in England is not to secure more political power for the people, but to persuade them to make any sensible use of the power they already have.

VIII.

Fabian Individualism

The Fabian Society does not suggest that the State should monopolise industry as against private enterprise or individual initiative further than may be necessary to make the livelihood of the people and their access to the sources of production completely independent of both. The freedom of individuals to test the social value of new inventions; to initiate improved methods of production; to anticipate and lead public enterprise in catering for new social wants; to practise all arts, crafts and professions independently; in short, to complete the social organization by adding the resources of private activity and judgment to those of public routine, is , subject to the above conditions, as highly valued by the Fabian Society as Freedom of Speech, Freedom of the Press or any other article in the charter of popular liberties.

IX.

Fabian Freedom of Thought

The Fabian Society strenuously maintains its freedom of thought and speech with regard to the errors of Socialist authors, economists, leaders and parties, no less than to those of its opponents. For instance, it insists on the necessity of maintaining as critical an attitude towards Marx and Lassalle, some of whose views must by this time be discarded as erroneous or obsolete, as these eminent Socialists themselves maintained towards their predecessors, St. Simon and Robert Owen.

X.

Fabian Journalism

The Fabian Society, in its relations with the Press, makes no such distinction as that indicated by the phrase "the Capitalist Press." In England all political papers without exception are conducted with private capital under the control of the owners of the capital. Some of them profess Socialist opinions, others Conservative opinions, others Liberal and Radical opinions, and so forth. The Socialists papers are in no way more independent of social pressure than the others; and the superiority of a Socialist paper from the Socialist point of view is of exactly the same nature as the superiority of a Conservative paper from the Conservative point of view. The Fabian Society, in securing journalistic expression for its ideas, has no preference, except for the largest circulation.

XI.

Fabians and the Middle Class

In view of the fact that the Socialist movement has been hitherto inspired, instructed, and led by members of the middle class or "bourgeoisie", the Fabian Society though not at all surprised to find these middle class leaders attacking with much bitterness the narrow social ideals current in their own class, protests against the absurdity of Socialists denouncing the very class from which Socialism has sprung as specially hostile to it. The Fabian Society has no romantic illusions as to the freedom of the proletariat from these same narrow ideals. Like every other Socialist society, it can only educate the people in Socialism by making them conversant with the conclusions of the most enlightened members of all classes. The Fabian Society, therefore, cannot reasonably use the words "bourgeoise" or "middle class" as terms of reproach, more especially as it would thereby condemn a large proportion of its own members.

XII.

Fabian Natural Philosophy

The Fabian Society endeavours to rouse Social compunction by making the public conscious of the evil condition of society under the present system. This it does by the collection and publication of authentic and impartial statistical tracts, compiled, not from the works of Socialists, but from official sources. The first volume of Karl Marx's *Das Capital*, which contains an immense mass of carefully verified facts concerning modern capitalistic civilization, and practically nothing about Socialism, is probably the most successful propagandist work ever published. The Fabian Society, in its endeavours to continue the work of Marx in this direction, has found that the guesses made by Socialists at the condition of the people almost invariably flatter the existing system instead of, as might be suspected, exaggerating its evils. The Fabian Society therefore concludes that in the natural philosophy of Socialism, light is a more important factor than heat.

XIII.

Fabian Repudiations

The Fabian Society discards such phrases as "the abolition of the wage system", which can only mislead the public as to the aims of Socialism. Socialism does not involve the abolition of wages, but the establishment of standard allowances for the maintenance of all workers by the community in its own service, as an alternative to wages fixed by the competition of destitute men and women for private employment, as well as to commercial profits, commissions, and all other speculative and competitive forms of remuneration. In short, the Fabian Society, far from desiring to abolish wages, wishes to secure them for everybody.

The Fabian Society resolutely opposes all pretentions to hamper the socialization of industry with equal wages, equal hours of labour, equal official status, or equal authority for everyone. Such conditions are not only impracticable, but incompatible with the equality of subordination to the common interest which is fundamental in modern Socialism.

The Fabian Society steadfastly discountenances all schemes for securing to any person, or any group of persons "the entire product of their labor". It recognises that wealth is social in its origin and must be social in its distribution, since the evolution of industry has made it impossible to distinguish the particular contribution that each person makes to the common product, or to ascertain its value.

The Fabian Society desires to offer to all projectors and founders of Utopian communities in South America, Africa, and other remote localities, its apologies for its impatience of such adventures. To such protectors, and all patrons of schemes for starting similar settlements and workshops at home, the Society announces emphatically that it does not believe in the establishment of Socialism by private enterprise.

XIV.

Finally

The Fabian Society does not put Socialism forward as a panacea for the ills of human society, but only for those produced by defective organization of industry and by a radically bad distribution of wealth. (Fabian Tract No. 70, 1896)

(f) *Fabian Society. Fabianism and the Empire* 1900

It may be conceded that to citizens and statesmen who are dominated by the morality of private property, the war must be demoralizing if they are on the side of the Empire, and shocking if they are on the side of the farmers. But it is impossible for a great Commonwealth to be bound by any such individualist superstition. However ignorantly its politicians may argue about it, reviling one another from the one side as brigands, and defending themselves from the other with quibbles from waste-paper treaties and childish slanders against a brave enemy, the fact remains that a Great Power, consciously or unconsciously, must govern in the interests of civilization as a whole; and it is not to those interests that such mighty forces as gold-fields, and the formidable armaments that can be built upon them, should be wielded irresponsibly by small communities of frontiersmen. Theoretically, they should be internationalized, not British-Imperialized; but until the Federation of the World becomes an accomplished fact, we must accept the most responsible Imperial federations available as a substitute for it. This is the best answer, for the purpose of excusing the war, to President Kruger's statement at Bloemfontein that, in demanding the franchise for the Outlanders, we were asking him to give the title-deeds of "his" land to the laborers on it. Sir Alfred Milner had no reply at all, because, not being a Socialist, he quite agreed with the President's fundamental position, and so had to argue in the manner of the wolf with the lamb. . . .

What we have to do in South Africa, having rightly or

wrongly shattered to pieces the governments of the South African Republic and the Orange Free State, is to guarantee a free constitution and responsible government within the Empire to the white inhabitants of these vast territories from the earliest moment at which it may be possible to make up the registers and summon a local Parliament (a necessary condition which will allow plenty of time for things to settle down), and in the meantime to restrict the powers of the military tribunals to committing persons for trial with the Habeas Corpus Act suspended, thereby relieving Lord Roberts from the odium of countenancing vindictive and irritating sentences on persons who, as everybody knows, will be amnestied when order is restored.

Pending the election of local Parliaments, the new provinces should be granted the following conditions:

I. Formal inclusion in the British Empire with the privilege of using its flag.

II. The charging of the mines and the land with a Royalty and a Land Tax to meet the expenses involved in setting up a new administration, and to make it clear that the incorporation into the Empire is a real one, and not merely an expedition to secure private property for European speculators at the public expense.

III. A provisional Factory and Mines Regulation Order, to secure the standard of life of the wage-earner, white or colored, in the way made plain to us by a century of experience.

IV. A Measure for the protection of the natives, to be administered by Imperial officials, not subject to local parliamentary authority.

The first three of these would be alterable by the local legislatures when elected, subject (since we have as yet no Imperial Council) to the Royal veto on legislation, which should be exercised so as to make inclusion in the British

Commonwealth mean a guarantee of certain constitutional rights to all its subjects, including regulation of the relations of capital and labor so as to maintain the British standard of life as the highest in the world. (*pp.* 23, 25–7)

(g) SIDNEY WEBB. *Twentieth Century Politics*

1901

. . . . . . To-day, in the United Kingdom, there are, Sir Robert Giffen tells us, not fewer than eight millions of persons, one-fifth of the whole population, existing under conditions represented by a family income of less than a pound a week, and constituting not merely a disgrace, but a positive danger to our civilization. These are the victims of "sweating" in one or other of its forms, condemned, as the House of Lords' Committee emphatically declared, to "earnings barely sufficient to sustain existence; hours of labour such as to make the lives of the workers periods of almost ceaseless toil; sanitary conditions injurious to the health of the persons employed and dangerous to the public."

The first and most indispensable step towards National Efficiency is the healing of the open sore by which this industrial parasitism is draining away the vitality of the race. There is no doubt about the remedy, no uncertainty among those who have really worked at the problem. We have passed through the experimental stage of factory legislation, and we now know that it is no mere coincidence that these eight million persons correspond almost precisely with the sections from whom we have hitherto withheld the effective protection of the Factory Acts. The statesman who is really inspired by the idea of National Efficiency will stump the country in favor of a "National Minimum" standard of life, below which no employer in any trade in any part of the kingdom shall be allowed to descend.

He will elaborate this minimum of humane order—already admitted in principle in a hundred Acts of Parliament with all the force that eloquence can give to economic science, into a new industrial charter, imperatively required, not merely or even mainly for the comfort of the workers, but absolutely for the success of our industry in competition with the world. With the widespread support which this policy would secure—not only from the whole Trade Union world and the two millions of organised co-operators, but also from ministers of religion of all denominations, doctors and nurses, sanitary officers and teachers, Poor Law administrators and modern economists, and even the employers themselves—he would be able to expand our uneven and incomplete Factory Acts into a systematic and all embracing code, prescribing for every manual worker employed a minimum of education, sanitation, leisure and wages, as the inviolable starting-point of industrial competition.

But factory legislation alone, however effective and complete, can secure a " moral and material minimum " only so far as the conditions of employment are concerned. Even more than in the factory, the Empire is rooted in the home. How can we build up an effective commonwealth—how, even, can we get an efficient army—out of the stunted, anaemic, demoralized denizens of the slum tenements of our great cities? Can we, even as a mere matter of business, any longer afford to allow the eight millions of whom I have already spoken—the " submerged fifth " of our nation—to be housed, washed, watered worse than our horses? Is it not clear that one of the first and most indispensable steps towards National Efficiency is to make really effective that " National Minimum " of sanitation which is already nominally compulsory by law? This means a great extension of municipal activity in town and country. It means a new point of view for the Local Government Board, which must cease to do evil and learn to do well, by dropping its lazy routine of obstruction and discouragement and rousing itself to be prompt with its stimulus, eagerly oncoming with its help and, when necessary, swift and ruthless with its compulsion. For the Local Government Board has, though no President seems to be aware of it, an even higher duty in sanitation than stimulus and help. It is the guardian of the National Minimum. To it is committed the great trust of seeing that no single family in the land is denied the indispensable conditions of healthy life. So far as house accommodation, ventilation, good drainage and pure water are concerned, Parliament has long ago embodied this National Minimum of sanitation in universally applicable Public Health Acts, which it is the duty of the Local Government Board to enforce upon local authorities just as drastically as these ought to do upon individuals. Can anything be more preposterous in a business nation than to allow (as a succession of Presidents of the Local Government Board have long allowed) one locality after another, merely out of stupidity, or incapacity, or parsimony, demonstrably to foster malignant disease and bring up its quota of citizens in a condition of impaired vitality? Why does not the Local Government Board undertake a systematic hurrying up of the backward districts, regularly insisting for instance, that all those having death rates above the average of the kingdom shall put themselves in order, improve their drainage, lay on new water supply, and insure by one means or another, a supply of healthy houses sufficient to enable every family to comply with the formula of "three rooms and a scullery" as the minium necessary for breeding an even moderately Imperial race? Every medical officer knows that it is quite possible, within a generation after the adoption of such a genuine enforcement of the

National Minimum of sanitation, to bring down the average death rate by at least 5 per 1,000, and the sickness experience by at least a third. The equivalent money gain to the community would be many millions sterling. A single friendly society, the Manchester Unity of Oddfellows, would, it has been calculated, save a quarter of a million annually in benefits alone. I measure my words when I say that the neglect of the Local Government Board to enforce even the existing legal National Minimum of sanitation causes, each year, more deaths than the most calamitous of our wars.

A Ministry really inspired with a passion for National Efficiency would, however, know how to use other instruments besides compulsion. The Government must set itself to raise the standard of life. This is specially the sphere of local initiative and corporate enterprise, of beneficent competition rigorously stopped by law from the downward way, but freed, stimulated and encouraged in every experiment on the upward way. We have seen how the Local Government Board has necessarily to be always coercing its local authorities to secure the National Minimum; for anything beyond that minimum the wise Minister would mingle premiums with his pressure. He would, by his public speeches, by his personal interviews with mayors and town clerks, and by the departmental publications, set on foot the utmost possible emulation among the various local governing bodies, as to which could make the greatest strides in municipal activity. We already have the different towns compared, quarter by quarter, in respect of their death-rates, but at present only crudely, unscientifically and perfunctorily. Why should not the Local Government Board avowedly put all the local governing bodies of each class into honorary competition with one another by an annual investigation of municipal efficiency, working out their statistical marks for excellence in drainage, water supply, paving, cleansing, watching and lighting, housing, hospital accommodation, medical service, sickness experience, and mortality, and publicly classifying them all according to the result of the examination? Nay, a Ministry keenly inspired with the passion for National Efficiency would call into play every possible incentive to local improvement. The King might give a "Shield of Honour" to the local authority which has made the greatest progress in the year, together with a knighthood to the Mayor, and a Companionship of the Bath to the clerk, the engineer, and the medical officer of health. On the other hand, the six or eight districts which stood at the bottom of the list would be held up to public opprobrium, whilst the official report on their shortcomings might be sent by post to every local elector in the hope that public discussion would induce the inhabitants to choose more competent administrators. (*pp.* 8–10)

12

INDEPENDENT LABOUR PARTY

The I.L.P. originated in the dissatisfaction of new unionists and others with the existing Socialist societies which centred on London. The inaugural conference (a), which met at Bradford early in 1893, was attended by delegates from many local Labour clubs which had sprung into existence in the previous year or two. There were also present representatives both of the Fabian Society and of the local S.D.F. branches, but the central organisations of these bodies refused to merge themselves in the new party.

The I.L.P.'s propaganda was of a simple, undogmatic type much more suitable for a working-class audience than that of the S.D.F. One of its most notable exponents was "Elihu" (Samuel Washington), who wrote several tracts in a popular, colloquial style (b). A similar but much more famous author was Robert Blatchford, editor of the *Clarion*, whose *Merrie England* (c), originally published serially in his paper, sold three-quarters of a million copies in a penny edition in the course of one year. Blatchford's politics contained an element of nationalism, as may be seen from the title of his second Socialist work, *Britain for the British*. On this and other issues, differences arose between him and the majority of the I.L.P.'s leaders, of whom the most notable was Keir Hardie. Hardie was virtually in control of the I.L.P. from 1894 onwards: his plain, rugged oratory and semi-religious approach to politics were especially popular with Nonconformist audiences (e). Other aspects of the I.L.P.'s interests here illustrated are its concern for the unemployed (d), its activity in local government (f) and its hostility to "imperialist" war (g), which aroused bitter popular feeling in 1914–18. Tom Mann, Secretary of the I.L.P. from 1894 to 1898, and F. W. Jowett, its chairman in 1909–10 and again in later years, were both of working-class origin, the former a leader of the London Dock strike in 1889, but an engineer by trade, the latter a Bradford man who helped to found the Bradford Labour Union and eventually became a Labour cabinet minister (1924).

(a) *Independent Labour Party.* Debate at the Inaugural Conference on the Object of the Party

13 January 1893

Mr. Bardsley, Heywood, moved:—

> That the object of the Independent Labour Party shall be to secure the collective and communal ownership of all the means of production, distribution and exchange.

(Similar resolutions had been sent in from the London Independent Labour Party (Central Executive), Nelson Social Democratic Federation, Bradford Labour Union, Glasgow Scottish Labour Party, and the Camberwell Independent Labour Party). Mr. Bardsley said that all the rest of the Labour Party's programme consisted only of steps towards the ultimate goal represented by the resolution.

Mr. Birch, Bury, seconded the resolution.

Mr. Johnson, Nelson, supported the resolution.

Mr. Mahon, Leeds, moved as an amendment that the resolution read as follows:—

> That the objects of the Independent Labour Party shall be to secure the separate representation and protection of Labour interests on public bodies.

Mr. Vickers, Leeds, seconded the amendment. He was of the opinion that the original resolution was simply pledging the party to co-operation.

Mr. Shaw Maxwell said labour representation was not an object, but a means to an object. Let them not blink the fact that the most earnest members of the party were Social

Democrats, and if they had made a concession as to title let it end there. They should not, by abandoning something of policy, run the risk of losing some of the best minds in the country.

Mr. Christie, Nottingham, thought that the Conference ought not to bind people, who were not then represented, to any policy whatever. Their purpose and duty was to organise themselves.

Mr. Mahoney, Middlesbro', supported the resolution.

Mr. Marles, Leeds, speaking as a Socialist, supported the amendment.

Mr. Kennedy, Carlisle, supported the resolution. He said that the effect of the amendment would be to collect an army to march them into chaos.

Another delegate who supported the resolution contended that if the amendment were passed a path would be opened by which more men, such as Mr. Fenwick and Mr. Broadhurst, would creep into the same offices and dam the Labour Party to all eternity.

Mr. Gazeby, Bradford, proposed an amendment for the insertion of the word " ultimate " before the word " object ". He said his aim was to make it clear that the party did not hope to get collective ownership in the means of production immediately, but as soon as possible.

Mr. Russell Smart, Plymouth, seconded the amendment.

Mr. A. K. Donald, supported the amendment, on the ground that it was the only proposition before them which contained a plain and definite policy. They would make up their minds that the party was going to be organised on a very simple, clear basis, that everybody could understand and agree with.

Mr. Burgess pointed out that if the Conference accepted anything less than the resolution, the Independent Labour Party would be behind its branches in point of policy.

Mr. G. Bernard Shaw said the important question before them was whether they should vote upon a programme at all. He should vote for the resolution as it stood, because he was a Socialist, and he suggested that everyman who was not a Socialist should vote against it, and then that would show the strength of Socialism in the Conference.

Mr. Mahon's amendment was then put, and defeated by 91 votes to 16 votes; and the suggestion for the insertion of the word " ultimate " was defeated by 56 votes to 36.

Alderman Tillett suggested the omission of the words " and communal ", and the amendment was passed by 56 votes to 23 votes.

The original resolution as amended was put, and carried almost unanimously. (*Inaugural Conference Report*, 1893, *p*. 4)

(b) "ELIHU" (SAMUEL WASHINGTON). *Milk and Postage Stamps*

1893

In the street in which I reside there are forty-three houses, John. Within a few minutes of eight o'clock every morning a person in uniform comes along, who by means of organisation, has laid hold of all the letters which happen to be in transit at the time intended for the inhabitants of this street. No matter from what diverse quarters of the country they may have come, or from what part of the world, every letter upon the wing directs its flight into this man's capacious bag, and in due course is deposited by him in its respective letter-box. He appears to spend some ten or twelve minutes in the street, from there passes to the next one, and so on over the district; and when he has passed, every person in the district has been served with his letters.

Organisation works so; now observe how private enterprise supplies the street with milk. At 7.30 a milk cart comes lumbering along and delivers milk at one house, and away again. Half-an-hour later another milk cart arrives and delivers milk first on this side the street, then on that, until seven houses are supplied, and he departs. During the next three hours four other milk carts put in an appearance at varying intervals, supplying a house here and another there until finally, as it draws towards noon, their task is accomplished and the street is supplied with milk.

The time actually occupied by one and another of these distributors of milk makes in all about an hour and forty minutes, six men and six horses and carts being required for the purpose; and these equipages rattle along, one after the other, all over the district, through the greater part of the day, in the same erratic and extraordinary manner.

Look now at some other advantages of an organised system of trade. It is a curious thing, John, but the price of these pieces of gummed paper does not fluctuate. You never hear of there being a scarcity of postage stamps or of the market being glutted with them. They are never quoted in the market reports. The capitalists never try to make a corner in postage stamps and bring them to a fictitious value. The manufacturers are never gobbled up by a syndicate for the purpose of "controlling the supply" and running up the price from 1d. to 2d. by "restricting the output". There are no "middlemen", no wholesale dealers contriving to live handsomely out of handling them. And the supply, you will observe, is always equal to the demand; the demand to the supply. These two deities who sway and totter about in so perilous a manner in your other branches of trade appear somehow to find a level bottom here, and go steadily along, hand in hand, as though both were perfectly sober and in their right senses.

By way of contrast with this, look now at the way in which "private enterprise" carries on another branch of trade. Your 38,000,000 of people, in addition to a supply of postage stamps, require a supply of soap; and, of course, you have neglected to make any arrangements for supplying them with that. Certain individuals, some hundreds of them in all, have consequently laid themselves out for making good your omission. Exactly how many firms are engaged in this business I do not know, but say 300. I firmly believe, John, that an examination of the manner in which these 300 individuals direct the production and distribution of soap will convince you their method is disgracefully wasteful, and causes your soap to cost more than is in any way necessary. . . .

Coming now to a consideration of the ultimate results of this system of private enterprise we find that its effects do not bear upon all members of the community in the same manner; on the contrary we find it divides the community into two classes, the system operating adversely to the one and favourably to the other. Singularly enough the line of division here is found to correspond exactly with the line of division previously arrived at, by which the community were divided into the "wage earning class" and the "capitalist class". It is a remarkable fact, John, that in making an incision in the body politic, no matter in what direction, this line of division is found, and your "wage earning class" is invariably found placed in a disadvantageous position in reference to the "capitalist class".

Bearing in mind that some 33,000,000 of your people are included in the larger class, while only some 5,000,000 are included in the smaller one, I want you now to consider how each is affected by your system of production and distribution by private enterprise. Each individual member of the wage earning class is in the employ of some capitalist, helping him to produce wealth, a portion of the wealth produced being told off to him each week, not in kind but in money. This money the wage earner may exchange for what various commodities he may require, and it is obviously to his interest, if it could be accomplished, to have each article without extraneous cost. But, as we have already seen, the average proportion of extraneous cost in anything purchased by retail amounts to one-half of the price paid, and, consequently, the first result which becomes visible to us is that this 33,000,000 of people *are taxed to the extent of half their income* to make good the waste expenditure arising from your competitive system of trading. (*pp.* 33–5, 43*f.*)

(c) ROBERT BLATCHFORD. *Merrie England* 1894

John Smith, do you know what Socialism is? You have heard it denounced many a time, and it is said that you do not believe in it; but do you know what it is?

Good or bad, wise or foolish, it is all I have to offer as a remedy of the many evils of which I have been complaining.

Good or bad, wise or foolish, Socialism is the only remedy in sight. None of its opponents, none of your friends, the members of Parliament, old trade union leaders, Tory and Liberal editors, parsons, priests, lawyers, and men of substance have any remedy to offer at all.

Some of them are sorry, or profess to be sorry, that there is so much misery in the land; some of them offer a little mild charity, some a little feeble legislation, but there is no great radical cure to be heard of except Socialism.

What is Socialism? I am going to tell you, and I ask you to listen patiently, and to judge fairly. You have heard Socialism reviled by speakers and writers. You know that the Pope has denounced it, and that the Bishop of Manchester has denounced it. You know that men like Herbert Spencer, Charles Bradlaugh, and John Morley have written and spoken against it, and doubtless you have got an idea that it is as unworthy, as unwise, and as unworkable as such men say it is. Now I will describe it for you and you shall draw your own conclusions.

But before I tell you what Socialism is, I must tell you what Socialism is not. For half our time as champions of Socialism is wasted in denials of false descriptions of Socialism; and to a large extent the anger, the ridicule, and the argument of the opponents of Socialism are hurled against a Socialism which has no existence except in their own heated minds.

Socialism does not consist in violently seizing upon the property of the rich and sharing it out amongst the poor.

Socialists do not propose by a single Act of Parliament or by a sudden revolution, to put all men on an equality, and compel them to remain so. Socialism is not a wild dream of a happy land where the apples will drop off the trees into our open mouths, the fish come out of the rivers and fry themselves for dinner, and the looms turn out ready-made suits of velvet with gold buttons without the trouble of coaling the engine. Neither is it a dream of a nation of stained-glass angels, who never say damn, who always love their neighbours better than themselves, and who never need to work unless they wish to.

No. Socialism is none of these things. It is a scientific scheme of national Government, entirely wise, just and practical. And now let us see.

For convenience sake, Socialism is usually divided into two kinds. These are called—

1. Practical Socialism.
2. Ideal Socialism.

Really they are only part of one whole; Practical Socialism being a kind of preliminary step towards Ideal

Socialism, so that we might with more reason call them Elementary and Advanced Socialism.

I am an Ideal Socialist, and desire to have the whole Socialist programme carried out.

Practical Socialism is so simple that a child may understand it. It is a kind of national scheme of co-operation, managed by the State. Its programme consists, essentially, of one demand, that the land and other instruments of production shall be the common property of the people, and shall be used and governed by the people for the people.

Make the land and all the instruments of production State property; put all farms, mines, mills, ships, railways, and shops under State control, as you have already put the postal and telegraphic services under State control, and Practical Socialism is accomplished.

The postal and telegraphic service is the standing proof of the capacity of the State to manage the public business with economy and success.

That which has been done with the post-offices may be done with mines, trams, railways, and factories.

The difference between Socialism and the state of things now in existence will now be plain to you.

At present the land—that is, England—does not belong to the people—to the English—but to a few rich men. The mines, mills, ships, shops, canals, railways, houses, docks, harbours and machinery do not belong to the people, but to a few rich men.

Therefore, the land, the factories, the railways, ships, and machinery are not used for the general good of the people, but are used to make wealth for the few rich men who own them.

Socialists say that this arrangement is unjust and unwise, that it entails waste as well as misery, and that it would be better for all, even for the rich, that the land and other instruments of production should become the property of the State, just as the post-office and the telegraphs have become the property of the State.

Socialists demand that the State shall manage the railways and the mines and the mills just as it now manages the post-offices and the telegraphs.

Socialists declare that if it is wicked and foolish and impossible for the State to manage the factories, mines and railways, then it is wicked and foolish and impossible for the State to manage the telegraphs.

Socialists declare that as the State carries the people's letters and telegrams more cheaply and more efficiently than they were carried by private enterprise, so it could grow corn and weave cloth and work the railway systems more cheaply and more efficiently than they are now worked by private enterprise.

Socialists declare that as our Government now makes food and clothing and arms and accoutrements for the army and navy and police, so it could make them for the people.

Socialists declare that as many corporations make gas, provide and manage the water-supply, look after the paving and lighting and cleansing of the streets, and often do a good deal of building and farming, so there is no reason why they should not get coal and spin yarn, and make boots, and bread, and beer for the people.

Socialists point out that if all the industries of the nation were put under State control, all the profit which now goes into the hands of a few idle men, would go into the coffers of the State—which means that the people would enjoy the benefits of all the wealth they create.

This, then, is the basis of Socialism, that England should be owned by the English, and managed for the benefit of the English, instead of being owned by a few rich idlers, and mismanaged by them for the benefit of themselves.

But Socialism means more than the mere transference of the wealth of the nation to the nation.

Socialism would not endure competition. Where it found two factories engaged in under-cutting each other at the price of long hours and low wages to the workers, it would step in and fuse the two concerns into one, save an immense sum in cost of working, and finally produce more goods and better goods at a lower figure than were produced before.

But Practical Socialism would do more than that. It would educate the people. It would provide cheap and pure food. It would extend and elevate the means of study and amusement. It would foster literature and science and art. It would encourage and reward genius and industry. It would abolish sweating and jerry work. It would demolish the slums and erect good and handsome dwellings. It would compel all men to do some kind of useful work. It would recreate and nourish the craftsman's pride in his craft. It would protect women and children. It would raise the standard of health and morality; and it would take the sting out of pauperism by paying pensions to honest workers no longer able to work.

Why nationalise the land and instruments of production? To save waste; to save panics; to avert trade depressions, famines, strikes, and congestion of industrial centres; and to prevent greedy and unscrupulous sharpers from enriching themselves at the cost of the national health and prosperity. In short, to replace anarchy and war by law and order. To keep the wolves out of the fold, to tend and fertilise the field of labour instead of allowing the wheat to be strangled by the tares, and to regulate wisely the distribution of the seed-corn of industry so that it might no longer be scattered broadcast—some falling on rocks and some being eaten up by the birds of the air.

I will now give you one example of the difference between Socialism and the existing system.

You remember my chapter on Salt and Waste. Under

existing conditions what was the state of the salt trade?

The mines and manufacture owned and carried on by a number of firms, each of which competes against all the rest.

Result: Most of the small firms ruined; most of the large firms on the verge of ruin. Salt-boilers, the workmen, working twelve hours a day for 3s., and the public wasting more salt than they use.

Put this trade under State control. They will cease to make salt to waste; they will establish a six-hours day, and they will raise the wages of the men to, say, two pounds a week.

To pay these extra wages they will abolish all the unnecessary middlemen and go-betweens. The whole industry will be placed under one management. A vast number of clerks, agents, travellers, canvassers, and advertisers will be dispensed with, the salaries of managers will be almost entirely saved, and the cost of distribution will be cut down by fully 75 per cent.

The same system would be pursued with other industries.

Take the soap trade. There is one firm which spends over £100,000 a year in advertisement and the head of that firm makes £100,000 a year in profits. Socialism would save all that advertisement, and would pay a manager a reasonable salary and produce the soap at less than its present cost, whilst paying the workers good wages for shorter hours than they now work.

You will observe that under Practical Socialism there would be wages paid; and, probably, the wages of managers would be higher than the wages of workmen; and the wages of artists, doctors, and other clever and highly-trained men would be higher than those of weavers or navvies.

Under Ideal Socialism there would be no money at all and no wages. The industry of the country would be organised and managed by the State, much as the post-office now is; goods of all kinds would be produced and distributed for use, and not for sale, in such quantities as were needed, hours of labour would be fixed, and every citizen would take what he or she desired from the common stock. Food, clothing, lodging, fuel, transit, amusements, and all other things would be absolutely free, and the only difference between a prime minister and a collier would be the difference of rank and occupation. (*pp.* 98–103)

(d) TOM MANN. *The Programme of the I.L.P. and the Unemployed*

1895

To solve THE UNEMPLOYMENT PROBLEM will really be to solve the Labour problem, and although all the various points previously emphasised are important in their place, to the Socialist the chief of all questions is this of the unemployed; therefore upon our capacity to deal with Clause 4 in the Industrial programme depends our capacity to raise the standard of life to the realisation of the democratic ideal.

Neither political nor trade union power is of any material service save in proportion as it enables us to solve the unemployed question, and it may be definitely stated that the very existence of the unemployed is proof positive of the helplessness of the democracy in any and every nation where the unemployed exist. It is difficult to conceive of any limit to the mental and social progress of a people whose industrial system affords opportunities of development for all alike; and it is difficult to see what real progress can be made by the workers of any nation whose industrial system is dependent entirely upon the awful fact that a percentage of its citizens must be in enforced idleness and therefore competing for work.

The control of industry to-day is left to the care of

individuals whose sole concern is to

MAKE PROFIT FOR THEMSELVES

and although life and death depend upon industry, never yet has there been any organized attempt by the nation to regulate the industry of the nation in the nation's interest. Raw material and tools having been monopolised by a few individuals, and the custom of society and the law of the land approving of the profit-making basis of industry, that which decides whether or not trade shall be conducted, and to what extent, is not the public necessity, but the capacity of the controllers of industry to make a satisfactory profit for themselves. Thus in the case of the general lock-out of miners in 1893, although 300,000 miners' homes were directly affected and a large number of other workers indirectly, it was considered that the mine owners were quite within their right to exercise the power they possessed of closing the mines, if in their judgment they were not making a satisfactory profit, and that was purely the reason why the mines were closed, nor were they opened again until higher profits could be made. It was exactly the same on the occasion of the lock-out of the Lancashire cotton operatives, and precisely the same a few months ago, when the employers in the boot and shoe trade locked out all the operatives connected with that industry.

The basis of modern trade, then, is *profit-making for individuals,* and satisfactory profit-making depends upon the power of the employers to decide what wages shall be paid, and the power of the employers to decide this item depends upon a proportion of operatives being in enforced idleness, and forcing the hands of their mates in work; and if by trade union or other action the workers get a power which when applied, entrenches upon what the employers consider their legitimate profit, then employers can close works and refuse to take part in trade, although by so doing hundreds or thousands of persons are reduced to starvation and death; nay, it is because it so brings the workers to starvation and therefore makes them powerless that this conduct is indulged in.

The workers have no real means of escape from this humiliating position short of providing the means of constant employment for themselves.

Now, what is especially called for from Socialists is that they shall dare to fight for this all-important question of the unemployed, thus affording the means of a livelihood for all, entirely irrespective of what effect it may have upon the profit-making system. All other questions are of secondary importance to this, not only because of the suffering endured by those who are out of work, but also from the fact that the making of profits is dependent upon the existence of the unemployed who make the employed relatively powerless; and the present system leaves it in the power of the capitalist employers to create any number of unemployed by their power to stop work by lock-outs. The way for us to proceed is to saddle the responsibility for providing

WORK FOR ALL WHO WANT IT

upon the Government. The way for the Government to proceed is to forthwith take over all lands not cultivated, and begin at once to cultivate them in the most effective way, providing food stuffs and sending them to market to compete with those supplies sent in by private enterprise profit-makers, and to do the same with all mines, and mills, and factories, etc., not in use, to produce commodities therein, and supply the market, and, if need be, underselling the profit-makers, giving to them a dose of the competition they have so liberally indulged in. If private enterprise men complain, as they certainly would, the reply would be, "If they did not like trade under such conditions they could give it up," and if they gave it up the Government would take it in hand forthwith; no prolonged strike or lock-out would be possible, as the Government would take over and conduct all establishments where the private enterprise people failed to cater for the well-being of the community. (*pp.* 9–11)

(e) J. KEIR HARDIE, Speech at Pendlebury 27 November 1898

ON Sunday afternoon, November 27th, at the Labour Hall, Pendlebury, Keir Hardie preached an eloquent sermon from the familiar text, "Consider the lilies how they grow". There was a large and appreciative audience.

The speaker at the outset declared that however much people differed regarding what were termed the Christian mysteries, all agreed that if the ethical principles of Christ were adopted to-day the world would be all the better. Religion was meant to apply more to life now than hereafter. If they went to church they would hear sermons and hymns the burden of which was that he who sacrificed most for his fellows pleased God most, but did they think it was pleasing to God, and pleased his will and his kingdom on earth, that in England four millions were living below the poverty line, and never had enough food and clothing? One million yearly received poor-law relief, and 11,000 were in gaols, having broken the law, but were those the conditions of the Kingdom of God which made it easier and pleasanter to break the law than to keep it? Socialists contended that so long as the conditions dragged people down they could not establish morality. Suppose Luther or some other earnest religious reformer could visit London and learn of its 80,000 certified prostitutes—what would he say when he found as a barrier to their reclamation that no room could be found for them as workers at good wages? This was akin to the mockery which Christ denounced in the Pharisees, who "cleansed the outside of the cup and platter, while within it was full of dead men's bones". The speaker then pictured the scene when Christ delivered the strange and wonderful doctrine that men should, considering the lilies of the field and the birds of the air, take no thought of the morrow. But they could not follow that out to-day. They could only live lives as beautiful as the flowers and free from anxious care as the sparrows by being free to grow—free from restricting conditions. The child born in the slums without sunshine and fresh air would grow up stunted and colourless, even as a plant which as a boy he (the speaker) had tried to grow in the mine. Suppose one giant master-lily were allowed to absorb all the moisture, could they expect the surrounding lilies to grow up healthy and beautiful? Yet they allowed a huge land-owning system to exist which created monopolists of leisure and luxury, and absorbed that which should sustain the workers in health and comfort. Mr. Hardie concluded with an earnest appeal to his hearers to work truly and nobly for their cause, and win at last as much chance to develop beautiful lives as the lilies of the field. (*Pendlebury Pioneer,* December 1898)

(f) F. W. JOWETT. *The Socialist and The City*

1907

THE machinery of city government exists for the purpose of ministering to the health, convenience, and well-being of its inhabitants; thoughtful people generally agree so far. When, however, we attempt to secure these very desirable objects, we separate; the Socialist is in one camp, and those who for want of a better word must be described as individualists, are in the other. In actual practice the individualist, so-called, accepts certain established services that are Socialistic in principle. He accepts them because they exist, and because he cannot deny the benefit the community derives from them, but his predecessors resisted their establishment, and he is opposed to further extension of the same principle.

As for the Socialist—his position is more clearly defined. He believes that the public should own and manage every service which provides for the common good. He believes that all should co-operate to supply their common needs, rather than leave the work of providing for those needs to the chance operations of the conflicting interests of individuals, whose sole object is the making of profit.

So far as his influence extends in public affairs it is clear, therefore, that it will be exercised in the direction of increasing the number and value of public possessions. The health, happiness, and well-being of the community can only, in his opinion, be attained that way. Private enterprise has failed in the domain of municipal life. It has driven the people into ugly, inconvenient, jerry-built dwellings. It provides adulterated food in such quantities that numerous officials have to be maintained by the public for its detection, and even these it will corrupt if it can.

Where the provision of water, light, and transit is left to private enterprise, charges are heavy, the service as a rule is bad, and the men employed work long hours for low wages. There may be much vague feeling amongst the members of the public that the conditions under which men are called upon to work are unjust; and it may be, and generally is acknowledged that the chief concern of competing firms, catering for the requirements of the community, is not the public welfare, but dividends and profit, yet the public conscience cannot be brought to bear on those responsible, and, except in cases where the law is actually broken, the offenders cannot be reached.

The Socialist believes that in extending the area of municipal co-operation he is making it possible for the best and most thoughtful elements in the community to exercise a powerful influence in favour of the production of sound goods, and honest description of the same; whilst unjust conditions of work, and low wages, are far less likely to remain the lot of the worker when he has public conscience to appeal to, instead of a managing director whose sole business it is to make dividends for his shareholders; or a private firm, actuated generally by motives of personal gain.

For these and other reasons, the Socialist seeks at every opportunity to replace private competitive enterprise by public co-operative ownership. To a certain extent Town and City Councils offer him opportunities in this direction, and these in his capacity as public representative on such bodies, he uses, within the scope of the Municipal Corporations Act, to the best of his ability. As I have said, he is restrained in his efforts by the difficulty of carrying the public with him, and I may also add, his best attempts are often brought to destruction by the wrecking policy adopted by other representatives, who use their position, not to extend the power and influence of municipal life, but to limit its functions to the mere protection of life and property, in the purely legal sense. (*pp*. 4–7)

(g) *Independent Labour Party*. Manifesto on the War

11 August 1914

It has long been earnestly urged by the Independent Labour Party that the diplomatic policies pursued by European rulers, including our own, and supported by the force of murderous armaments, would lead inevitably to universal war or universal bankruptcy—or both. That prediction, based upon facts and tendencies, has been only too swiftly and tragically fulfilled.

The Cause of the War

Instead of striving to unite Europe in a federation of States, banded together for peace, diplomacy has deliberately aimed at dividing Europe into two armed, antagonistic camps, the Triple Entente and the Triple Alliance. Diplomacy has been underground, secret, deceitful, each Power endeavouring by wile and stratagem to get the better of its neighbour. Diplomats have breathed the very air of jealousy, deception, and distrust. Each country, in turn, largely through the influence of its Jingo Press, has been stampeded by fear and panic. Each country has tried to outstrip other countries in the vastness and costliness of its war machine. Powerful armament interests have played their sinister part, for it is they who reap rich harvest out of havoc and death. When all this has been done, any spark will start a conflagration like the present.

It is difficult and perhaps futile to try to apportion at this moment the exact measure of responsibility and blame which the various countries must bear. It is just as untrue to say that British policy has been wholly white and German policy wholly black as to say that German policy has been entirely right and British policy entirely wrong. Simple undiscriminating people in both countries may accept unreservedly one or other of these alternatives, but, as past experience shows, history will tell a different story.

Secret Diplomacy

For the present Sir Edward Grey issues his White Paper to prove Germany the aggressor, just as Germany issues a White Paper to prove Russia the aggressor, and Russia to prove Austria the aggressor. Even if every word in the British White Paper be admitted, the wider indictment remains. Let it be acknowledged that in the days immediately preceding the war, Sir Edward Grey worked for peace. It was too late. Over a number of years, together with other diplomats, he had himself dug the abyss, and wise statesmanship would have foreseen, and avoided, the certain result.

It was not the Servian question or the Belgian question that pulled this country into the deadly struggle. Great Britain is not at war because of oppressed nationalities or Belgian neutrality. Even had Belgian neutrality not been wrongfully infringed by Germany we should still have been drawn in.

If France in defiance of treaty rights had invaded Belgium to get at Germany, who believes we should have begun hostilities against France? Behind the back of Parliament and people, the British Foreign Office gave secret understandings to France, denying their existence when challenged. That is why this country is now face to face with the red ruin and impoverishment of war. Treaties and agreements have dragged Republican France at the heels of despotic Russia, Britain at the heels of France. At the proper time all this will be made plain, and the men responsible called to account.

We desire neither the aggrandisement of German militarism nor Russian militarism, but the danger is that this war will promote one or the other. Britain has placed herself behind Russia, the most reactionary, corrupt, and oppressive Power in Europe. If Russia is permitted to gratify her territorial ambitions and extend her Cossack rule, civilisation and democracy will be gravely imperrilled. Is it for this that Britain has drawn the sword?

Tens of thousands of our fellow-workers are in the front of battle, knowing not if they will ever return again. Already many have fallen, and soon the death-roll will mount appallingly and the wounded lie suffering on the battlefield, on the decks of ships, and in the hospitals. Among those who are bravely facing this fate are many of our Socialist comrades serving in the regular forces, the reserves, and the territorials.

Hardly less dread is the position of the women and children at home who are dependent on those who are under arms, and the countless workers and their families who are plunged into unemployment and destitution by the war. Almost no conceivable effort—even if the food supply of the country holds out—will prevent the occurrence of fearful privation amongst them.

German Workers Our Comrades

And what is true of the soldiers and the workers and their families of our own country is no less true of those of France, Belgium, Germany, and other lands. Is it not right that we should remember this?

To us who are Socialists the workers of Germany and Austria, no less than the workers of France and Russia, are comrades and brothers; in this hour of carnage and eclipse we have friendship and compassion to all victims of militarism. Our nationality and independence, which are dear to us, we are ready to defend; but we cannot rejoice in the organised murder of tens of thousands of workers of other lands who go to kill and be killed at the command of rulers to whom the people are as pawns.

The war conflagration envelops Europe; up to the last moment we laboured to prevent the blaze. The nation must now watch for the first opportunity for effective intervention.

As to the future, we must begin to prepare our minds for the difficult and dangerous complications that will arise at the conclusion of the war.

The People must everywhere resist such territorial aggression and national abasement as will pave the way for fresh wars; and, throughout Europe, the workers must press for frank and honest diplomatic policies, controlled by themselves, for the suppression of militarism and the establishment of the United States of Europe, thereby advancing toward the world's peace. Unless these steps are taken

Europe, after the present calamity, will be still more subject to the increasing domination of militarism, and liable to be drenched with blood.

Socialism Will Yet Triumph

We are told that International Socialism is dead, that all our hopes and ideals are wrecked by the fire and pestilence of European war. It is not true.

Out of the darkness and the depth we hail our working-class comrades of every land. Across the roar of guns, we send sympathy and greeting to the German Socialists. They have laboured unceasingly to promote good relations with Britain, as we with Germany. They are no enemies of ours but faithful friends.

In forcing this appalling crime upon the nations, it is the rulers, the diplomats, the militarists who have sealed their doom. In tears and blood and bitterness the greater Democracy will be born. With steadfast faith we greet the future; our cause is holy and imperishable, and the labour of our hands has not been in vain.

Long live Freedom and Fraternity. Long live International Socialism. (*I.L.P. Report*, 1915, *pp.* 115*f.*)

13

INDUSTRIAL UNIONISM AND SYNDICALISM

The Socialist Labour Party, founded in 1903 on Clydeside by a group of seceders from the S.D.F., took the idea of industrial unionism from the American Daniel De Leon and his organisation the Industrial Workers of the World (a). The movement received a fresh impetus as a result of the return to Britain in 1910 of Tom Mann, the former I.L.P. leader, who had for some years been involved in labour politics in Australasia. Tom Mann, under the influence of French Syndicalism as well as of the American movement, plunged into syndicalist propaganda among the unions, and issued a monthly pamphlet-journal, designed to fit easily into the pocket of a workman's overalls (b). The movement had some success among the transport workers and also among the South Wales miners, who were dissatisfied with their leaders and who set up an Unofficial Reform Committee to demand more militant action against the employers. The programme approved by this Committee, *The Miners' Next Step* (c), was drafted by Noah Ablett.

(a) *Platform of the Socialist Labour Party*

1905

THE Socialist Labour Party is a political organization seeking to establish political and social freedom for all, and seeing in the conquest by the Socialist Working Class of all the governmental and administrative powers of the nation the means to the attainment of that end.

It affirms its belief that political and social freedom are not two separate and unrelated ideas, but are two sides of the one great principle, each being incomplete without the other.

The course of society politically has been from warring but democratic tribes within each nation to a united government under an absolutely undemocratic monarchy. Within this monarchy again developed revolts against its power, revolts at first seeking to limit its prerogatives only, then demanding the inclusion of certain classes in the governing power, then demanding the right of the subject to criticise and control the power of the monarch, and finally, in the most advanced countries this movement culminated in the total abolition of the monarchical institution, and the transformation of the subject into the citizen.

In industry a corresponding development has taken place. The independent producer, owning his own tools and knowing no master, has given way before the more effective productive powers of huge capital, concentrated in the hands of the great capitalist. The latter, recognising no rights in his workers, ruled as an absolute monarch in his factory. But within the realm of capital developed a revolt against the power of the capitalist. This revolt, taking the form of trade unionism, has pursued in the industrial field the same line of development as the movement for political freedom has pursued in the sphere of national government. It first contented itself with protests against excessive exactions, against all undue stretchings of the power of the capitalist; then its efforts broadened out to demands for restrictions upon the absolute character of such power, i.e., by claiming for trade unions the right to make rules for the workers in the workshop; then it sought to still further curb the capitalist's power by shortening the working day, and so limiting the period during which the toiler may be exploited. Finally, it seeks by Boards of Arbitration to establish an equivalent in the industrial world for that compromise in the political world by which, in constitutional countries, the monarch retains his position by granting a parliament to divide with him the duties of governing, and so hides while securing his power. And as in the political history of the race the logical development of progress was found in the abolition of the institution of monarchy, and not in its mere restriction, so in industrial history the culminating point to which all efforts must at last converge lies in the abolition of the capitalist class, and not in the mere restriction of its powers.

The Socialist Labour Party, recognising these two phases of human development, unites them in its programme, and seeks to give them a concrete embodiment by its demand for a Socialist Republic.

It recognises in all past history a preparation for this achievement, and in the industrial tendencies of to-day it hails the working out of those laws of human progress which bring that object within our reach.

The concentration of capital in the form of trusts at the same time simplifies the task we propose that society shall undertake, viz. the dispossession of the capitalist class, and the administration of all land and instruments of industry as social property, of which all shall be co-heirs and owners.

As to-day the organised power of the State theoretically guarantees to every individual his political rights, so in the Socialist Republic the power and productive forces of organised society will stand between every individual and want, guaranteeing that right to life without which all other rights are but mockery.

Short of the complete dispossession of the capitalist class which this implies there is no hope for the workers.

SPEED THE DAY. (*The Socialist,* Edinburgh, November, 1905)

(b) TOM MANN. *Forging the Weapon*

1910

SLOWLY but surely it is coming to be realised in the Labour Movement that economic organisation is more than merely helpful to the attainment of better conditions; that it is not only a means, but the chief means, whereby progress can be made.

The present day degradation of so large a percentage of the workers is directly due to their economic enslavement; and it is economic freedom that is demanded.

Now Parliamentary action is at all times useful, in proportion as it makes for economic emancipation of the workers. But Socialists and Labour men in Parliament can only do effective work there in proportion to the intelligence and economic organisation of the rank and file.

True, a thorough going, fearless, revolutionary group in the House of Commons might succeed in being a nuisance to the plutocratic members, even though there were no industrial organisation at all. But there is no possibility of achieving economic freedom, nor even of taking any steps towards that end, unless the workers themselves are conscious that what they suffer from, as a class, is economic subjugation and consequent exploitation by the capitalists.

Moreover, unless the workers themselves, protest against this subjugation and exploitation, and themselves form organisations for the specific purpose of persistently fighting the enemy until freedom shall be won—then all else is as nothing. The strong right arm of the Labour Movement is direct economic organisation. This alone makes possible concerted action, whereby the workers may be enabled to decide the conditions under which production shall be carried on.

But it must be made clear that neither industrial organisation, nor Parliamentary action, nor both combined, can achieve the emancipation of the workers unless such emancipation is definitely aimed at.

Unionism that aims only at securing peace between employers and men is not only of no value in the fight for freedom, but is actually a serious hindrance and a menace to the interests of the workers.

Political and industrial action direct must at all times be inspired by revolutionary principles. That is, the aim must ever be to change from capitalism to Socialism as speedily as possible. Anything less than this means continued domination by the capitalist class. . . .

The struggles of the future will have to be fought scientifically. The relationship of union to union for Syndicalist purposes must be equal to an amalgamation of all unions in any one industry. Without this the capitalists are certain to win—and only fools would think of fighting them when we know that they are organised by whole industries and not, as we are at present, by small ineffectual sections.

Industrial Syndicalism, therefore, and not sectional trade unionism, must be the basis of all future industrial activity for fighting purposes.

In an industry there may be fifty trades. For each trade there may be one or more unions, each designated a "trade union" because it consists of the men connected with that trade. When, for the purpose of waging the Class War, these unions coalesce into one compact organisation for the whole industry, this union of unions is properly termed an "Industrial Union". As the title implies, the workers of all trades and occupations connected with the industry are represented, including, of course, the labourers.

It is this union of unions, inspired with the revolutionary spirit of Syndicalism, that will do the fighting of the future. (*Industrial Syndicalist*, September 1910)

(c) *Unofficial Reform Committee of the South Wales Miners Federation. The Miners' Next Step*

1912

The Elimination of the Employer

This can only be obtained gradually and in one way. We cannot get rid of employers and slave-driving in the mining industry, until all other industries have organised for, and progressed towards, the same objective. Their rate of progress conditions ours, all we can do is to set an example and the pace.

Nationalisation of Mines

Does not lead in this direction, but simply makes a National Trust, with all the force of the Government behind it, whose one concern will be, to see that the industry is run in such a way, as to pay the interest on the bonds, with which the Coalowners are paid out, and to extract as much profit as possible, in order to relieve the taxation of other landlords and capitalists.

Our only concern is to see to it, that those who create the value receive it. And if by the force of a more perfect organization and more militant policy, we reduce profits, we shall at the same time tend to eliminate the shareholders who run the coalfield. As they feel the increasing pressure we shall be bringing on their profits, they will loudly cry for Nationalization. We shall and must strenuously oppose this in our own interests, and in the interests of our objective.

Industrial Democracy the Objective

To-day the shareholders own and rule the coalfields. They own and rule them mainly through paid officials. The men who work in the mine are surely as competent to elect these, as shareholders who may never have seen a colliery. To have a vote in determining who shall be your fireman, manager, inspector, etc., is to have a vote in determining the conditions which shall rule your working life. On that vote will depend in a large measure your safety of life and limb, and your freedom from oppression by petty bosses, and would give you an intelligent interest in, and control over, your conditions of work. To vote for a man to represent you in Parliament, to make rules for, and assist in appointing officials to rule you, is a different proposition altogether.

Our objective begins to take shape before your eyes. Every industry thoroughly organized, in the first place, to fight, to gain control of, and then to administer that industry. The co-ordination of all industries on a Central Production Board, who, with a statistical department to ascertain the needs of the people, will issue its demands on the different departments of industry, leaving to the men themselves to determine under what conditions and how, the work should be done. This would mean real democracy in real life, making for real manhood and womanhood. Any other form of democracy is a delusion and a snare.

Every fight for, and victory won by the men, will inevitably assist them in arriving at a clearer conception of the responsibilities and duties before them. It will also assist them to see, that so long as shareholders are permitted to continue their ownership, or the State administers on behalf of the shareholders, slavery and oppression are bound to be the rule in industry. And with this realization, the age-long oppression of Labour will draw to its end. The weary sigh of the over-driven slave, pitilessly exploited and regarded as an animated tool or beast of burden: the mediaeval serf fast bound to the soil, and life-long prisoner on his lord's domain, subject to all the caprices of his lord's lust or anger: the modern wage-slave, with nothing but his labour to sell, selling that, with his manhood as a wrapper, in the world's market for a mess of pottage : these three phases of slavery, each in their turn inevitable and unavoidable, will have exhausted the possibilities of slavery, and mankind shall at last have leisure and inclination to really live as men, and not as the beasts which perish. (*pp.* 28–30)

14

GUILD SOCIALISM

Guild Socialism originated in the same suspicions of the bureaucratic tendencies in State Socialism that animated the Syndicalists. It developed as an attempt, by a number of intellectuals, to synthesise the concepts of Collectivism and Syndicalism, so that the achievement of nationalisation might be followed at once by decentralisation and the assumption of a wide measure of control in industry by the producers themselves. Its ideas which owe much to Ruskin and Morris are foreshadowed in A. J. Penty's *Restoration of the Gild System* (a), but some years elapsed before the movement began to spread, as a result of the propaganda of S. G. Hobson and A. R. Orage in the weekly, the *New Age* (b), and of the work of the Oxford don, G. D. H. Cole (c). The National Guilds League was founded in 1915, but was broken up by the dissensions arising from the fresh issues raised by the Russian Revolution. Although certain Building Guilds were formed and functioned for a time just after the war, Guild Socialism failed to maintain its separate organisation. It has, however, had a marked influence on British Socialist thought, which has been augmented by the ability of exponents such as Cole and another Oxford intellectual, R. H. Tawney, a historian and a pioneer of workers' education (d).

(a) A. J. PENTY. *The Restoration of the Gild System*

1906

For the sake of clearness, therefore, we will define the terms competition and commercialism as follows: Commercialism means the control of industry by the financier (as opposed to the master craftsman) while competition means the rivalry of producers.

Viewing Collectivism in this light, we find that it seeks to eliminate, not commercialism, but competition. In so doing it establishes more securely than ever the worst features of the present system. The mere transference of the control of industry from the hands of the capitalist into those of the state, can make no essential difference to the nature of the industry affected. In Belgium, for example where the bread-making and shirt-making industries have been nationalized, it has been found impossible to abolish sweating, or to introduce a shorter working day. This abandonment of the principle of social justice at the outset doubtless foreshadows its abandonment for ever; since, as Collectivists become more and more concerned with practical politics, the difficulties of asserting their ideals, together with the establishment of their system of organization, will likewise be more and more increased. Moreover, after its establishment, the difficulties of reforming any State Department are well known; and how shall society be prevented from acquiescing in the present commercial abuses, under a collectivist régime, and treating them as inevitable evils?

This question is a very pertinent one, since, according to the economics of Collectivism, every industry nationalized must be made to pay, and a Government charged with the administration of any industry would become interested in its continuance as a business, quite apart from its usefulness or otherwise, or whether or no it had been called into existence by some temporary and artificial need of modern civilization. Thus the Government at the present time, having nationalized the telegraphs, becomes interested in the continuance of gambling, the use of the system being its real basis of support, and not the comparatively insignificant percentage of work undertaken in respect to the more human agencies which require it. Again, were existing railways nationalized, Government would become interested in the continuance of wasteful cross distribution, called into existence by the competition of traders. Similarly, the gradual development of municipal trading and manufacture would tend to militate against the depopulation of towns. And this conservative tendency is inevitable, since Collectivism can only maintain its ground as a national system so long as it justifies the claims of its advocates to financial soundness.

Co-operation in its inception aimed at the establishment of an ideal commonwealth, but the co-operative ideal has long since departed from the movement, and little but a scramble for dividends remain. In like manner it is not unreasonable to suppose that Collectivism, having made its appeal for popular support on the grounds of its capacity to earn profits for the public, would suffer a similar degeneration. The electorate, in their profit-making zeal, would certainly not remedy abuses if their dividends were to be lowered, for they would still retain the superstition that only by producing dividends could their finances be kept in a healthy condition. Inasmuch as the ultimate control of industry would rest in the hands of the financier, production for profit and not for use would continue. For what other test can there be of a financier's skill except his ability to produce profits?

In a word Collectivism means State Commercialism.

So long as the people are attached to their present habits of life and thought, and possess the same ill-regulated tastes, a State Department, charged with the administration of industry, would be just as much at the mercy of supply and demand as at present, while the fluctuations of taste would be just as disturbing to them as the fluctuations of public opinion are to the politician.

This brings us to the great political fallacy of the Collectivist doctrine—namely, the assumption that Government should be conducted solely in the interests of man in his capacity as consumer—a superstition which has survived the Manchester School; for a little consideration will convince us that in a true social system the aim of the Government would not be to exalt either producer or consumer at the expense of the other, but to maintain a balance of power between the two.

The policy of exalting the consumer at the expense of the producer would be perfectly sound, if the evils of the present day were caused by the tyranny of the producer. But is it so? It is true that trade is in such a hopeless condition that the consumer is very much at the mercy of unscrupulous producers. The cause of this, however, is not to be found in the preference of producers generally for crooked ways, but in the tyranny of consumers which forces the majority of producers to adopt malpractices in self-defence. Doubtless all trade abuses have in their origin been the work of individual producers. They grow, in the first place, because without privileges the more honourable producers are powerless to suppress them, and secondly, because consumers generally are so wanting in loyalty to honest producers, and are so ready to believe that they can get sixpennyworth of stuff for threepence, that they deliberately place themselves in the hands of the worst type of producer. In every department of life the successful man is he who can lead the public to believe they are getting something for nothing, and generally speaking, if consumers are defrauded by producers, it is because they deserve to be. The truth of this statement will be attested by all who, in any department of industry, have made efforts to raise its tone. Everywhere it is the tyranny of the consumer that blocks the way. For example, anybody who has followed the history of the Arts and Crafts movement, and noted the efforts which have been made to raise the quality of English production must be convinced that this is the root of the difficulty. If the public were capable of a tenth part of the sacrifice which others have undertaken on their behalf, we might see our way out of the industrial quagmire.

The evil would not be remedied by bringing industry under State Control. Rather would it be intensified. Art in the past had its private patrons, and while these continue some good work may still be done. But the artist is powerless when face to face with a public body whose taste recognized no ultimate standard, but taken collectively is always the reflection of the vulgarity its members see around them. As we may assume that private patrons would cease under Collectivism, so Art's last support would disappear also. Whatever good work has been done for the public during the past century has been in the main the result of accident. Collective control foreshadows, not the abolition of poverty in our midst, by the direction of industry passing into the hands of wise administrators, but the final abandonment of all standards of quality in production, owing to the complete subjection of all producers to the demoralizing tyranny of an uninstructed majority. (*pp.* 3–10)

(b) *The Bondage of Wagery.* An Open Letter to the Trades Union Congress

1913

During the past two years we have been at great pains in elaborating a constructive programme to be followed after the wage-earners had repudiated wagery. . . . We will endeavour briefly to summarise our argument. Let us suppose that labour in this country were so completely organised as to constitute a monopoly. On one side we should have the profiteers possessing the machinery and the land; on the other, the army of workers in complete possession of the labour. Obviously, a dead-lock. What would be done? The State Socialists would contend that the way out would be for the State to purchase the assets and to work them. But the amount of money involved in the purchase would remain a permanent charge upon labour equivalent to the existing rent, interest and profits. Labour would be no better off. Worse remains: the State would have to maintain the wage-system because there would be no other means to pay the interest on the purchase price. Does that puzzle you? It is really quite simple. All rent, interest and profits come out of the difference between the price of labour as a commodity and the selling price of the finished product. If, therefore, Labour had organised itself to abolish wagery, it would naturally reject the overtures of the State to continue the wage system. There would, therefore, be no fund out of which to pay interest to the discharged profiteers. This is the fatal objection to State Socialism. It predicates purchase, the purchase price to be a national debt, paying interest in the usual way. It must therefore equally predicate the continuance of the wage system. Worse still remains to be told: the State would find that the cost of production would so seriously increase as to put it out of action in the world's market. Every serious student has now finally discarded State Socialism, either as an economic improvement upon existing capitalism, or as a cure for the ills of wagery. Nevertheless, the present owners of the plant and machinery are entitled to recompense. Our own proposal in this regard is to pay them a reasonable annuity for two generations. It is, at least, rough and ready justice.

We fear that our argument seems to you to tend towards Syndicalism. Fundamentally, we do not accept Syndicalism because it argues for the possession by every union of its own land and machinery. To this we do not assent, because all wealth—particularly plant and machinery—belongs to the community, and does not, and ought not to, belong to any particular group. We would accordingly vest all industrial assets in the State, to be leased by the State to the appropriate guilds. This lease would be in the nature of a charter.

We can now see the beginnings of a new order of society from which the wage-system has been eliminated. In this new society the Trades Union Congress may become the nucleus of an industrial parliament—the plenary committee of the federated guilds.

You, perhaps, are now curious to know what we mean by a guild. A guild is the combination of all the labour of every kind, administrative, executive and productive in any particular industry. It includes those who work with their brains and those who contribute labour power. Administrators, chemists, skilled and unskilled labour, clerks—everybody who can do work—are all entitled to membership. This combination clearly means a true labour monopoly. The State, as trustee for the whole community, by charter (the terms being mutually agreed upon) hands over to this guild all the plant, material and assets generally cognate to the industry. The guild must be national in its organisation and ramifications. In mediaeval times the guilds were local. The railway and telegraph and telephone have annihilated time and space and killed the old sense of locality. Thus we have a labour monopoly married to the mechanical means of wealth production. In our opinion there ought to be about fifteen of these guilds covering the vast majority of the working population. They would mutually exchange their products, referring all difficulties and all questions of policy to the general committee of the federated guilds, a body which ought to descend direct from the Trades Union Congress.

What, in these new circumstances, would be the substitute for wagery? Has it ever struck you that soldiers never receive wages? They receive pay—officers and men of all ranks.

What is the distinction? Mainly in this: so long as a soldier belongs to the Army, he receives pay whether playing or working. He does not sell his labour as a commodity; his labour is not marketable, and there is no profit on it. In like manner, every member of a guild would receive pay whether working or playing, employed or unemployed. (It is only in this direction that any solution of the unemployed problem can be found.) The guilds would be absolute masters of their own economic affairs. They would themselves undertake certain duties now clumsily undertaken by the State—insurance, compensation for injury, sickness and old-age pensions. It would not be wise to elaborate here too many of the details of guild organisation. Our present purpose is to urge you to concentrate upon the wage-system and to understand the evils that flow out of it. We have felt it necessary to go one step further to prove that modern capitalism, founded as it is upon wagery, is by no means the last word in social or industrial organisation.

The transition from wagery to the national guilds will be a period of thrilling interest far transcending in its intensity the artificial excitement of present Parliamentary politics. The work calls for men of strong will and clear judgment. There is a coterie of thinkers who now assert that capitalism has finally subdued our population into a servile state. We have not only intellectually combated that view but have passionately resented it. Our belief in the principles of democracy remains unshaken. We believe that out of the mass of the working population can be developed genius and character as great as can be found under any aristocratic or autocratic system of life and government. Above all, we know that the British worker is the finest fighter in the world when once his interest has been touched, his passions aroused, and his imagination quickened. In the struggle that lies before you, all these qualities will be requisitioned. When you are convinced that what we have here written is substantially true, we have no doubt of the issue. (*New Age*, 28 August, 1913)

(c) G. D. H. COLE. *Self-Government in Industry* 1917

WHAT, I want to ask, is the fundamental evil in our modern Society which we should set out to abolish?

There are two possible answers to that question, and I am sure that very many well-meaning people would make the wrong one. They would answer POVERTY, when they ought to answer SLAVERY. Face to face every day with the shameful contrasts of riches and destitution, high dividends and low wages, and painfully conscious of the futility of trying to adjust the balance by means of charity, private or public, they would answer unhesitatingly that they stand for the ABOLITION OF POVERTY.

Well and good! On that issue every Socialist is with them. But their answer to my question is none the less wrong.

Poverty is the symptom: slavery the disease. The extremes of riches and destitution follow inevitably upon the extremes of license and bondage. The many are not enslaved because they are poor, they are poor because they are enslaved. Yet Socialists have all too often fixed their eyes upon the material misery of the poor without realising that it rests upon the spiritual degradation of the slave.

I say they have not realised this, although they have never ceased to proclaim that there is a difference between social reform and Socialism, although they have always professed to stand for the overthrow of the capitalist system. For who among our evolutionary Socialists can explain wherein this difference consists, and who of our revolutionists understands what is meant by the overthrow of Capitalism?

It is easy to understand how Socialists have come so to insist upon the fact of poverty. Not one of them, at least until he has eaten of the forbidden fruit of office in the political Garden of Eden, but is moved by an intense conviction that our civilisation is beyond measure degrading and immoral. His first object, then, is to make others see that he is right. What more natural than to exhibit, before the eyes of all men, the open sore of physical misery? Even the least imaginative can see the evils of poverty, and the majority are supposed to lack imagination. We, therefore, confront the world with the incontrovertible fact that the few are rich and the many poor. The idea that the fundamental aim of Socialism is the abolition of poverty begins in an *argumentum ad hominem*.

I have not time to describe the effect of this attitude on the practice of Socialists in the political field. I can only say, in a few words, why I believe it to have been disastrous. Our preoccupation with poverty is the cause of our long wanderings in the valley of the shadow of reformism: it is the cause of that dragging of Labour into a Liberal alliance which has wrecked every chance of successful political action for a generation to come. There are too many to whom Socialism has come to mean a steeper graduation of the income-tax, the nationalisation of mines and railways and the break-up of the poor law, together with a shadowy something behind all these to which they can give neither name nor substance. The very avidity with which we clung like drowning men, to the somewhat bulky straw of the Minority Report was a clear indication of our bankruptcy in the realm of ideas. To many of us, that very adroit and necessary adjunct to the capitalist system seemed the crowning expression of the constructive Socialism of our day. Our generation was seeking for a sign; but there was no sign given it save the sign of the prophet Jonah. And Jonah, if my memory serves, was a minor prophet.

The biblical Jonah once had the fortune to be swallowed by a whale. In our days, the tables have been turned, and, instead of the Labour movement swallowing its Jonah, Jonah has swallowed the Labour movement.

Inspired by the idea that poverty is the root evil, Socialists have tried to heal the ills of Society by an attempt to redistribute income. In this attempt, it will be admitted that they have hitherto met with no success. The gulf between rich and poor has not grown an inch narrower; it has even appreciably widened. It is the conviction of Guild-Socialists that the gulf will never be bridged, as long as the social problem is regarded as pre-eminently a question of distribution.

Idle rich and unemployed poor apart, every individual has two functions in the economic sphere—he is both a producer and consumer of goods and services. Socialists, in seeking a basis on which to build their ideal Society, have alternated between these two aspects of human activity. The Fourierists, the Christian Socialists and the Communists, with their ideals of the phalangstery, the self-governing workshop, and the free Commune, built—and built imperfectly—upon man the producer. Collectivism, on the other hand, which includes most modern schools of Socialism, builds upon man the consumer. It is our business to decide which, if either, of them is right.

It is the pride of the practical social reformer that he deals with "the average man in his average moments". He repudiates, as high falutin nonsense, every attempt to erect a new social order on a basis of idealism; he is vigilantly distrustful of human nature, human initiative and human freedom; and he finds his ideal in a paternal govenmentalism tempered by a preferably not too real democratic control. To minds of such a temper, Collectivism has an irresistible appeal. The idea that the State is not only supreme in the last resort, but also a capable jack of all trades, offers to the bureaucrat a wide field of petty tyranny. In the State of to-day, in which democratic control through Parliament is little better than a farce, the Collectivist State would be the Earthly Paradise of bureaucracy.

The Socialist in most cases admits this, but declares that it could be corrected if Parliament were democratised. The "conquest of political power" becomes the Alpha and Omega of his political method: all his cheques are post-dated to the Greek Kalends of the first Socialist Government. Is, then, his ideal of the democratic control of industry through Parliament an ideal worthy of the energy which is expended in its furtherance?

The crying need of our days is the need for freedom. Machinery and Capital between them have made the worker a mere serf, with no interest in the product of his own labour beyond the inadequate wage which he secures by it. The Collectivist State would only make his position better by securing him a better wage, even if we assume that Collectivism can ever acquire the driving power to put its ideas into practice: in other respects it would leave the worker essentially as he is now—a wage-slave, subject to the will of a master imposed on him from without. However democratically minded Parliament might be, it would none the less remain, for the worker in any industry, a purely external force, imposing its commands from outside and from above. The postal workers are no more free while the Post Office is managed by a State department than Trade Unionists would be free if their Executive Committees were appointed by His Majesty's Minister of Labour. (New ed., 1919, *pp.* 34–8)

(d) R. H. TAWNEY. *The Acquisitive Society*

1921

Economic science has never escaped from the peculiar bias received from the dogmatic rationalism which presided at its birth. Man seeks pleasure and shuns pain. He desires riches and hates effort. A simple, yet delicate, hedonistic calculus resides in the bosom of "employer" and "labourer"; so that they will respond with the precision of a needle to the magnetic pole, and they will respond to nothing else. That doctrine has been expelled from psychology and political science: the danger to-day is that these studies should lay too little stress upon reason, not too much, and forget that however unreasonable human beings may be proved to be, the principal moral to be drawn is that at any rate they should be as reasonable as they can. But mere crude eighteenth century rationalism still works havoc with the discussion of economic issues, and, above all, of organization. It is still used as a lazy substitute for observation, and to suggest a simplicity of motive which is quite foreign to the facts.

All that type of thought belongs to the dark ages. The truth is that we ought radically to revise the presuppositions as to human motives on which current presentations of economic theory are ordinarily founded, and in terms of which the discussion of economic questions is usually carried on. The assumption that the stimulus of imminent personal want is either the only spur, or a sufficient spur, to productive effort is a relic of a crude psychology which has little warrant either in past history or in present experience. It derives what plausibility it possesses from a confusion between work in the sense of the lowest *quantum* of activity needed to escape actual starvation, and the work which is given, irrespective of the fact that elementary wants may already have been satisfied, through the natural disposition of ordinary men to maintain, and of extraordinary men to improve upon, the level of exertion accepted as reasonable by the public opinion of the group of which they are members. It is the old difference, forgotten by society as often as it is learned, between the labour of the free man and that of the slave. Economic fear may secure the minimum effort needed to escape economic penalties. What, however, has made progress possible in the past, and what, it may be suggested, matters to the world to-day, is not the bare minimum which is required to avoid actual want, but the capacity of men to bring to bear upon their tasks a degree of energy, which, while it can be stimulated by economic incentives, yields results far in excess of any which are necessary merely to avoid the extremes of hunger or destitution.

That capacity is a matter of training, tradition and habit, at least as much as of pecuniary stimulus, and the ability to raise it of a professional association representing the public opinion of a group of workers is, therefore, considerable. Once industry has been liberated from its subservience to the interests of the functionless property-owner, it is in this sphere that trade unions may be expected increasingly to find their functions. Its importance both for the general interests of the community and for the special interests of particular groups of workers can hardly be exaggerated. Technical knowledge and managerial skill are likely to be available as readily for a committee appointed by the workers in an industry as for a committee appointed, as now, by the shareholders. But it is more and more evident to-day that the crux of the economic situation is not the technical deficiencies of industrial organization, but the growing inability of those who direct industry to command the active good will of the *personnel*. Their co-operation is promised by the conversion of industry into a profession serving the public, and promised, as far as can be judged, by that alone.

Nor is the assumption of the new and often disagreeable obligations of internal discipline and public responsibility one which trade unionism can afford, once the change is accomplished, to shirk, however alien they may be to its present traditions. For ultimately, if by slow degrees, power follows the ability to wield it; authority goes with function. The workers cannot have it both ways. They must choose whether to assume the responsibility for industrial discipline and become free, or to repudiate it and continue to be serfs. If, organized as professional bodies, they can provide a more effective service than that which is now, with increasing difficulty, extorted by the agents of capital, they will have made good their hold upon the future. If they cannot, they will remain among the less calculable instruments of production which many of them are to-day. The instinct of mankind warns it against accepting at their face value spiritual demands which cannot justify themselves by practical achievements. And the road along which the organized workers, like any other class, must climb to power, starts from the provision of a more effective economic service than their masters, as their grip upon industry becomes increasingly vacillating and uncertain, are able to supply. (*pp.* 198–201)

15

COMMUNIST PARTY

The Communist Party of Great Britain was founded in 1920 and survives to the present day with much the same principles and attitude. In origin it was a combination of members of the Socialist Labour Party and the British Socialist Party (a body based on the old S.D.F., but deprived of the collaboration of Hyndman and his immediate following because it had reversed his policy of supporting the allied war effort). Its *raison d'être* and tactics derived from the Bolshevik revolution in Russia, and the maintenance of the Bolshevik regime there and the establishment of a similar system here have been its principal aims. Its requests for affiliation to the Labour Party though repeatedly put forward since the first attempt in 1920 (a), have never been acceded to. J. T. W. Newbold, an early Communist Member of Parliament, took the opportunity of Snowden's debate on the failure of the capitalist system to explain the differences between the Communist strategy and that of the Labour Party (b). He himself, however, resigned from the Communist Party in 1924. Harry Pollitt, on the other hand, has been the party's General Secretary almost consistently since 1929. Together with other prominent leaders of the party, he was sent to prison for twelve months in 1925 for Seditious Libel and Incitement, in spite of an eloquent speech in his own defence (c).

(a) *Communist Party of Great Britain.* Letter to the Secretary of the Labour Party

10 August 1920

DEAR SIR,

At a National Convention held in London on Saturday and Sunday, July 31st and August 1st last, the Communist Party of Great Britain was established. The resolutions adopted by the Convention defining the objects, methods and policy of the Communist Party read as follows:

(a) 'The Communists in conference assembled declare for the Soviet (or Workers' Council) system as a means whereby the working class shall achieve power and take control of the forces of production; declare for the dictatorship of the proletariat as a necessary means for combating the counter-revolution during the transition period between Capitalism and Communism, and stand for the adoption of these means as steps towards the establishment of a system of complete Communism wherein all the means of production shall be communally owned and controlled. The Conference therefore establishes itself the Communist Party on the foregoing basis and declares its adherence to the Third International.

(b) 'The Communist Party repudiates the reformist view that a Social Revolution can be achieved by the ordinary methods of Parliamentary Democracy, but regards Parliamentary and electoral action generally as providing a means of propaganda and agitation towards the Revolution. The tactics to be employed by representatives of the Party elected to Parliament or local bodies must be laid down by the Party itself according to national or local circumstances. In all cases such representatives must be considered as holding a mandate from the Party and not from the particular constituency for which they happen to sit. Also that in the event of any representative violating the decision of the Party as embodied in the mandate which he or she has accepted, or as an instruction, that he be called upon to resign his or her membership of Parliament or municipality and also of the Party.

(c) 'That the Communist Party shall be affiliated to the Labour Party.'

At a meeting of the Provisional Executive Committee held on Sunday last, we were directed to send you the foregoing resolutions and to make application for the affiliation of the Communist Party to the Labour Party.

Yours faithfully,

Arthur MacManus, Chairman.

Albert Inkpin, Secretary.

(*Labour Party Annual Report*, 1921, *pp.* 18*f.*)

(b) J. T. W. NEWBOLD. Speech in Debate on the Failure of the Capitalist System (Motion by Mr. Snowden), House of Commons

16 July, 1923

It might be said that, in effect, the argument that is put forward vehemently in all these discussions from the standpoint of the Labour party is to accept the inevitability of gradualness rather than wait for the wrath that is to come. The Labour party is using the enthusiasm generated throughout the working-class ranks of the world to push forward its little barque from this side of the Table to the other side of the Table. The alternative to revolution is undoubtedly an attempt on the part of the Labour party to establish a Socialism by constitutional means, and if it be possible for the Labour party to establish Socialism by constitutional means, there will be no one better pleased than the hon. Member for Motherwell,[1] I can assure the House. But there is very little reason to believe that it will be possible to establish it in such a way, for when it comes to be a case, not merely of restraining aspects of capitalism, not merely of making extensions of public control, but a case of overthrowing capitalism entirely, there is no likelihood that the governing classes will be any more friendly disposed to the rule of a Labour Government than they are to the rule of a Labour majority in the Borough of Poplar, or than they were in Italy to the capture of the municipal communes by Socialists and Communists. Wherever an attempt at Socialism has been made during the course of the last few years, there has immediately sprung up within the State, or within society, a movement known as *Fascisti*. We have the equivalent of that movement in this country. We had one of these reactionary movements, presided over by an hon. Member opposite, stating last week that it was intended to remain constitutional as long as possible, making it quite clear that as soon as constitutionalism failed, they were quite prepared to go outside the constitutional limits. There is not the slightest likelihood that it will be possible to carry the expropriation of the capitalist class by peaceful means. If it can be done, well and good; but the whole lesson of history in this country and other countries is that no governing class ever abdicates power unless compelled to do so by force exerted in a much more strenuous manner than passing through and having your names ticked off in the Division Lobby.

I notice that the supporters of this Motion are very kindly pointing out that they do not believe in Socialism without compensation and I notice that there is tacked on to this Motion, though it has been very little discussed in this Debate, a Bill for the nationalisation of land, providing

[1] Mr. Newbold.

for the payment of £150 for £100—5 per cent for a period of 30 years. I am not coming to that aspect of it immediately, but I would like to point out that the hon. Member for Colne Valley,[1] when he first appeared in this House, was pledged definitely to the elimination of the capitalist by means of taxation. I read as a youth with tremendous enthusiasm, and re-read it until I knew it almost line by line, an interesting little book entitled " Socialist Budget ". Therein it was the intention of the hon. Member for Blackburn, as he was then, to tax the capitalist out of existence. Now, in his mellow middle age, he comes forward with a proposal, not for confiscating the property of the capitalist in crude ways, as hon. Members opposite might be inclined to think that he would, but by means of the capital levy, and the capital levy, I take it, will be appreciated by the governing class of this country as a confiscation, whether it so seems to hon. Members on this side or not, and in the event of the governing class refusing to allow their capital to be taken away from them by one means of taxation or another, what is then to ensue?

Apparently, nothing is to ensue, because we have been informed that the Labour party is not in favour of use of force. Consequently they have told the governing class that they will not have their property taken away. Nothing further will happen except a series of resolutions, and the governing class will say: " We will keep our capital in our pocket, for nothing is going to occur." I have heard the argument put forward time after time on the Labour side of the House that once they capture the House of Commons, which seems to them to be the same thing as capturing the State—though it is a very far cry from capturing one third of Parliament to capturing the whole State—they will have the police force in their hands, the Army under their control, the Navy at their command, and they

[1] Mr. Snowden.

will be prepared to use these institutions for the furtherance of their aims. It may be that it appeals more to the hon. Member for Colne Valley or the hon. Member for Aberavon[1] to say that once force is directed by the competent authority it ceases to be force. That sort of argument may sound perfectly good at a Labour party conference when you are endeavouring to prevent the Communist party from affiliating, but it is not the kind of thing that is calculated to carry conviction to the majority of people who have no particular axe to grind for the moment.

The Labour party, I do not think will succeed in convincing the governing classes that they are so lamblike that they can be quite safely allowed to take over the land, the mines, and the other capital, hand over the script for it, and then tax the script-holders to extinction—that they can be allowed to do it merely because of the casuistical argument that once force is held by the State it ceases to be force, that it is only force when it is exercised against the constitution; not when it is exercised as it was exercised in the barrack yard in May, 1916, when on the authority of the right hon. Gentleman the Member for East Newcastle[2] a bullet was sent through James Connolly's heart. It is force, whether used by the State or otherwise, and consequently the argument that the Labour party is not in favour of using force falls to the ground, and the whole of the case for carrying through Socialism peacefully falls to the ground. (*Parliamentary Debates,* 5th Series, vol. 166, c. 1979–81)

[1] Mr. J. R. MacDonald.

[2] Mr. Arthur Henderson.

(c) HARRY POLLITT. Speech for the Defence, Trial for Seditious Libel and Incitement, Old Bailey

October 1925

Does this Party believe that it can only achieve its object by force or does it not? Members of the jury, the question of wars can only be decided when the circumstances are actually at hand. Experience has had so many lessons for us that we cannot neglect them, and we would be failing in our duty to the working classes of this country if we did not explain those lessons to them. The Communist Party believes that force is inevitable, not because we want to believe this, but our past and our present experiences have convinced us. You have only got to take the history of the past 200 years. This belief in progress—that society develops as a result of peaceful persuasion—is it good? It is very plausible, but it is not in accord with facts. Under the regime of militarism itself, what has happened? The chartist agitation in England, the Revolution in '48, the French Revolution in '79, and the South African War, the Russo-Japanese War and the Imperialist War from 1914 to 1918—are these peaceable advancements under ordinary conditions of capitalism? Did they not all occur under circumstances which necessitated the use of force by the ruling classes? The abolition of slavery in America, for example, was never brought about as a result of peaceable persuasion. As a result of the last War, there was a revolution in Russia. The trouble in Russia only came after the revolution, and not before, when those who had previously been the dominant class endeavoured to regain their supremacy. They not only endeavoured to gain it themselves, but they relied upon the sympathy and munitions, the men and the money of every capitalist country in the world.

Members of the jury, you know, as a matter of common knowledge, that this country spent 100 million pounds trying to smash the Russian Government. The lesson of history is that whatever ruling class is in power, it will retain that power peaceably and constitutionally, if it can, and if it cannot it will resort to other methods. This is not simply the view of one or two hot-heads who are now in the dock; it is very prevalent among people in this country. It is very prevalent in the Labour movement all over the world. We work to get our candidates on the local councils and boards of guardians and in Parliament. No one is more delighted than the members of the Communist Party to bring this about, but we have a right to warn the working classes of what happened in the past, and what is happening now before our very eyes.

The facts with which we are surrounded are justifying this point of view. You have the development of the *Fascisti*, you have the development of a new strike-breaking organisation called the Organisation for Maintaining Supplies, and you have the Conservative newspapers telling the people that if a Labour Government endeavoured to do anything that was only in the interests of the working class they would be smashed. Now, members of the jury, I just want to sum up the points I have endeavoured to make. First, to give the historical association and development of the Communist theory which is now on trial; secondly, to endeavour to give you a correct idea, from our point of view, of course, of what we are after; to try to clear away this conception that we are some secret bunch of conspirators meeting in dark corners, and now and again crawling up secret channels, and to show you that we are a working-class political organisation who have a point of view, and who endeavour to establish that point of view in exactly the same way as the rest of the political working class in this country. It has been suggested by innuendo that when we are talking about our immediate demands it is only for a material motive. Members of the jury, nothing that Lenin ever wrote or Marx ever found in the British Museum made a Communist; it was the conditions under which we lived. When I see it suggested that we stand here accused of uttering seditious libel calculated to bring, I think it is, "ill-will, hostility and hatred and disaffection" amongst the various classes of the people, members of the jury, you will pardon me if I say that that is not seditious libel at all. I saw the best woman in the world carry two children out, morning after morning, while I went with her to work: that made me a Communist.

Mr. Justice Swift: You must not tell facts to the jury which you are not going to prove.

Pollitt: It was the experience all of us in this dock have gone through and had, which made us devote our lives to working for the cause which we believe in. The Prosecution has not been able to produce anyone who has been affected and has shown ill-will, hatred and disaffection; they have not been able to produce a single worker in the forces incited to mutiny as the result of anything he had heard any Communist Party man saying, or anything the Communist Party has written. I say the party is a political party carrying out its political ideas. No jury for seventy years has been empanelled which has to take such a serious verdict as you have to take in this case. Our ideals may be distasteful to you, they may be repulsive to you, but they are our ideals, and it is these ideals which are on trial. I would like my last appeal to you to be this: to remember while you are endeavouring to arrive at your verdict what was the nature and circumstances of the Act of 1797 under which you are trying us. Believe me, members of the jury, this cause to which we belong, this Party, this Communist

International of which I am an accepted member, and proud to acknowledge the fact, is now a permanent factor of current political life; that the ideals for which we are to be convicted here are ideals which have inspired and will inspire more and more in the future, millions of the very best of the working class.

We are looked upon as the vanguard of the working-class movement. Progress can be hindered and can be retarded, but it can never be stopped. Communism to-day is a general political issue which cannot be wiped out by persecution or repression.

I confidently ask you, members of the jury, to return a verdict of 'Not Guilty'. (Pollitt, *Serving My Time*, 1940, *pp.* 245–8)

PART II

ASPECTS OF THE TRADITION

16

SOCIAL EQUALITY

The Socialist is emphatic that political equality of itself does not guarantee social equality. In Britain severe inequalities of wealth in the past, together with a long-established class system, appear to have rendered the attainment of social equality a distant goal even to-day. H. G. Wells's pamphlet, *This Misery of Boots,* first published by the Fabian Society, provides a good instance of Socialist propaganda directed to the feeling of injustice aroused by economic inequality and the distress of the poor (a). In the excerpt from Shaw's *Intelligent Woman's Guide* (b) we find an unusual plea for complete equality of incomes—an ideal that few Socialists would regard as attainable in the foreseeable future, owing to the loss of economic incentive involved (the same grounds as those on which William Thompson criticised the Owenite ideal: 3a above). The more practicable object of equality of opportunity, coupled with measures to avoid undue disparity of incomes, is ably set forth in R. H. Tawney's *Equality* (c); and both this passage and that from George Orwell (d) attach special importance to the need for transforming the educational system, in order to break down the barriers of social class that at present, it is felt, it helps to maintain. Orwell, who is best known for his satires of the totalitarian state, *Animal Farm* and *1984,* was also a bitter opponent of social inequality, as his works *The Road to Wigan Pier* and *The Lion and the Unicorn* strongly testify.

(a) H. G. WELLS. *This Misery of Boots*

1907

Everybody does not suffer misery from boots.

One person I know, another friend of mine, who can testify to that; who has tasted all the miseries of boots, and who now goes about the world free of them, but not altogether forgetful of them. A stroke of luck, aided perhaps by a certain alacrity on his own part, lifted him out of the class in which one buys one's boots and clothes out of what is left over from a pound a week, into the class in which one spends seventy or eighty pounds a year on clothing. Sometimes he buys boots and shoes at very good shops; sometimes he has them made for him; he has them stored in a proper cupboard, and great care is taken of them; and so his boots and shoes and slippers never chafe, never pinch, never squeak, never hurt or worry him, never bother him; and when he sticks out his toes before the fire, they do not remind him that he is a shabby and contemptible wretch, living meanly on the dust heaps of the world. You might think from this that he had every reason to congratulate himself and be happy seeing that he has had good follow after evil; but, such is the oddness of the human heart, he isn't contented at all. The thought of the multitudes so much worse off than himself in this matter of foot-wear, gives him no sort of satisfaction. Their boots pinch him vicariously. The black rage with the scheme of things that once he felt through suffering in his own person in the days when he limped shabbily through gaily busy, fashionable London streets, in split boots that chafed, he feels now just as badly as he goes about the world very comfortably himself, but among people whom he knows with a pitiless clearness to be almost intolerably uncomfortable. He has no optimistic illusion that things are all right with them. Stupid people who have always been well off, who have always had boots that fit, may think that; but not so, he. In one respect the thought of boots makes him even more viciously angry now, than it used to do. In the old days he was savage with his luck, but hopelessly savage; he thought that bad boots, ugly uncomfortable clothes, rotten houses, were in the very nature of things. Now, when he sees a child sniffing and blubbering and halting upon the pavement, or an old countrywoman going painfully along a lane, he no longer recognizes the Pinch of Destiny. His rage is lit by the thought, that there are fools in this world who ought to have foreseen and prevented this. He no longer curses fate, but the dullness of statesmen and powerful responsible people who have neither the heart, nor courage, nor capacity, to change the state of mismanagement that gives us these things.

Now do not think I am dwelling unduly upon my second friend's good fortune, when I tell you that once he was constantly getting pain and miserable states of mind, colds for example, from the badness of his clothing, shame from being shabby, pain from the neglected state of his teeth, from the indigestion of unsuitable food eaten at unsuitable hours, from the unsanitary ugly house in which he lived and the bad air of that part of London, from things indeed quite beyond the unaided power of a poor overworked man to remedy. And now all these disagreeable things have gone out of his life; he has consulted dentists and physicians, he has hardly any dull days from colds, no pain from toothache at all, no gloom of indigestion. . . .

I will not go on with the tale of good fortune of this lucky person. My purpose is served if I have shown that this misery of boots is not an unavoidable curse upon mankind. If one man can evade it, others can. By good management it may be altogether escaped. If you, or what is more important to most human beings, if any people dear to you, suffer from painful or disfiguring boots or shoes, and you can do no better for them, it is simply because you are getting the worst side of an ill-managed world. It is not the universal lot.

And what I say of boots is true of all the other minor things of life. If your wife catches a bad cold because her boots are too thin for the time of the year, or dislikes going out because she cuts a shabby ugly figure, if your children look painfully nasty because their faces are swollen with toothache, or because their clothes are dirty, old, and ill-fitting, if you are all dull and disposed to be cross with one another for want of decent amusement and change of air —don't submit, don't be humbugged for a moment into believing that this is the dingy lot of all mankind. These people you love are living in a badly-managed world and on the wrong side of it; and such wretchednesses are the daily demonstration of that.

Don't say for a moment: 'Such is life.' Don't think their miseries are part of some primordial curse there is no escaping. The disproof of that is for any one to see. There are people, people no more deserving than others, who suffer from none of these things. You may feel you merit no better than to live so poorly and badly that your boots are always hurting you; but do the little children, the girls, the mass of decent hard-up people, deserve no better fate? (*pp.* 14–18)

(b) BERNARD SHAW. *The Intelligent Woman's Guide to Socialism and Capitalism*

1928

So far we have not found one great national institution that escapes the evil effects of a division of the people into rich and poor: that is, of inequality of income. I could take you further: but we should only fare worse. I could shew you how rich officers and poor soldiers and sailors create disaffection in the army and navy; how disloyalty is rampant because the relation between the royal family and the bulk of the nation is the relation between one rich family and millions of poor ones; how what we call peace is really a state of civil war between rich and poor conducted by disastrous strikes; how envy and rebellion and class resentments are chronic moral diseases with us. But if I attempted this you would presently exclaim "Oh, for goodness' sake don't tell me everything or we shall never have done". And you would be quite right. If I have not convinced you by this time that there are overwhelming reasons of State against inequality of income, I shall begin to think that you dislike me.

Besides, we must get on to the positive reasons for the Socialist plan of an equal division. I am specially interested in it because it is my favourite plan. You had therefore better watch me carefully to see that I play fairly when I am helping you to examine what there is to be said for equality of income over and above what there is to be said against inequality of income.

First, equal division is not only a possible plan, but one which has been tested by long experience. The great bulk of the daily work of the civilized world is done, and always has been done, and always must be done, by bodies of persons receiving equal pay, whether they are tall or short, fair or dark, quick or slow, young or getting on in years, teetotallers or beer drinkers, Protestants or Catholics, married or single, short tempered or sweet tempered, pious or worldly; in short, without the slightest regard to the differences that make one person unlike another. In every trade there is standard wage; in every public service there is a standard pay; and in every profession the fees are fixed with a view to enable the man who follows the profession to live according to a certain standard of respectability which is the same for the whole profession. The pay of the policeman and soldier and postman, the wages of the laborer and carpenter and mason, the salary of the judge and the member of Parliament, may differ, some of them getting less than a hundred a year and others five thousand; but all the soldiers get the same, all the judges get the same, all the members of Parliament get the same; and if you ask a doctor why his fee is half a crown or five shillings, or a guinea or three guineas, or whatever it may be, instead of five shillings or ten shillings, or two guineas or six guineas or a thousand guineas, he can give you no better reason than that he is asking what all other doctors ask, and that they ask it because they find they cannot keep their position on less.

Therefore when some inconsiderate person repeats like a parrot that if you gave everybody the same money, before a year was out you would have rich and poor again just as before, all you have to do is to tell him to look round him and see millions of people who get the same money and remain in the same position all their lives without any such change taking place. The cases in which poor men become rich are most exceptional; and though the cases in which rich men become poorer are commoner, they also are accidents and not ordinary everyday circumstances. The rule is that workers of the same rank and calling are paid alike, and that they neither sink below their condition nor rise above it. No matter how unlike they are to one another, you can pay one of them two and sixpence and the other half a crown with the assurance that as they are put so they will stay, though here and there a great rogue or a great genius may surprise you by becoming much richer or much poorer than the rest. Jesus complained that he was poorer than the foxes and birds, as they had their holes and nests whilst he had not a house to shelter him; and Napoleon became an emperor; but we need take no more account of such extraordinary persons in forming our general plan than a maker of readymade clothes takes of giants and dwarfs in his price list. You may with the utmost confidence take it as settled by practical experience that if we could succeed in distributing income equally to all the inhabitants of the country, there would be no more tendency on their part to divide into rich and poor than there is at present for postmen to divide into beggars and millionaires. The only novelty proposed is that the postmen should get as much as the postmasters, and the postmasters no less than anybody else. If we find, as we do, that it answers to give all judges the same income, and all navy captains the same income, why should we go on giving judges five times as much as navy captains? That is what the navy captain would like to know; and if you tell him that if he were given as much as the judge he would be just as poor as before at the end of a year he will use language unfit for the ears of anyone but a pirate. So be careful how you say such things.

Equal distribution is then quite possible and practicable, not only momentarily but permanently. It is also simple and intelligible. It gets rid of all squabbling as to how much each person should have. It is already in operation and familiar over great masses of human beings. And it has the tremendous advantage of securing promotion by merit for the more capable. . . .

Between persons of equal income there is no social distinction except the distinction of merit. Money is nothing: character, conduct, and capacity are everything. Instead of all the workers being levelled down to low wage standards and all the rich levelled up to fashionable income standards, everybody under a system of equal incomes would find her and his own natural level. There would be great people and ordinary people and little people; but the great would always be those who had done great things, and never the idiots whose mothers had spoiled them and whose fathers had left them a hundred thousand a year; and the little would be persons of small minds and mean characters, and not poor persons who had never had a chance. That is why idiots are always in favor of inequality of income (their only chance of eminence), and the really great in favor of equality. (*pp.* 68, 70*f.*)

(c) R. H. TAWNEY. *Equality*

1931

WHEN the ground is littered with the remains of an obsolete social tradition, which impedes the free movement of the national energies, and breeds confusion in place of understanding, what surer way can be found of burying the thing decently without violent commotion or the strife of tongues, than to let the young understand that, in the eyes of all sensible people, it is already dead? The English educational system will never be, what it should be, the great uniter, instead of being, what it has been in the past, a source of disunion, until children of all classes of the community attend the same schools. Indeed, while it continues to be muddied by absurd social vanities, it will never even be efficient as an educational system; for it is only when all parents are equally interested in its progress that a common effort to improve it will take the place of demands for increased expenditure on the part of some classes and resistance to increased expenditure on the part of others. The time will come when the scheme of English education, which hitherto has followed and heightened the lines drawn by social divisions, will be the symbol and cement of social unity, and the idea that differences of wealth should produce differences of educational opportunity will seem as grotesque and repulsive as that they should result in differences of personal security and legal status. The primary school will become in such conditions what it should be, and what in some countries it already is, the common school, so excellent and generally esteemed that all parents desire their children to attend it. It will be the preparatory school, from which all normal children, and not merely a favoured minority, pass on to secondary education, and which, since the second stage succeeds the first as a matter of course when children are ripe for it, will be free from the pressure to train them for a competition, which cramps it to-day. Special schools for the rich, if they still survive, will form one minor category within the national system, offering curative treatment, perhaps, to such children as require it.

A spendthrift's utopia or a hell of mediocrity? Is the alternative, then, so practical and inspiring? As a society sows, so in the long run it reaps. If its schools are sordid, will its life be generous? Will it later unite by an appeal to economic interests those whom in nurture and education it has taken pains to put asunder? If it sacrifices its children to its social conventions and its economic convenience, is it probable that, when men, they will regard it with affection? The principle to be followed is, after all, simple. What a wise and good parent would desire for his own children, that a nation, in so far as it is wise and good, must desire for all children. Educational equality consists in securing it for them. It is to be achieved in school, as it is achieved in the home, by recognizing that there are diversities of gifts, which require for their development diversities of treatment. Its aim will be to do justice to all, by providing facilities which are at once various in type and equal in quality.

Is it necessary to rehearse once more the familiar catalogue, every item of which has been thrashed bare in the last ten years, of the measures required to create the mere skeleton and mechanism into which the spirit may later breathe life? The establishment of open-air nursery schools in all urban areas, and the development of the school medical service and the extension of school meals; the staffing and equipment of primary schools on a scale which may make possible initiative and experiment, and a large measure of practical work, and an atmosphere of freedom and humanity; the provision of different kinds of secondary education, not merely in name, but in fact, for all children from eleven to sixteen; the abolition of the ridiculous distinction between schools which are secondary and schools which are merely post-primary, and the amendment of the Board's regulations in such a way as to establish common standards of staffing and equipment for all; the abolition of fees at grant-aided secondary schools, and the creation of a system of maintenance allowances on a scale sufficiently ample to break the vicious circle which binds poverty in one generation to lack of educational opportunity in the next; the removal of the absurd barriers which at present divide different branches of the teaching profession, and the general recognition that the provision of a liberal education for the future primary teacher is among the most vital of a university's functions—what trifles to advance as a contribution to equality, and through what a den of lions the humblest of them must be dragged! A blink, a yawn, a growl, a heavy paw, and the most timid of improvements fluttering in tatters! How few have escaped the majestic creatures since 1918! (*pp.* 204–7)

(d) GEORGE ORWELL. *The English People*

1947

The English are probably less irked by class distinctions, more tolerant of privilege and of absurdities like titles, than most peoples. There is nevertheless, as I have pointed out earlier, a growing wish for greater equality and a tendency, below the £2,000 a year level, for surface differences between class and class to disappear. At present this is happening only mechanically and quite largely as a result of the war. The question is how it can be speeded up. For even the change-over to a centralised economy, which, except, possibly, in the United States, is happening in all countries under one name or another, does not of itself guarantee greater equality between man and man. Once civilisation has reached a fairly high technical level, class distinctions are an obvious evil. They not only lead great numbers of people to waste their lives in the pursuit of social prestige, but they also cause an immense wastage of talent. In England it is not merely the ownership of property that is concentrated in a few hands. It is also the case that all power, administrative as well as financial, belongs to a single class. Except for a handful of "self-made men" and Labour politicians, those who control our destinies are the product of about a dozen public schools and two universities. A nation is using its capacities to the full when any man can get any job that he is fit for. One has only to think of some of the people who have held vitally important jobs during the past twenty years, and to wonder what would have happened to them if they had been born into the working class, to see that this is not the case in England.

Moreover, class distinctions are a constant drain on

morale, in peace as well as in war. And the more conscious, the better educated, the mass of the people become, the more this is so. The word " They ", the universal feeling that " They " hold all the power and make all the decisions, and that " They " can only be influenced in indirect and uncertain ways, is a great handicap in England. In 1940 " They " showed a marked tendency to give place to " We ", and it is time that it did so permanently. Three measures are obviously necessary, and they would begin to produce their effect within a few years.

The first is a scaling-up and scaling-down of incomes. The glaring inequality of wealth that existed in England before the war must not be allowed to recur. Above a certain point—which should bear a fixed relation to the lowest current wage—all income should be taxed out of existence. In theory, at any rate, this has happened already, with beneficial results. The second necessary measure is greater democracy in education. A completely unified system of education is probably not desirable. Some adolescents benefit by higher education, others do not, there is need to differentiate between literary and technical education, and it is better that a few independent experimental schools should remain in existence. But it should be the rule, as it is in some countries already, for all children to attend the same schools up to the age of twelve or at least ten. After that age it becomes necessary to separate the more gifted children from the less gifted, but a uniform educational system for the early years would cut away one of the deepest roots of snobbery.

The third thing that is needed is to remove the class labels from the English language. It is not desirable that all the local accents should disappear, but there should be a manner of speaking that is definitely national and is not merely (like the accent of the B.B.C. announcers) a copy of the mannerisms of the upper classes. This national accent—

a modification of Cockney, perhaps, or of one of the northern accents—should be taught as a matter of course to all children alike. After that they could, and in some parts of the country they probably would, revert to the local accent, but they should be able to speak standard English if they wished to. No one should be " branded on the tongue ". It should be impossible, as it is in the United States and some European countries, to determine anyone's status from his accent. (*pp.* 42–4)

17

FREEDOM AND SOCIAL POWER

The historical development of the Socialist movement in opposition to existing authority has given it a traditional interest in the freedom of the individual. Nevertheless, the Socialist is inclined to regard liberty not as a purely abstract right but as a series of practical problems in social organisation, where one man's liberty may threaten another's. If the individual has free access to economic and social power over his fellows, this may—and in historical experience does—lead to the loss of effective freedom by the many.

Fred Henderson, a Norwich Socialist prominent in local politics from the time of the Socialist League to the present day, expresses this point of view in his *Case for Socialism* which is based on lectures originally delivered to the Norwich Labour Church (a). Bertrand Russell, the well-known philosopher and political writer, who suffered for his support of pacifism in the 1914–18 war, presents a strongly anti-statist attitude, coupled with a pessimistic view of human nature which world events of the last generation would seem to have justified (b).

A very different position is taken up by John Strachey, writing as a Communist spokesman[1] at a time when the severe economic depression of 1929 to 1933 and the collapse of the second Labour Government in 1931 had driven a large section of the Labour movement to favour drastic action along Marxist–Leninist lines (c). Yet this was never the majority view; and in the milder and more responsible tones of Clement Attlee, Leader of His Majesty's Opposition from 1935, we again find a high value placed on the British tradition of freedom (d). A. D. Lindsay, the Master of Balliol and an important

[1] Mr. Strachey dissociated himself from the Communists at the beginning of the war, and was a Minister in the Labour Governments of 1945–51.

Socialist political philosopher, sought in his work *The Modern Democratic State* to reconcile the concepts of democracy and liberty along the lines of pluralism (e). Finally, Kingsley Martin, editor of the *New Statesman,* is quoted to emphasize the Socialist interest in the maintenance of freedom in a world in which, in spite of the defeat of Fascism, large-scale organisation continues to threaten the rights of the individual (f).

(a) FRED HENDERSON. *The Case for Socialism*

1911

If the absence of restraint upon the exercise of a man's faculties is the merely negative aspect of liberty then surely the positive aspect of liberty is the presence of actual opportunity for the exercise of those faculties.

It is not enough that a man should have the right to use his earnings as he thinks best. To enjoy liberty in the full sense, he must first of all have the positive opportunities to get those earnings. He must have access to opportunity before he can exercise his power of initiative or his free play of intelligence upon it.

If a civilized community is to safeguard effectively the liberty of its members, it has, therefore, a twofold duty; the negative duty of refraining from coercion or restraint except so far as is necessary to prevent men from encroaching on the liberty of others or becoming a nuisance or a danger to the community; and the positive duty of providing and keeping open the widest possible range of opportunity, and guaranteeing to its citizens the right of access to that opportunity.

Thus liberty in its negative aspect means what the State is to refrain from doing; while liberty in its positive aspect means constructive civilization, and finds its expression in the activities of the State.

The whole worth and meaning of civilization is to make men secure in the possession and enjoyment of this opportunity, this ever widening range of opportunity. Our advance in civilization depends upon the extent to which the individual is set free from the individual gamble against the chances and accidents of life. Progress consists in men ceasing to have to struggle for their old objects, and so being set free to work for new ideals; achieving security in lower things, and going on to higher things. The difference between civilization and savagery is just in that. The savage makes no progress so long as he has to be constantly occupied, constantly alert in the business of defending himself from the possible attacks of other savages like himself. Civilization begins when men come together into a tribe and make collective provision for defence. The individual is thus relieved of the individual struggle for safety, and is set free for other things. Having attained to some degree of security in this respect, the tribe is free to think about other matters; and the settled cultivation of the soil begins, the foundations of a civilized order appear. The law of the evolution of human society is that all progress, all human advancement in civilization, comes about by men being set free from being wholly absorbed in the individual struggle for the satisfaction of their lower wants, and so enabled to pursue higher aims in security.

And how are they so set free? By co-operation and collective action. The old parable of the bundle of sticks holds good. It is the business of a civilized community to set its members free in this way; constantly to gather up the attainment of the race and embody it in secure collective provision,—in other words in access to opportunity,—so that individual gambling and uncertainty ceases in connection with that attainment; the struggle being constantly raised to the next higher level of human endeavour until that in time and turn becomes part of the secure and completely mastered human heritage. That is the inner process of all civilization,—constantly to widen the range of that provision for human needs within which struggle ends and uncertainty ceases, and men stand secure within the shelter and guarantee of the collective life.

That is constructive civilization; the positive as distinguished from the negative aspect of liberty; the " something more " than the mere absence of restraint.

And if, at this point in the argument, it should be suggested that human life is a continual struggle having a disciplinary value in developing the strength and quality of the race, I agree; but I put it to you that the value of the struggle as a means of human advancement depends upon what it is you are struggling for. To keep men in a state of struggle and uncertainty about their animal satisfactions, about such elementary needs as food, clothing, and shelter, is to keep them in bondage to their lower wants; a bondage which prevents them from advancing to a human life distinguishable in its qualities from the life of brutes. Apes and tigers are under the discipline of that sort of struggle. There is no educational value to any human end, there is only hindrance to progress, in keeping men absorbed in the individual struggle for things which are within the general attainment of the race. To give educational value to the struggle it must constantly be pushed outwards to new frontiers of human endeavour not yet securely occupied. Civilization should extend all ways just in the rear of this struggle, gathering up and assimilating into secure collective provision what has been gained, establishing a settled order of life, and assured access to the widened opportunity in the regions thus explored and cleared and made habitable.

That is the positive aspect of liberty: Not merely to say to each new generation as it comes into manhood and womanhood and responsible citizenship, " You shall not be interfered with in the exercise of your faculties," but " Here is your positive heritage of widened opportunity, widen it again further for those who will come after you all."

I assert, therefore, that the very first condition necessary to personal liberty in this positive sense is the social organisation of the supply of the primary material needs of life, so as to guarantee to every citizen, with absolute security, access to the opportunity of providing for his life in respect of the needs. That, surely, is one of the primary purposes for which a civilized organisation of society exists at all.

And I further assert—and here we get to the direct Socialist issue—that society can only carry out this purpose by collective ownership and control of the land and of the machinery needed to produce and distribute the material resources which are essential to the life and convenience of its citizens. (*pp.* 65–9)

(b) BERTRAND RUSSELL. *Roads to Freedom*

1918

Respect for the liberty of others is not a natural impulse with most men: envy and love of power lead ordinary human nature to find pleasure in interference with the lives of others. If all men's actions were wholly unchecked by external authority, we should not obtain a world in which all men would be free. The strong would oppress the weak, or the majority would oppress the minority, or the lovers of violence would oppress the more peaceable people. I fear it cannot be said that these bad impulses are *wholly* due to a bad social system, though it must be conceded that the present competitive organization of society does a great deal to foster the worst elements in human nature. The love of power is an impulse which, though innate in very ambitious men, is chiefly promoted as a rule by the actual experience of power. In a world where none could acquire much power, the desire to tyrannize would be much less strong than it is at present. Nevertheless, I cannot think that it would be wholly absent, and those in whom it would exist would often be men of unusual energy and executive capacity. Such men, if they are not restrained by the organized will of the community, may either succeed in establishing a despotism, or, at any rate, make such a vigorous attempt as can only be defeated through a period of prolonged disturbance. And apart from the love of political power, there is the love of power over individuals. If threats and terrorism were not prevented by law, it can hardly be doubted that cruelty would be rife in the relations of men and women and of parents and children. It is true that the habits of a community can make such cruelty rare, but these habits, I fear, are only to be produced through the prolonged reign of law. Experience of backwoods communities, mining camps, and other such places seems to show that under new conditions men easily revert to a more barbarous attitude and practice. It would seem, therefore, that, while human nature remains as it is, there will be more liberty for all in a community where some acts of tyranny by individuals are forbidden, than in a community where the law leaves each individual free to follow his every impulse. But, although the necessity of some form of government and law must for the present be conceded, it is important to remember that all law and government is in itself in some degree an evil, only justifiable when it prevents other and greater evils. Every use of the power of the State needs, therefore, to be very closely scrutinized, and every possibility of diminishing its power is to be welcomed provided it does not lead to a reign of private tyranny. (*pp.* 121–3)

(c) JOHN STRACHEY. *Theory and Practice of Socialism*

1936

It is interesting to speculate upon the problems which will face the British and American workers when they come to the job of building up a free life for themselves. In this matter also they possess great advantages which the Russian workers lacked. The measure of liberty which they have enjoyed under capitalism will undoubtedly help them rapidly to create the basis of a free life. The existence of a tradition of relative self-government, self-reliance, and independence will be of great assistance to them in building up a socialist society. In this respect also they will start out from a point of development to which the Russians had laboriously to climb.

But here, too, the British and American people will face a special difficulty. Our traditions of relative civil liberty will no doubt be used by the dispossessed British and American capitalists to demand their " right " to combine for the overthrow of the workers' State and the re-acquisition of the means of production. They will, no doubt, make both night and day hideous with their outcry at the " monstrous, outrageous violation of liberty " of which the workers' government will be guilty when it protects itself against their implacable hostility. Their complaints will seem to themselves perfectly justified, for they really did enjoy liberty under capitalism; and they really will have that liberty severely curtailed under socialism.

Moreover, their specious agitation is only too likely to take in a number of quite sincere and disinterested people. For the level of political education is so low in Britain and America that some people will be quite unable to detect the fallacy of their plea. Our minds have been so bemused with centuries of talk about liberty in the abstract, without any rational attempt to discover what this great word means, or to ascertain the conditions under which alone effective liberty for the greater part of the population can be achieved, that a considerable amount of confusion is only too likely to occur.

And this confusion will, paradoxically enough, necessitate a more considerable temporary curtailment of the liberty of some sections of the population than would otherwise be necessary. If everyone could be relied upon to see clearly that when the dispossessed capitalists cried out that they were the champions of the immortal cause of human freedom, they were merely crying for their lost dividends, then there would be little need to restrict their liberty to cry out; for they would be crying for the moon. But if certain sections of the population are still confused enough to take them at their word, then it will become necessary to restrain the outcry.

Thus we must face the fact that, for a period, the British and American workers will almost certainly be compelled to restrict the civil liberties of the dispossessed classes to an extent that these classes will consider outrageous. But even during that period the degree of liberty enjoyed by incomparably the greater part of the population will have been enormously extended. It will still be restricted and imperfect compared to the liberty which will be possible when a truly classless society will have emerged. But it will be incomparably fuller and richer than are those partial, if precious, liberties which we possess in Britain and America to-day. (*pp.* 209*f.*)

(d) C. R. ATTLEE. *The Labour Party in Perspective*

1937

. . . THE aim of Socialism is to give greater freedom to the individual. British Socialists have never made an idol of the State, demanding that individuals should be sacrificed to it. They have never accepted the beehive or the ants' nest as an ideal. They leave that to the advocates of the Corporate State. They have never desired that men and women should be drilled and regimented physically and mentally so that they should be all of one pattern. On the contrary, they appreciate that the wealth of a society is in its variety, not its uniformity. Progress is not towards, but away from the herd. It is no part of the Socialist idea that there should be in every human activity an orthodox pattern to which all must conform.

This is well illustrated by considering the attitude of the Labour Party towards religion. In the Labour Party are found active adherents of many religious creeds, and also men and women who do not conform to any denomination. There has never been any attempt to impose on members of the Party a creed of materialism, any more than there has been any imposition of a religious test. Within the Labour Party everyone is entitled to hold what religious views he will. Where legislation impinges upon religious questions, the individual member is accorded complete freedom of action. It is recognised that religion is a sphere which should be left to the individual.

Again, in education, while Socialists have protested against a bias in favour of the existing order being maintained in education, they have not sought to twist education into a means of imposing upon all a rigid orthodoxy. They have such faith in the rightness of their views that they desire the utmost freedom of enquiry and discussion. The action of the Nazi Government in Germany in turning their universities into parrot cages for the repetition of the catchwords of Fascism evokes only contempt. The tendency observable among Communists to try to reduce all history to an economic formula has always been rejected. The conception of a proletarian art and literature which must be sharply distinguished from anything hitherto accomplished in those fields is quite alien to true Socialism. It results from a sense of inferiority. British Socialists recognise very clearly the danger that exists in the tyranny of the reformer who wishes to make all men in his own image. The very differences which arise in the Labour movement are an earnest that in the Socialist State of the future there will be constant vigilance to prevent loss of freedom.

State action is advocated by Socialists not for its own sake, but because it is necessary to prevent the oppression of an individual by others, and to secure that the liberty of the one does not restrict that of others, or conflict with the common good of society.

Those who attack Socialism on the ground that it will mean the enslavement of the individual belong invariably to the class of people whose possession of property has given them liberty at the expense of the enslavement of others. The possession of property in a Capitalist society has given liberty to a fortunate minority who hardly realise how much its absence means enslavement. The majority of the people of this country are under orders and discipline for the whole of their working day. Freedom is left behind when they 'clock in' and only resumed when they go out. Such liberty as they have got as workers has been the fruit of long and bitter struggles by the Trade Unions. But a far greater restriction on liberty than this is imposed on the vast majority of the people of this country by poverty. There is the narrowing of choice in everything. The poor man cannot choose his domicile. He must be prepared at the shortest notice to abandon all his social activities, to leave the niche which he has made for himself in the structure of society, and to remove himself elsewhere, if economic circumstances demand it. This is called 'transfcrcncc.' How littlc would those who so easily recommend this to the workers appreciate being transferred from their pleasant homes in Surrey or Buckinghamshire to Whitechapel or the Black Country. Yet this is an ordinary incident of working class life. The poor man is restricted in his food, his clothing, his amusements, and his occupation. The liberty which it is feared Socialism may restrict is the liberty of the few. Moreover, in modern Capitalist society, the power of wealth is such as to affect the lives of the people in thousands of ways. The whole organisation of the country is based on the superior rights of the wealthy. Nothing is sacred to the profit maker. The beauty and amenities of the country are at his mercy. The life of whole communities may be ruined at his will. . . .

My conclusion is that men and women will be more free, not less free, under Socialism. Freedom will be more widely disseminated. There will be no attempt made to impose rigid uniformity. There will be no forcible suppression of adverse opinion. The real change will be that a man will become a citizen, with the rights of a free man during his hours of labour just as in his leisure time. This does not mean that he will have the right to do just as he will. He will have freedom within the necessary restraints which life in a complex society imposes. (*pp.* 139–44)

(e) A. D. LINDSAY. *The Modern Democratic State*

1943

We continually discuss whether certain social activities

should or should not be taken over by government, or be done by voluntary effort There are certain advantages in having things done by government and thereby having compulsion behind them. Statutory administration is more uniform and regular: it is on the whole more reliable than voluntary effort; it can be made to apply to everybody, while voluntary effort usually only affects a fraction of those you want to affect. But any action backed by compulsion has the defects of its qualities: it tends to be stiffer, to be more routine, and special safeguards are needed to prevent officials using their power in an arbitrary and tyrannical way. Dickens's account of the Circumlocution Office in *Little Dorrit* is, like all Dickens's satire, exaggerated, but true enough to have a sting in it. On the other hand we have come to recognize that experiments and pioneer work are much more likely to come from voluntary associations and from individuals. The informality, the lack of administrative routine, the absence above all of compulsion or sanctions, make a different atmosphere which produces results of a certain kind. The ordinary man quite sensibly thinks that there is more liberty in working with voluntary associations than in working under government orders. So, normally, there is.

Liberty is a note of a democratic society in so far as such a society believes that voluntary association, informal uncompelled relations between man and man, should play a large part in society. This is only another way of saying what was said in the last chapter that the end of the state, i.e. of the compulsory organization, is to serve, foster, harmonize, and strengthen the free life of the community. Freedom of speech, freedom of meeting, freedom of association—these are all necessary conditions of this general freedom.

Democratic liberty then is a mean between two extremes —between the extreme view that society has no need of a compulsion and that there can be no place for compulsion in a democratic society, and the other extreme that government, the organization with force behind it, should control all social activities, and that this may well be quite compatible with liberty. Democratic liberty is incompatible with any kind of totalitarianism.

If the strength of voluntary associations and informal relations is that they are more likely to produce initiative, experiment, and invention, the view that the compulsory organization—the state—should be the servant and not the master of the voluntary associations implies a belief in the value of experiment and initiative. That goes back to the principle which, as we have seen, was introduced into society by Christianity, the belief in infinite moral progress. If we really believed that a full and complete understanding of the purposes and meaning of life were not attainable, we ought to have a state on Plato's model, appoint the wisest men available to formulate and expound those purposes, and then use all the power of the state to 'put them across'. If on the other hand we have any belief in 'The wind bloweth where it listeth. . . . so is every one that is born of the Spirit', we are bound to regard the free life of the spirit as something which it is the essential task of the state to safeguard.

Democracy is a revolutionary form of government. For its aim is to find a place for continual change within government. Its law exists to foster freedom: its form exists to protect law. It is an organization to preserve, leave room for, these precious things of the spirit which in their nature cannot be organized. This may seem a high-flown statement of democracies as we know them. No doubt men and women abuse liberty and we must all be prevented from using our own liberty to destroy the liberty of others. Nevertheless the steady insistence in democratic government that there is always a strong *prima facie* case against interference with free association, that there ought to be spheres of life which government does not control, is based on the conviction of the value of change and experiment and initiative.

If equality and liberty, so conceived, are the marks of a democratic community, it will be the task of the government of such a community to be sensitively aware of the conditions which are making equality and liberty hard to maintain. There are of course certain elementary minimum conditions which will have to be laid down and provided. These are of the kind which can at least be defined in a list of rights—minimum legal rights and a minimum standard of economic security, as was suggested in the last chapter. There are some obvious and outstanding evils like widespread unemployment which can so poison the life of a community that they make equality and liberty and true democratic life impossible. The diagnosis of such evils is not difficult. But just because true equality and liberty are not mechanical conceptions and not standardized articles, a successful democratic government will, as we have said above, have to be sensitively aware of the conditions in society which prevent the community from being a community.

It will never be its business to construct a complete plan for society, nor to run and dominate or plan the community. A democratic government has to take the community for granted, to recognize, as we saw in the last chapter, that there are activities essential for the health of the community which cannot be the state's activities—must be done by independent and free organizations or not done at all. The democratic state may support such activities but cannot perform them. (*pp.* 264–7)

(f) KINGSLEY MARTIN. *Socialism and the Welfare State*, a lecture to the Fabian Society

1951

As we look at the world today the tendency is clearly towards a vast increase of state control. In one form or another the Managerial State seems inescapable. One of the main reasons for the recoil from the Socialist conception is that people fear that, in practice and in time, the world might be governed, as we are told it is in the Soviet Union, or even as it is depicted in the nightmares of Aldous Huxley or George Orwell. The trend is as clear in free America, which one can only too easily imagine developing into a society such as H. G. Wells pictured in *The Sleeper Awakes*, or Jack London in *The Iron Heel.* The simple fact is that the development of a central control by force, by propaganda, and by the technique of mass production is so strong as to seem in our day irresistible. The Socialists are right in striving to ensure that this new "Statism" should be Socialist and not Fascist. That is, that the central control should be in the hands of people who represent the masses and desire their well-being, and not those who are the servants of a private and privileged ruling class. Clearly that is vital.

Marx rightly prophesied the end of private Capitalism, and rightly demanded a proletarian victory in the class war. What we have learnt is that this historical determinism inevitably takes us to the destruction of old-fashioned Capitalism, and its supersession by a monopolist state, but it does not tell us whether the result will be good or bad. That is within human will. For the goodness or badness of the society depends only in part on its structure. We might end the evils of private property and substitute for them a new set of evils which would make us hate our Socialism. The peculiar—and I think unique quality of British Socialism—is that it contains in it a greater faith in the power of the individual and group to fashion its own destinies within the Socialist structure. There is nothing written in history, for instance, to show that if the State takes over the means of distribution, production and exchange then the administration must be completely centralised. On the contrary: we need small units of administration with local "participation" to the utmost within a general, central framework. The alternative, as a Frenchman said, is "apoplexy at the centre and anaemia at the extremities." The Welfare State, which involves far more attention to the private lives of citizens than the Englishman has been accustomed to relish, can nevertheless be compatible with the rights of free speech, personal and civil freedom. It is because British Labour has maintained this conception—and to some extent put it into practice—that one meets all over the world today anxious people who will tell you that they fear both Soviet Communism and the American way of life. Their hopes, they say, hang on the survival and development of the British Welfare State. They fear that it too may become too centralised, that the acquisition of the new social and economic rights may be allowed to endanger the personal and civil ones. The answer to these questions is not to be found in Marx, who dealt only with the structure of society, and who knew what modern Communists are apt to deny—that the superstructure is not mechanically determined. Within the limits of the structure, the superstructure depends on our wills. I remember years ago asking Tawney how he conceived Socialism. He replied "A society in which everyone can say 'Go to hell' to everyone else, but no one wants to." (*pp.* 19*f.*)

18

DEMOCRACY AND THE TRANSITION TO SOCIALISM

For Ramsay MacDonald, the first leader of a Socialist party in Parliament, there was never any doubt that the path to power must lie along the lines of constitutional political action (a). Closely sympathetic as he was to Liberalism, he believed in the evolutionary progress of society towards the Socialist goal, and was an opponent of the idea of class-conflict. For many of the younger generation of Socialists, even for an ex-Liberal like H. N. Brailsford (editor of the *New Leader*, organ of the I.L.P.) this was too unrealistic an attitude. In Brailsford we see the influence of the war and the revolutionary acts that it occasioned on the continent (b). The realities of naked power which these events revealed gave force to the Leninist conception of the transition to Socialism—that no ruling class would hesitate to resort to force in order to maintain its ascendancy. The collapse of the second Labour Government in 1931, which appeared to be due in part at least to the hostility of the City, increased the tendency of the remaining Socialist leaders to view the transition period as a problem in revolutionary tactics, in which democratic forms might well have to be abandoned. Stafford Cripps, the future Chancellor of the Exchequer, advocated revolutionary measures in order to safeguard an elected Socialist government (c). The spread of Fascism on the continent and the appearance of a Fascist movement in this country raised fresh doubts about the future of the British parliamentary tradition, as may be seen from Professor Laski's comment (d).

Yet the immediate reaction to the events of 1931 was something exceptional; and Laski, though influential, did not express the views of more than a small minority. E. F. M. Durbin, the Oxford economist, who served as a junior minister in the 1945 Labour Government, was representing the deeper feeling of British Socialists in reasserting the primacy of the democratic method (e).; and the good fortune of the 1945 Government in taking over the state machine with controls already imposed stilled—at least temporarily—the debate on the problems of democracy in the transition.

The experience of that government and its aftermath, however, showed that the whole concept of the 'transition to Socialism' has a certain unreality about it even to the middle-of-the-road ethical Socialists who compose the newly-founded Socialist Union (f).

(a) J. RAMSAY MACDONALD. *Socialism and Society* 1905

THE industrial and economic inevitability of Socialism is a mere fancy. It is inevitable only if intelligence makes it so. It is inevitable only if we are to develop on rational lines; it is inevitable, not because men are exploited or because the fabric of capitalism must collapse under its own weight, but because men are rational. It is the action of reason alone which makes our evils a cause of progress and not the beginning of final deterioration. Intelligence and morality set out the goal which makes effective struggles to escape the existing purgatory. Human evolution is a stretching out, not a being pushed forward. Acorns produce oaks, grubs grow into beetles, tadpoles into frogs, but slums, industrial crises, poverty, trusts, do not in the same way grow into Socialism. Man was "inevitable" so soon as the amoeba appeared, but in the struggle for life which has taken place in the world of nature since life began, many species have been exterminated, many evolutions have been completed. Arrested development is as conspicuous as finished processes.

The workmen who vote Liberal and Unionist to-day are

perfectly conscious of the drawbacks of a life of wage-earning; they are also quite conscious that they belong to a separate economic and social class—and a great many of them would like to belong to another. In short, in any natural meaning of the words, they are class conscious. But they are not Socialists because they are not convinced that the intellectual proposals of Socialism should receive their support.

In order, therefore, that the social organism may perfect itself, there must be the will for perfection and the definite idea as to what changes are required. The life of the organism is continued through change, and the organism itself is ever in a state of reorganisation. Nation after nation has arisen and fallen, others have risen, have attained to a certain civilization and there have stuck. But stagnation is impossible for our own Western peoples. They may fall. Political combinations may crush them; the canker of poverty may drive them down into degeneracy. But if they are to continue to grow and to adapt themselves to new circumstances, if they are to carry on their development from stage to stage, it must be by the organisation of opinion and the operations of a constructive genius which sees the stage ahead and teaches the people how to attain to it. The Socialist appeal, therefore, is to all who believe in social evolution, who agree that the problem which Society has now to solve is that of the distribution of wealth, who trust in democracy, who regard the State not as antagonistic to but as an aspect of individuality, and who are groping onwards with the co-operative faith guiding them. That appeal may find some people in poverty, and they may follow because it offers them economic security; but it will find others in wealth, and they will follow because it brings order where there is now chaos, organisation where there is now confusion, law where there is now anarchy, justice where there is now injustice.

Socialism marks the growth of Society, not the uprising of a class. The consciousness which it seeks to quicken is not one of economic class solidarity, but one of social unity and growth towards organic wholeness. . . .

I reject what seems to me to be the crude notion of a class war, because class consciousness leads nowhere, and a class struggle may or may not be intelligent. But still, we turn our hopes first of all to the wage earners. They are the most certainly doomed victims of the present chaos; they suffer most from the inability of the present system to provide employment, wages, life; they are least buoyed up by elusive hopes that a lucky turn of the wheel of fortune will pitch them up on the backs of others; they are the helpless spills tossing on the troubled waters of present day strife; their attempts to share in the benefits of an efficient method of production result in little but turmoil, hunger and poverty; and above all, their needs have now become the chief concern of Society, because in fulness of time social organisation is being tested by its human results, and because the economic enfranchisement of the people naturally treads upon the heels of their political emancipation. (*pp.* 125–8)

(b) H. N. BRAILSFORD. *Socialism for To-day*

1925

DEMOCRACY is a great instrument for orderly change, and yet it would be fatal to exaggerate the omnipotence of Parliament. A majority which tried to nationalise everything at a stroke, or drove the possessing class to desperation by refusing compensation, would soon provoke civil war. The quality of the support behind us will count no less than the quantity. For success we need intelligent consent; we must first educate the manual workers. Even then we shall not go far, until we win a part of the professional and managerial class. Nor will political power alone suffice. Behind the Parliamentary party must stand the industrial army organised in trade unions. In the end, the unanswerable argument for fundamental change will be the increasing reluctance of the organised workers in mine and factory to tolerate the present distribution of wealth and power. When all these conditions are satisfied, we shall still avoid civil war only by a combination of great skill with unflinching resolution. We shall not glide comfortably into Socialism. The first open step which a Labour Government takes towards Socialism will at once arouse an embittered and unflinching will to resist. We may have to answer with emergency measures and war-time precautions. But even then it would be folly to abandon Parliamentary forms.

History has placed an admirable lever in our hands, such as no other people possesses. If we ever have to face the challenge of armed force, it is the English and not the Russian precedent which should inspire us. If ever we have to fight to impose our will, our most hopeful course would be to fight with the Parliament behind us, as the Puritan middle-class fought against Charles I. In defence of a threatened Parliament, Labour in power would repeat the revolution of the seventeenth century, and rally the nation against any Fascist attempt. It is well to start with the constitutional right to call on the obedience of magistrates and soldiers, even though we may expect that some of them will disobey. There is, moreover, a modern weapon at our service which the Parliament could not use under the Stuarts. The general strike may be useless for any positive or aggresive purpose. It has never in fact availed to gain any new right. But once, at least, in the recent history of Europe it proved itself a formidable weapon of defence against a sudden use of force by the reaction. It sufficed, after the mutinous troops and irregulars had seized Berlin during the Kapp revolt in 1920, to save the German Republic. (*pp.* 66–8)

(c) STAFFORD CRIPPS. *Problems of a Socialist Government*

1933

WHEN the decision has been taken by the Party as to whether they will accept office, it will have to be made clear to the country that it is the Party that is going to accept power and not some individual or individuals. Under existing circumstances the Prime Minister is theoretically and practically free to choose his own colleagues, and his primary responsibility is as an individual minister to the Crown.

The political Party to which the Prime Minister belongs has no right or power to recall the Prime Minister and replace him by some person more able and willing to direct policy along the lines required by the Party. In a Socialist Party this power is I believe essential, and more especially so during its early days of power. I do not propose to deal here with the method of selecting Party leaders or Cabinet ministers, as that is a political rather than a constitutional question. But however the selection is made the constitutional position of the Party must be clearly laid down. The formation of a Government must be the work of the Party, and the Party must have the right at any time to substitute fresh ministers in the places of any it desires to recall.

When the Party has come to a decision upon these two matters the list of ministers will be submitted to the Crown and their appointment will follow. The Socialist Government will then be in control of the country. The time between the decision to accept office and the actual appointment of ministers must be reduced to a minimum, as it will be a time of great danger in which saboteurs will be able to crystallise their plans for opposition and to concentrate their forces.

From the moment when the Government takes control rapid and effective action must be possible in every sphere of the national life. It will not be easy to detect the machinations of the capitalists, and, when discovered, there must be means ready to hand by which they can be dealt with promptly. The greatest danger point will be the financial and credit structure of the country and the Foreign Exchange position. We may liken the position that will arise somewhat to that which arose in August, 1914, but with this difference, that at the beginning of the war the capitalists, though very nervous and excited, were behind the Government to a man, whereas when the Socialist Government takes office they will not only be nervous and excited but against the Government to a man. The Government's first step will be to call Parliament together at the earliest moment and place before it an Emergency Powers Bill to be passed through all its stages on the first day. This Bill will be wide enough in its terms to allow all that will be immediately necessary to be done by ministerial orders. These orders must be incapable of challenge in the Courts or in any way except in the House of Commons.

This Bill must be ready in draft beforehand, together with the main orders that will be made immediately upon its becoming law.

It is probable that the passage of this Bill will raise in its most acute form the constitutional crisis.

It will be necessary—if constitutional forms are to be complied with—to obtain the consent of the House of Lords to this Bill, and that consent must be given immediately, as otherwise the Socialist Government cannot be responsible for the safety of the country or the continued supply of foodstuffs and raw material from overseas.

It is most probable that the House of Lords—the stronghold of capitalism—will either reject or more likely delay the passage of such a Bill. The Commons will be in a strong position as the election will have so recently taken place, and it may be that guarantees as to the passage of such a Bill may have been obtained as a condition of the taking of office.

If this is not so, then immediate application will have to be made to the Crown to resolve the conflict by the creation of Peers, and although this will necessitate some delay, it is better to risk this delay, which need not be excessive, than to adopt any unconstitutional alternative. Should the Crown refuse there would then be two alternative lines of action open to the Government, first, immediate resignation, throwing the responsibility back upon the capitalists, or second, an unconstitutional continuance in power with a total disregard of the Lords. This latter course would lead to an immediate conflict not only with the Crown and the Lords, but with the Judiciary, who would then refuse to recognise the Acts of the House of Commons unconfirmed by the House of Lords and the Crown. Such a conflict would throw the country into confusion and would almost certainly result in an uprising of the capitalists which would have to be quelled by force, and would lead to the very difficulties that it is most desired to avoid.

Returning therefore to the first alternative, the capitalist Government in a minority would have to accept office, or an immediate second General Election would ensue, on the sole issue of the right of the Lords to obstruct the emergency legislation. On such an issue the Socialist Party would, I think, be in a strong position, and—provided they could " beg, borrow or steal " the funds to fight the election —would have a second and perhaps even greater success.

In this event the capitalists would have to yield; if they did not, the Socialist Government, reassured of the country's support, would be justified in overriding any obstruction it found placed in its way.

There is perhaps one other possibility that we should envisage in the case of such a conflict and that is a dictatorship. The Crown has the right constitutionally only to accept advice from the Prime Minister, or such other person as the Prime Minister advises the Crown to consult. If once the Socialist Government resigned and advised the Crown to send for one of the leaders of the other parties, it might happen that none of them were prepared to take office and that eventually some stop-gap Ministry might be found which would rely upon the support of the armed forces of the Crown rather than upon any popular mandate, as indeed has happened in other countries. To throw the power into the hands of such a military dictatorship would be the worst possible thing for the country.

If the Socialist Government came to the conclusion that there was any real danger of such a step being taken, it would probably be better and more conducive to the general peace and welfare of the country for the Socialist Government to make itself temporarily into a dictatorship until the matter could again be put to the test at the polls. (*pp.* 41–6)

(d) H. J. LASKI. *Parliamentary Government in England*

1938

THE Russian Revolution has had on our own day a psychological influence at least as great as that of the French Revolution almost a century and a half ago. Like its predecessors, it has thrown the propertied class into a panic; its members have become persuaded that ideas and voluntary associations, which they once regarded with indifference, now constitute a challenge to their privileges. They move out to battle against them exactly as in the earlier time; old-time Jacobin has become new-time Bolshevik and he is similarly suppressed in the name of law and order. But by these terms are meant not a framework of principles in application for which there is general agreement. What is meant is the defence of the old order from the danger of change. There is even less reason, in so much more interdependent a world, to suppose that Great Britain will remain free from the pressure of these ideas. Its insular position, its historic traditions, its great wealth with its consequential capacity to set the limits of concession wider than elsewhere, are all of them, of course, important safeguards against extreme measures. But they are no more final safeguards here than they have proved elsewhere. They are all subject to the fundamental condition that men care so much more for social peace than for the rights of private property, as the present system views those rights, as to accept without counter-attack whatever disposition of their content the mass of the electorate may choose to make.

There is, this is to say, more room for compromise within the framework of the British system that has been found to be the case in other countries, though it must be added that room for compromise is a hope, rather than an assurance, of its successful attachment. The variables in the equation of social peace are as delicate as they are complex. It is not merely a matter of wisdom and self-restraint on the part of our governors. At least as important is the existence of the objective conditions which make possible their wisdom and self-restraint. They need international peace and economic recovery as the essential postulates of the conditions of successful compromise. These give men confidence, and, where they are confident, there is the prospect of mutual understanding. But there is no certain prospect of peace in an international situation which visibly deteriorates before our eyes. There is little prospect of permanent economic recovery when, all over the world, vested interests stand in the way not merely of Socialism, but of the very habits of successful intercourse which capitalism itself requires. It has its own inherent and inescapable logic. The world of vested interest cannot continue to deny that logic without paying the price for it. And there can, in the light of the post-war years, be no possibility of mistaking what that price is.

To put it briefly, that price is the war of creeds. Established expectations become armed philosophies, and they go out to do battle with one another. Men whose feet are set on the path of war, whether internal or external, do not speak the same language; how then can they hope to understand one another? To assume, in this kind of atmosphere, that they will accept as "binding and sacred" principles so delicate as those upon which the conventions of the British Constitution rest is to go contrary to everything we know from historic experience. In the circumstances we confront, what they do is either to suspend the conventions—a direct challenge to those whose hopes depend upon their continuing operation; or they retain their form while altering the spirit which lies behind that form. In Great Britain, it is the latter danger by which we are threatened. Political parties feel the strain of the pressures to which they are subjected. They seek as best they can the formulae of peaceful adjustment. They emphasize the special character of our conditions; they urge us to remember that violent solutions are out of accord with the national genius of the people. But the sense of strain is there; and its appeasement depends upon the arrest of that deterioration of the world-position which the wisest of national statesmen are not, of themselves, in a position to secure.

Peace, in fact, depends upon our ability to bring the relations of production into a new harmony with the forces of production. That new harmony means, as in the past it has always meant, a wholesale invasion of the privileges built upon vested interests. They have to be persuaded or coerced into giving way. And, historically, on any large scale and within any brief period of time, they have never, so far, been persuaded. For that persuasion requires a volume of mental adjustment which wholly contradicts the basic *weltanschauung* of those who have to be persuaded. Their lives have been tempered to the medium in which they live. Their conception of right is limited by the horizon of that medium. The State they built they conceived as an assurance of their purposes. Its apparatus of coercion was intended for nothing so much as to protect those purposes from invasion. They are asked to see that same State, that same apparatus of coercion, used for the denial of those purposes. And they are, more profoundly than any other, the religion by which they live. It is the religion which enshrines all that has made life pleasant for them. They no more doubt its principles than a good Mohammedan can doubt the promises of the Koran. It represents for them all the certainties that give colour and hope to their lives. Are they to admit, if regretfully, yet still freely, that all for which it stands is in fact grave error? Such an admission has not been the previous habit of mankind. Nor do we know of any change which should predispose us to believe that a change has taken place in the mental constitution of mankind. (*pp.* 61–4)

(e) E. F. M. DURBIN. *Politics of Democratic Socialism*

1940

DEMOCRACY is a *method* of taking political decisions, of compromising and reconciling conflicting interests. The method is more important, more formative of the resulting social order, than the disputes so resolved.

When individuals or groups disagree—including nations and classes and Parties within the state—the most important question is not what they disagree about, but the method or methods by which their disputes are to be resolved. If force is to be the arbiter between them, international war, civil war, cruelty and persecution are the inevitable consequences. Civilization cannot be built upon these crises of destruction.

There are two great principles at struggle in the hearts of men—friendliness and aggressiveness, co-operation and struggle. The lives of us all, and the slow growth of reason and kindliness between us, depend upon the victory of the first principle over the second. It is only if men will agree at least in this, that their disputes shall not be resolved by force, that culture and justice can slowly develop in our midst. The vital question is the question of method. The method will determine the end.

This is not a pacifist conclusion—not in the very least. I am not contending that it is the duty of any man to surrender his own purpose simply because other persons or groups use force, or threaten to use force, against him. That appears to me to be nonsensical, and to offer prizes to the unreasonable and to the aggressive. It may very well be our duty to repel force with force, and to see that—once the peace is broken—the group to which we owe our loyalty is victorious in the struggle that ensues.

My point, then, is not that we should be pacifist or believe in non-resistance, but that we should be pacific and believe in compromise. It is our supreme social duty to aid contending groups to agree not to use force in the settlement of their disputes. To set the maintenance of such agreements first in the sequence of our social values.

It is of the first importance to notice that the principle

of pacific settlement and of mutual compromise must be accepted by all the parties within a democracy. The obligation not to use force, and the obligation to compromise, is not restricted to one party. No party within the state is called upon to contemplate its own liquidation or to surrender its own objectives, simply because its opponents threaten to use force against it. . . .

With these further explanations of it, my central point now stands. I wish to maintain that the question of method is prior to the substance of the dispute between any pair of groups, including economic classes. If the method is to be that of warfare, then the hope of justice must be indefinitely postponed. Terror and cruelty must rule the affairs of men, and we must walk for ever in the shadow of fear. It may be that as individuals we shall belong to the group that is victorious in the struggle, or it may be that we shall be with those who are defeated. In victory or defeat we shall live in fear and see blood upon our hands. The victorious will live in fear of the oppressed, and the defeated in terror of the victors. And all those who fight must carry the guilt of destruction in their hearts. It may be our duty to join in such a battle—for it is often impossible to be indifferent to the outcome of a fight, however savage or irrational its origins may have been. But the basis of social justice, of friendliness between persons, of happiness and security in society, cannot be founded upon a regime of warfare. It can only be founded upon the principles of compromise and peace, and upon the restriction of force to the single task of coercing the aggressive minorities who will not accept the rule of law.

The authoritarian architects of Utopia all start by building the upper floors of their buildings. They try to build insubstantial 'castles in the air'. Social justice is the spire and the crown of the human habitation. But there is only one foundation for it. Common security and common happiness can only be founded upon common consent—men must come freely to their own salvation—justice can only spring from liberty. Democracy is the foundation and corner-stone of the temple. (*pp.* 271–3)

(f) *Socialist Union. Socialism: A new Statement of Principles*

1952

JUST because we have not always recognised that socialist programmes may vary in time and place, and even in name, the belief took root that there is somewhere, even if only in our imaginations, a "socialist system" with its own unique set of institutions. For European socialists in the nineteenth century the position seemed simple. Capitalism was to be overthrown; something known as socialism would naturally replace it. A straight choice was proclaimed between two clear-cut antithetical systems—destroy the one and the other would supersede it.

Today we know that this is a myth. There are no two distinct and opposing systems, only an infinite series of gradations. No one defines British society today as "socialism", yet it is also not nineteenth century capitalism. All the changes we have seen in our lifetime—full employment, planning, controls, housing programmes, social security, the national health service, progressive taxation—have produced a structure to which no ready-made label can be tagged. It may be said that these changes are a part of the transition to socialism. But have any of us knowledge of a system of institutions which would mark the end of the transition? And if we had, would there be any agreement on their nature?

Obviously no such knowledge and no such agreement

exists. Our agreement lies deeper—in our ideals, and in a readiness to take the axe to the root causes of social injustice. The essence of socialism is the perpetual struggle to realise its ideals, whenever and wherever possible. From this one statement a number of vital truths flow. Ideals, by their very nature, are never fully realised, but we can strive all the time for their fuller realisation. What is more, just because they are ideals involving the human spirit, their fulfilment cannot depend only upon changes in the social structure; there must be changes in human attitudes and relationships as well. Further, since institutions are means to an end, their exact form will certainly vary in time and place. No one pattern is sacrosanct. Nor can we ever assert the inevitable success of any new institution; it must always be subject to trial and error. In other words, we must come to the making of institutions with an empirical and not a doctrinaire attitude, for there is no accepted institutional blueprint called "socialism".

Are these statements mere platitudes? Although no one of them is original, yet taken together they may dispel some of the anxieties which cloud socialist thinking today. They deny the dogmas of the past, the failure of which has sapped our confidence. They glorify no particular institution which is bound, like all human creations, to be imperfect. They save us from the disillusionment which is the price of a faith in panaceas. And they show us, with an unflinching certainty, where our own tasks lie. Our first responsibility is to be aware of the implications of our own ideals, and to try to shape society and human attitudes accordingly. After all, society is always in a state of transition. Socialists should strive, unremittingly, for its betterment and not shirk current problems by waiting for the miraculous arrival of a Utopia.

Just as the myth of a "socialist system" took hold of men's minds, so did the illusion that to achieve it the "class struggle " must be intensified. Class struggle is an inevitable feature of class society, but its elevation into the supreme rule of socialist action is another of those doctrines which have not stood the test of events. . . .

The class struggle is no more a fixed pattern of action for the achievement of socialism than socialism itself is a fixed set of institutions. It is true that those who suffer from the class structure are more likely to fight against it than those to whom it brings advantages. But members of the privileged classes have also played an important part in the struggle for a better society; and some of the underprivileged have, at times, rebelled only in order to gain new privileges for themselves. Classes cannot be divided off into sheep and goats. Even if they could, to pit class against class in the end leads to a naked struggle for power and advantage, destroying the very values which socialists wish most to uphold.

Do we even wish, in a democratic country, deliberately to foster class hatred? There are dangers enough in this sort of hostility, as socialists have experienced in office. Democracy demands a willingness to compromise, an attempt to reconcile conflicting interests. Some common standards of behaviour must be accepted. In any community, interests conflict and power may determine the outcome. But what socialists want are civilised methods for resolving conflicts; power alone must not be the arbiter. Strike action was used to gain recognition and respect for the trade unions, but industrial conflict is not an end in itself. On the contrary, the unions have consistently tried to avoid it through agreed and peaceful methods of settling disputes. The concept of advancing towards our ideal society through hatred and schism has already, at least in this country, been largely discarded in practice. (*pp.* 40–4)

19

PUBLIC OWNERSHIP

Socialists of the late nineteenth and early twentieth centuries have almost all been committed to the aim of public ownership, in one form or another, of 'the means of production, distribution, and exchange'; and except for Syndicalists, this has meant nationalisation in the first instance. The main question in early discussions of nationalisation was whether, and if so how, to compensate the previous owners. Most British Socialists agreed that it would be invidious to nationalise without compensation. Keir Hardie's abortive Mines Nationalisation Bill, put forward by him when he was the only parliamentary representative of the I.L.P., contains provision for compensation (a), and similar arrangements are accepted as desirable by R. B. Suthers, a member of the *Clarion* staff and a well-known Socialist writer of the early years of this century (b).

Keir Hardie's Bill ignored the possibility that the workers might be interested to have a direct share in the control of their industry. This aspiration only came to the fore as a result of the Syndicalist and Guild Socialist movements. Although the Webbs were strong opponents of both these movements at first, they modified their views considerably as a result, as is evident in their *Constitution for the Socialist Commonwealth* (c) in which they advocate considerable participation by producers in the management of production. The Russian Revolution and the failure of the General Strike in 1926 tended on the whole to discredit Syndicalist theories, and the orthodox view was that expressed by Herbert Morrison, Minister of Transport in the second Labour Government of 1929–31 and chief organiser of the nationalisation programme of the third Labour Government of 1945–50. Morrison argued in favour of the independent public corporation, responsible to a minister but without direct participation by the trade unions on the board of management. The opposition that he had to overcome inside the Labour movement is indicated by the quotations here given from the debate at the 1932 Labour Party Conference (d). The sections of the Party's 1945 election programme in which the vital nationalisation proposals are made contain no mention of producers' participation (e). Perhaps it is natural that subsequent Socialist criticism of nationalised industries has concentrated on the failure, so far, to transform the status of the worker and to give him a share in running his industry (f).

(a) J. KEIR HARDIE. Nationalisation of Mines Bill 1893

A BILL

To Nationalise the Mines and Minerals of Great Britain and Ireland, and to provide for the working of the same.

PREAMBLE

Whereas coal having become an essential factor in the manufacturing industries and transport service of the nation, any interference with a regular and continuous supply is fraught with gravest dangers to our commercial supremacy:

And whereas the supply of coal is limited, and when exhausted can never be replaced:

And whereas the present system of working mines as private concerns leads to great waste of our material supplies, and to strikes and lock-outs, thereby imposing great hardship on the mining community and trades dependent on a mineral supply for their continuance:

And whereas the nationalisation of the minerals and mines would secure the economical working of the same, the just treatment and consequent contentment of the mining population, and a continuous and cheap supply of coal and other minerals:

BE IT THEREFORE ENACTED by the Queen's most Excellent Majesty, by and with the advice and consent of the Lords Spiritual and Temporal, and Commons, in this Parliament assembled, and by the authority of the same, as follows:

1. On and after the *first day of January One Thousand Eight Hundred and Ninety-Five* all mines and minerals within the United Kingdom of Great Britain and Ireland shall be transferred, in fee simple, to the Crown, and shall thereupon become the property of the nation.

2. All persons who are owners in whole or in part of the said mines or minerals shall on or before the *first day of May One Thousand Eight Hundred and Ninety-Four* make a full and complete return to the Secretary of State for the Home Department showing the extent and nature of their pecuniary interest in the said mines or minerals.

3. (1) The Secretary of State for the Home Department shall appoint duly qualified valuers who shall assess the present value of the said mines or minerals without regard either to the amount of capital invested or prospect of profits on the working of the same.

(2) The said valuers shall carefully inquire into the present value as above defined of the mines and minerals of Great Britain and Ireland, and report to the Home Secretary, who shall thereupon issue an order upon the Treasury for the amount of the value so ascertained.

(3) *The Lords of the Treasury shall, on receipt of the said order, issue to the persons who have established their claim to be reckoned owners in whole or in part of said mines or minerals, consols to the amount of their interests as found to exist at the date of the transfer to the Crown. The said consols shall bear interest at the current rates, plus three per centum on the capital amount to form a sinking fund for the redemption of the capital sum.*

(4) The interest on the mining consols together with the sinking fund shall form a first charge upon the working of the mines.

4. (1) Previous to the *first day of January One Thousand Eight Hundred and Ninety-Five*, the Government shall create a special Mining Department with a President, who must be a member of the House of Commons, invested with full powers for the direct working and conducting of the mining industry of Great Britain and Ireland, without the intervention of any contractor or lessee, in such a way as will supply the legitimate demands for coal and other minerals, and ensure the safety and comfort of the persons employed.

(2) The said Mining Department shall also pay such wages to persons employed in and about the mines as will ensure a healthy and comfortable existence to the said persons and their dependants.

(3) No woman, nor any young person under *fifteen years* of age, shall be employed under ground, nor shall any person be allowed to work alone in a mine until he has first served an apprenticeship of *three years'* duration.

(4) No person shall be employed in a mine for a longer period than *eight hours* in any twenty-four hours, the time to be reckoned from the hour of descent to the hour of ascent from the mine.

(5) In the case of accident, fatal or otherwise, to any person employed in or about a mine, and sustained while in the performance of their duty as a workman, or persons unable to follow their occupation from old age, sickness, or other cause, over which they have no control, compensation or provision shall be made in terms of Schedule I of this Act.

(6) The cost of such compensation or provision shall be a charge upon the working of the mines.

5. On the establishment of a local parliament for any

part of the United Kingdom of Great Britain or Ireland, the powers conferred upon the Mining Department under this Act shall, in so far as they relate to the country over which such local parliament has control, be transferred to and vested in the Executive Government responsible to such local parliament.

SCHEDULE. . . . (*Labour Leader*, 26 May 1900)

(b) R. B. SUTHERS. *Common Objections to Socialism Answered*

1909

We shall most probably begin by nationalising the foundation industries of the nation, land, railways, mines, insurance, banking, and so on.

We shall also put an increasing tax on incomes received for idleness, on rent, and interest, and monopoly.

By this means we shall accumulate national Capital for starting State industries, and so solve the unemployed problem.

If we take over, say, the railways, we could give the shareholders Government stock like Consols, in return for their shares, and pay a fixed interest for a certain number of years at any rate.

This interest would be paid out of the earnings of the railways, as it is to-day, but it is probable that under State management the railways would yield higher profits, which would go into the public treasury. So with the banks and insurance companies, the mines and other industries.

A Socialist Government would naturally not desire to impoverish the poor man who happened to be a little "capitalist". The Duke of Westminster and John Smith might conceivably have, the first one million and the second £20 in the same land company.

Well, if the land company were nationalised and the dividends were reduced to a fixed rate of interest, it might hurt John Smith, while the Duke of Westminster would not feel the reduction. Such an injustice would be provided for. John Smith might have his tobacco and food taxes and his rates reduced, so that he would not lose on the whole.

The working man with £20 in the bank, or a house of his own, need have no fear. His position would certainly improve under these conditions. He would for one thing be getting an old age pension, which he could not buy for £100 to-day, and he would have regular employment, which would be worth at least £20 a year to him.

And by the time the next steps come to be taken you will be dead, and all your anxiety about your savings will be as a tale that is told.

I wonder if any of you will feel sorry, when you arrive in the next world, that you fought against Socialism for fear of losing your savings? O, my Christian friends, *what* an argument!

" I will say unto my soul, 'Soul, thou hast much goods laid up for many years; take thine ease, eat, drink, and be merry.' But God said unto him, 'Thou foolish one, this night is thy soul required of thee; and the things which thou hast prepared, whose shall they be?' "

Socialists would not be unjust or harsh. But they would not forget, when dealing out Compensation, the millions who have so long suffered from the Confiscation of the present system, and it would always be their aim to hasten the time when that Confiscation should cease.

We see, then, that Compensation in our opponents' sense *is* impossible, because it would be unjust; but Compensation in our sense is possible, because it would be just. (*pp*. 27–9)

(c) SIDNEY and BEATRICE WEBB. *A Constitution for the Socialist Commonwealth of Great Britain*

1920

Two fundamental conclusions stand out. The minimum participation of Democracies of Citizen-Consumers must be the ownership of the instruments of production. The minimum participation of Democracies of Producers is control over the conditions under which the producers by hand or by brain fulfil their vocation. But both these highly generalised phrases demand specific interpretation.

It is plainly necessary to include with the ownership of the instruments of production what has usually gone with property rights, namely, the power to decide, subject to the limits prescribed by the law of the land, what disposition shall be made of these instruments, what commodities or services shall be produced, and in what quantities and qualities, and how the product shall be disposed of. It is thus not a bare legal ownership of land and raw materials, or of buildings and plant, that is here in question, but the actual power of deciding to what use the instruments of production shall be put, and to what end each productive process shall be directed. On the other hand, what is referred to as instruments of production is not, pedantically, every tool or accessory by which production is assisted—there is no suggestion that a carpenter should not individually own his kit of tools, the seamstress her needle, or the clerk his fountain-pen—but merely what is commonly included by the business man as capital, such as is provided by a joint-stock company engaged in manufacture or commerce.

Similarly, there must be included in the conditions under which the producers by hand or by brain fulfil their vocation, and over which they must exercise control (though not necessarily dictatorship or exclusive control) not merely their pay, their working hours, and the sanitation, safety and amenity of their places of employment, but also the character of the operations that they are called on to perform, and the persons with whom they are required to associate in work, their intellectual liberty both inside and outside of their employment, and—what is often forgotten—their practical freedom or opportunity to exercise their vocation in an efficient way.

It is exactly at this point that the great mass of productive workers, probably nine-tenths of the whole, are under the Capitalist System most restricted, and it is here that the Socialist Commonwealth will seek to provide for the greatest development. Exactly as a nation feeling itself to have a common heritage in a distinct culture is morally entitled to self-determination in matters of government (and cannot with advantage be denied it), so each vocation that is conscious of itself as a distinct vocation, with its own training, its own standard of qualification, its own technique, its own code of honour among the fellow-members and towards the community, and an interest in the development of its own science and the promotion of its own art or craftsmanship, is equally entitled to its own measure of self-determination in the specialised service that it renders to the community. The most disastrous of all the effects of the Capitalist System has been the destruction of this "instinct of workmanship" among nine-tenths of the people. With relentless pressure the Capitalist System is always seeking, whilst magnifying the sphere of the brain-working specialist, to "unspecialise" the wage-earner, or, what amounts to much the same thing in terms of individual development, to reduce the workman's function to one endless repetition of a purely mechanical task, under the direction, not of his own but of another's brain and will.

It will be one of the functions of vocational organisation in the Socialist Commonwealth—to be described in a subsequent chapter—to restore to the manual worker his "instinct of workmanship."

Now it is obvious that these various minimum requirements of the different sections of producers, of the consumers of different commodities and of the citizens as a whole, not only impinge on one another theoretically, but must, in practice, often lead to a clashing of decisions. It follows, therefore, that every constitution for a socialised industry or service must include, as an indispensable feature, not only a well-balanced constitution for carrying on the day-by-day administration, but also well-devised machinery for consultation, for accommodation and, in fact, for bargaining, between the representatives of the Citizen-Consumers and those of the various grades or sections of the producers in the particular industry or service. (*pp.* 163–6)

(d) Debate on National Planning of Transport, Labour Party Conference

5 October 1932

Rt. Hon. Herbert Morrison (National Executive):
. . . I beg of you not to move from that point—that the final test of appointment should be individual capacity—and you will then remove the possibility of the appointment being such that it could be said we are going to do somebody a good turn. We have no right to do anybody a good turn at the expense of the socialised industries. Now, suppose I concede that point, and give the Transport Workers' Union the substance of what they ask for, what happens? I commit the Executive of the Party to it. We are there in the House of Commons for our own Party, and Labour leader-

ship is the most difficult form of political leadership of any political Party in the civilised world. You get your Bill. You have got this one statutory provision of the right of the workers of the industry to representation, and what happens? You have given away the case for the Board of capacity and ability. . . . Labour in the industry, and only in the industry, is to have its representation. The Order Paper will be flooded with amendments to secure the representation of other interests. . . . What you would have in the end is a Board of interests, and some of these organisations—not the Trade Unions—would put old men upon the Board, third-rate men, people they wanted to do a good turn to. In that case you would run the risk of the whole show being run by dead-heads no better than the guinea pigs who now run the railway companies of Great Britain. I beg of this Conference not to snatch at the shadow of control but to take the substance. Let us find our own people who are best fitted for the work that has to be done; and remember that everyone on the Board will divest themselves of any financial interest they may have. Once they are there, what will they be thinking about? Certainly our Trade Union friends will be thinking of the well-being of the undertaking, but at the back of their heads they will be thinking of the interest of the Union that nominated them for appointment to the Board. Once you concede to any industry the right of representation, your Board will be run by interests, thinking of their interests with sectional minds, scratching each other's backs, "pull devil, pull baker", and your Socialist undertaking will be in danger of failure. It is not good for Socialism that it should be mixed up with things that are failures. . . .

Mr. H. E. Clay (*Transport and General Workers' Union*): . . . When Mr. Morrison says this is the Socialist solution, we are definitely in opposition to him. We are not opposing the resolution to set up a Transport Board, we are not opposing the idea of a Public Corporation, but we want to make it perfectly clear that we do not regard this as the solution of the transport problem along definite Socialist lines. . . . I want to suggest that the proposals which Mr. Morrison puts forward stratifies industrial society. The workers are workers, and you doom them to remain hewers of wood and drawers of water under the perpetual control of their bosses. They are to have no real effective power under the proposals put forward in this Report. This Report provides for an efficient bureaucracy being placed in control with no effective check upon it. You have a public corporation now in the B.B.C. What effective control have you there? . . .

I do not happen to be a Syndicalist. I went through that movement like many others. I am a Socialist. I believe in political democracy, but I do not believe that can become complete until you have industrial democracy. One of my difficulties in reading this Report is that it appears to assume the permanency of the purely commodity status of labour. That, I think, is a fundamental objection. It assumes that the Board will be a kind, benevolent sort of thing that will give to labour an opportunity to learn more about the job. Good heavens! we can teach them more about the job than they ever knew. I have been dealing lately with the development of Company Unions, welfare schemes and things of that sort. That kind of thing is not good enough for us. Finally, this Report pays no regard to what I may term the humanities of labour. I would like to have the spirit which animated Tawney when he wrote his *Acquisitive Society*. After all, industry has a purpose, and if that purpose is going to be finally achieved, then the workers within the industry must have full citizen rights. They have not only to be efficient wealth producers, but they have to realise that in doing their job, and doing it well, they are ministering to the community as a whole and rendering service to a great ideal. . . . (*Labour Party Report*, 1932, *pp.* 213–6)

(e) *Labour Party. Let Us Face the Future*

1945

By the test of war some industries have shown themselves capable of rising to new heights of efficiency and expansion. Others, including some of our older industries fundamental to our economic structure, have wholly or partly failed.

To-day we live alongside economic giants—countries where science and technology take leaping strides year by year. Britain must match those strides—and we must take no chances about it. Britain needs an industry organised to enable it to yield the best that human knowledge and skill can provide. Only so can our people reap the full benefits of this age of discovery and Britain keep her place as a Great Power.

The Labour Party intends to link the skill of British craftsmen and designers to the skill of British scientists in the service of our fellow men. The genius of British scientists and technicians who have produced radio-location, jet propulsion, penicillin, and the Mulberry Harbours in wartime, must be given full rein in peacetime too.

Each industry must have applied to it the test of national service. If it serves the nation, well and good; if it is inefficient and falls down on its job, the nation must see that things are put right.

These propositions seem indisputable, but for years before the war anti-Labour Governments set them aside, so that British industry over a large field fell into a state of depression, muddle and decay. Millions of working and middle-class people went through the horrors of unemployment and insecurity. It is not enough to sympathise with these victims: we must develop an acute feeling of national shame—and act.

The Labour Party is a Socialist Party, and proud of it. Its ultimate purpose at home is the establishment of the Socialist Commonwealth of Great Britain—free, democratic, efficient, progressive, public-spirited, its material resources organised in the service of the British people.

But Socialism cannot come overnight, as the product of a week-end revolution. The members of the Labour Party, like the British people, are practical-minded men and women.

There are basic industries ripe and over-ripe for public ownership and management in the direct service of the nation. There are many smaller businesses rendering good service which can be left to go on with their useful work.

There are big industries not yet ripe for public ownership which must nevertheless be required by constructive supervision to further the nation's needs and not to prejudice national interests by restrictive anti-social monopoly or cartel agreements—caring for their own capital structures and profits at the cost of a lower standard of living for all.

In the light of these considerations, the Labour Party submits to the nation the following industrial programme:

1. *Public ownership of the fuel and power industries.*—For a quarter of a century the coal industry, producing Britain's most precious national raw material, has been floundering chaotically under the ownership of many hundreds of independent companies. Amalgamation under public ownership will bring great economies in operation and make it possible to modernise production methods and to raise safety standards in every colliery in the country. Public ownership of gas and electricity undertakings will lower charges, prevent competitive waste, open the way for

co-ordinated research and development, and lead to the reforming of uneconomic areas of distribution. Other industries will benefit.

2. *Public ownership of inland transport.*—Co-ordination of transport services by rail, road, air and canal cannot be achieved without unification. And unification without public ownership means a steady struggle with sectional interests or the enthronement of a private monopoly, which would be a menace to the rest of industry.

3. *Public ownership of iron and steel.*—Private monopoly has maintained high prices and kept inefficient high-cost plants in existence. Only if public ownership replaces private monopoly can the industry become efficient.

These socialised industries, taken over on a basis of fair compensation, to be conducted efficiently in the interests of consumers, coupled with proper status and conditions for the workers employed in them.

4. *Public supervision of monopolies and cartels* with the aim of advancing industrial efficiency in the service of the nation. Anti-social restrictive practices will be prohibited.

5. *A firm and clear-cut programme for the export trade.*—We would give State help in any necessary form to get our export trade on its feet and enable it to pay for the food and raw materials without which Britain must decay and die. But State help on conditions—conditions that industry is efficient and go-ahead. Laggards and obstructionists must be led or directed into better ways. Here we dare not fail.

6. *The shaping of suitable economic and price controls* to secure that first things shall come first in the transition from war to peace and that every citizen (including the demobilised Service men and women) shall get fair play. There must be priorities in the use of raw materials, food prices must be held, homes for the people must come before

mansions, necessities for all before luxuries for the few. We do not want a short boom followed by collapse as after the last war; we do not want a wild rise in prices and inflation, followed by a smash and widespread unemployment. It is either sound economic controls—or smash.

7. *The better organisation of Government departments* and the Civil Service for work in relation to these ends. The economic purpose of government must be to spur industry forward and not to choke it with red tape. (*pp.* 5–7)

(f) *Keeping Left*, by a Group of Members of Parliament

1950

WHILST maintaining the need to expand continuously the public sector of our economy, we cannot disguise the fact that the public corporations have not, so far, provided everything which socialists expected from nationalised industries. Very largely, of course, this is due to the fact that the take-over was so recent and that some of these industries were taken over in very poor condition. But even allowing for this, they do not yet make us all feel that it's our own property we're dealing with. And until that happens we have only the letter of public ownership and not the spirit, only the establishment of the fact and not the fulfilment of the purpose.

Largely this is due to the decision to put each nationalised industry under a public corporation with a large degree of autonomy and with the prime duty of balancing its accounts. Relieved in this way from detailed parliamentary control, and ordered to operate on a "strictly business" basis, some of the corporations have been able to show good results within the confines of their own industry, and have thus converted many people who were formerly sceptical about public ownership.

So far, so good; but the question remains whether we are not paying too high a price for the autonomy of the public corporations. For one thing, we are prevented by it from integrating their price-policies into national economic planning. Since they must sell their products or services at just enough to break even, they cannot be used to influence the price mechanism according to social priorities. We thus rob ourselves of a flexible and useful tool in the task of correlating demand with supply.

The argument for making the public corporations autonomous is that it takes them out of politics. But the inhibiting effect of parliamentary control can be greatly exaggerated; witness the Post Office, which, though subject to the parliamentary question, is a good deal more efficient than (say) the British Overseas Airways Corporation—and without paying its chief executive £7,500 a year plus expenses. On the other hand, the lack of parliamentary control over the public corporation is a great loss in a social democracy.

One of the effects of the fear of making losses is that the corporations have not shown any great keenness for consumers' councils. This is not altogether their fault. Consumer representation in many industries is not easy to organise, and the public itself has so far shown little interest in the consumers' councils that have been set up. Nevertheless, a really socialised industry would actively encourage the expression of customers' opinions, and would be more sensitive to them than our nationalised industries have been so far.

Nor can it be pretended that the workers have obtained from nationalisation that greater share in the running of their industries which they had a right to expect. It is true that some of these industries have had only a very short time to set up effective joint consultative machinery, and some of them have made a great deal of progress in that time. But most of that progress has been between the corporations and the national executives of the trades unions, and it has not penetrated down to the manager and the worker at the workplace level.

To some extent this is because the National Boards, who have a real desire for their workers to participate in management, have failed to inculcate that desire in their subordinate managers. But chiefly it is due to a large and widening gap between the national officers of trades unions and their lay members.

This gap shows itself more clearly in the public sector than in private industry. In the latter the worker rarely gets any chance to participate in effective joint consultation, and so he accepts it as the natural order of things that his national officers shall meet the employers on his behalf. But in the nationalised industries, unlike the private sector, joint consultation is now a statutory obligation, and it operates at all levels. Because of this, the rank-and-file worker has had a taste of doing his own consultation at the factory level—often with a great deal of success—and so he wants to take part in all the joint machinery right up to the top. He is not allowed to, partly because national officers are unwilling to entrust large-scale and intricate wage negotiations to inexperienced lay members, but chiefly because they are tender about their own authority and prestige. The result is that national consultation and local consultation are two quite separate things with no points of contact, and the two-way channel of information between the corporation and the workers, which is the first essential of good industrial relations and the only safeguard against workers' frustration, does not exist.

An equally serious result of this gap between national and local levels is that joint consultation in the nationalised industries, contrary to what we had all hoped, has been confined (except to some extent in coal) to the negotiation of wages and working conditions, and has hardly penetrated into the sphere of participation in management. In the nationalisation Acts we carefully inserted a provision that the unions must be consulted not merely on wages, working conditions, health, welfare and safety, but also on "efficiency in the operation of the corporation's services." But no one can be consulted on this subject unless he takes the time and trouble to study each issue as it crops up. The trades-union officers don't know the issues and, because they're nearly all heavily overworked, have not the time to study them. The rank-and-file workers do know, but they're kept off the national committee.

In the main the solution to this problem must come from within the unions. Indeed, there are already signs of rank-and-file pressure to that end—in demands that members of the national committee should visit workplace committees, and vice-versa; that the national members shall consist of, or at least include, elected rank-and-file workers; and that national agreements shall not be concluded without a referendum. But the Government, too, since it has nationalised these industries, has a duty to take a hand in the solution of this problem. Labour Ministers have an influence with the Unions that no Conservative Minister could ever command; and they should use it to give a lead in making joint consultation fully effective. (*pp.* 29–31)

20

SOCIALISM AND WELFARE

Although 'palliative' measures have sometimes been ignored on the ground that they diminish the ardour for complete revolution, the bulk of the Socialist movement including, as we have seen, Marx and Engels themselves have taken up with enthusiasm various issues of immediate welfare, not only for their own sake, but also because it has been possible to associate them with propaganda of a more general nature.

The Socialist attitude towards welfare legislation is based, first of all, on the view that poverty is primarily due not to the faults of the individual but to those of society as a whole. This finds simple expression in Jowett's speech for the Liberal Bill to allow local authorities to provide meals for schoolchildren (a); it can also be seen in a larger context in the Minority Report of the Poor Law Commission (1909), drafted by the Webbs.

An additional important argument in favour of raising the lower income levels was that the underconsumption caused by poverty was responsible for the economic crises of the capitalist system. This was first put forward as an economic theory by J. A. Hobson in 1889, but hints of it are to be found in Ruskin and in several of the early Socialists. Philip Snowden's argument in a Commons debate of 1908 is based on this theory (b); twenty-five years later as Chancellor of the Exchequer he had abandoned it, in spite of the I.L.P.'s official acceptance of the theory in the Report on *The Living Wage*, in which Hobson and another able economist, E. F. Wise, the pioneer of bulk buying, personally participated (c).

The final quotation, from Aneurin Bevan on the National Health Service, the greatest of the social welfare schemes of the Labour Government, shows an advance from the old Webb principle of the National Minimum (making the best of

Capitalism) to the fully egalitarian and Socialist concept of uniform facilities for all (d).

(a) F. W. JOWETT. Speech on Education (Provision of Meals) Bill, Second Reading, House of Commons

2 March 1906

. . . The Committee upon Physical Deterioration found that :—

> "It was a subject of general agreement that as a rule no purely voluntary association could successfully cope with the whole extent of the evil."

With those words he heartily agreed. Much was often said about sapping the independence of the people, but he knew of nothing which so much sapped that independence as the wild charity which created so much trouble by indiscriminate giving without having the power to see what was done with the gift. It seemed to him that, underlying some remarks made during the discussion by previous speakers, there was an idea that if they were to do something to relieve the material necessity under which people had to struggle, the desire to struggle would cease, and that, therefore, a greater mistake could not be made. But what was civilization if it was not directed to freeing the people from material necessities; and if they could do that, surely the result would be that the struggle would be transferred to a higher plane, and the people would have the opportunity to fight for better things. Any Member of the House who had come to close quarters with the question would bear him out when he said that those portions of the community which were most subject to material uncertainty were the least responsive to any message coming from any man or woman who cared for the uplifting of humanity. It was only by setting the people free from material necessities that they were able to keep their attention on those matters which really concerned them more than material necessities. Therefore, he asserted that if this Bill could free human beings from some part of the material struggle, that struggle would still go on, but it would be a better and nobler struggle than before. The question whether or not this step should be taken was a plain and simple one, and any Member of the House representing an industrial constituency who asked himself how many of the families in the constituency which he represented were in the enjoyment of an income sufficient to enable them to feed and clothe themselves would feel bound to give an answer to the question in the affirmative. He was able to speak for Bradford, and he anticipated that London was in an even worse position. But what were the facts so far as Bradford were concerned? Whole industries and trades were there carried on permanently under such conditions that the wage-earner could not maintain himself, his wife, and his bairns in comfort. He might take the case of the wool-combers; in this industry there were some 4,000 persons employed on the night turns, and he would like to ask what opportunity had they to maintain their families? Their wages, when fully employed, ranged from 18s. to 21s. per week, so far as a large majority of them were concerned. But there was no such thing as continuity of employment in their case. . . . What could be done for them? In his opinion there was one thing could be done, and that was to say to the parents, "You are not responsible for the system of society under which you live; the economic conditions have not been created by you; your children must be looked after and they must be fed," if we are to lift our heads among the nations of the earth, and if we desire to keep our place in the civilized world. (*Parliamentary Debates*, 4th Series, vol. 152, c. 1,409–11)

(b) PHILIP SNOWDEN. Speech in Debate on the King's Speech, House of Commons

30 January 1908

. . . Let them apply all the root causes suggested by the Parliamentary secretary and they had not touched at all the root cause of unemployment, which, as the President of the Local Government Board had said, was deep down in our capitalistic system. Upon this point John Stuart Mill said—"The deep root of the evils which fill the industrial world is the subjection of labour to monopoly, and the enormous share which the possessors of the instruments of production are able to take from the produce." He thoroughly agreed with the hon. Member for Preston when he said that this was a question of poverty. Even old age pensions was a question of poverty. He would venture to describe it also as a question of the unequal distribution of wealth. The hon. Member for Preston had said they could not increase wages without increasing the amount of the country's wealth. In his opinion, the root cause of unemployment was monopoly. It was a question of the standard of living and the purchasing power of money. He did not expect a solution of the unemployed question from one or from a hundred Acts of Parliament, but it was important to understand the nature of the problem to avoid by blunders aggravation of the situation. Any proposal which in its results would add to the amount of wealth at the disposal of the working-class population would increase the volume of employment. A time of bad trade followed a period of good trade, but the purchasing power of the people during the late period of good trade was less than it had been in preceding years. In the Lancashire weaving trade the rate of wages was the same as in 1859, the cost of living had increased, but there had been no corresponding increase in wages. The Board of Trade returns showed that in each year, from 1901 to 1905, the wages of the people went down, and yet during the whole time the cost of living was going up. Each succeeding year the workers were able to buy a less proportion of the production, and yet the production increased. No wonder, then, that in a short time we were confronted with that curious phenomenon of modern civilization, over-production—too much of cotton goods and men without shirts, too many boots and children with bare feet. It was really a question of under-consumption, not of over-production. It was not for himself and his hon. friends to put forward proposals to reform the present economic conditions. They were not the Executive Government of the country. The devising of the plan of campaign lay with the men who were paid for it. A right hon. Gentleman speaking from the front Opposition Bench had said that Socialists had never put their proposals into definite and practical forms. They were not there to defend Socialism. It was not Socialism but capitalism which was on its trial. It was for others to defend a system under which the men who did not work grew richer day by day, and the harder a man worked the poorer he was. Some reforms a Government might introduce and carry into law in a comparatively short time. The shortening of the hours of labour had been advocated as a means of increasing employment, but economic students had given up that point. The improved efficiency of workmen would in a short time bring up the output of the shorter to that of the longer day. He drew a distinction between productive and non-productive occupations. The shortening of the hours of labour on railways would require the employment of 100,000 additional men and have a far-reaching effect. It would reduce dividends, but it would increase the spending power of those engaged in the industry.

It would not only add to the purchasing power of the 100,000 workers directly employed, but their increased purchasing power would stimulate other trades as well. So with the case of the mines and other industries ripe for public control. They could only increase the amount of employment, as the hon. Member for Preston said, by increasing the demand for labour and increasing consumption. He believed that public management of the railways would enable economies to be effected by which the cost of transit would be considerably reduced and that would have its effect on every trade which used the railways. The thing to keep in mind was that they must effect a more equal and just distribution of wealth. They must carry out reforms which would add to the purchasing power of the people, for after all, it was on their spending power that trade relied. (*Parliamentary Debates*, 4th Series, vol. 183, c. 325–7)

(c) H. N. BRAILSFORD, J. A. HOBSON, A. CREECH JONES and E. F. WISE. *The Living Wage, a Report to the I.L.P.*

1926

Two lines of thought converge upon this problem of achieving a Living Income for every worker.

One of them is ethical. The gross inequalities of income which prevail to-day forbid a great part of the population to attain, in its mental and even in its physical growth, the full stature of humanity, and condemn it to a life of care and privation, if not actual want. A society which allows generation after generation of its children to grow up in this condition, violates morality in its very structure.

The other line of reasoning is economic. Low wages mean a limitation of the home market. The benefits of mass production cannot be realised to the full, because the power of the masses to consume fails to keep pace with the power of the machines to produce. The wrong division of the product of industry involves in this way a limitation of the output. We produce less wealth than our technical resources would enable us to create, because the mass of the wage-earners lack " effective demand ". The owning class has misused the advantage of its position. Too much, proportionately, of the product of industry, has been accumulated and applied to the creation of fresh instruments of production: too little, proportionately, has gone in wages to make a market for the product of these new machines. The recent experience of America confirms this diagnosis. Great national resources and high technical efficiency are only part of the explanation of the present prosperity of the United States. Much is explained by the fact that the restriction of immigration and the consequent scarcity of labour compelled the employers to resort to a policy of high wages. That gave them a vast home market, and enabled them to develop the full possibilities of mass production.

The practical conclusion from this familiar analysis of the vices of the industrial system, as we know it in this country, is that by one expedient or another we must aim at a general and simultaneous increase in the purchasing power of the masses. The bootmaker will demand high wages with success, if his factory is working economically, at its full capacity, to satisfy an assured and constant demand. But that will happen only if the wages of the engineers and agricultural labourers permit them to buy more boots, and to buy them steadily. The agricultural labourer, in his turn, would find himself in this fortunate position, if an increase in the wages of every poorly-paid trade enabled working-class mothers to increase the inadequate quantity of milk which their children at present drink.

In thinking out any constructive policy, we would urge that the Labour Movement must base itself upon this fact of "under-consumption." We are far from disputing the reasoning of thinkers who insist that higher production is necessary in order that the national income may be increased. That is self-evident. But it is equally necessary to insist that higher production is in the long run unattainable, or can at best be only spasmodic and temporary, unless there goes with it a parallel increase in the purchasing power of the mass of the consumers. Every improvement and expansion in production, whether it comes from fresh investment, better organisation or new inventions, must be accompanied by a corresponding expansion of the market. We can, however, ensure the observance of this axiom only within that part of the market which we can control—in other words the home market.

The expansion of the market will be found to have two aspects:—

1. The necessary expansion of credit and currency to keep pace with the growth in the output of goods and services, with which we deal in the next section.
2. The wider distribution of this expanded purchasing power.

It is not sufficient to ensure that the nation's total purchasing power shall be increased. Care must be taken, in distributing it, to ensure that a due proportion shall be observed, in its probable destination, between saving and spending, or in other words between expenditure on reproductive instruments and on consumable goods and services. This means that a higher proportion than is customary in our society must go to the wage-earning masses, and a lower proportion to the owning and investing class. Failing this readjustment in the distribution of the national income, the inevitable glut will recur periodically as the result of under-consumption, and the process of production will be subject to the jerks, the interruptions and the waste of the trade cycle.

There are two sources from which this fresh stream of mass purchasing power can be provided. The simpler of these two methods is by a re-distribution of the existing national income, through the instrument of direct taxation. This occurs whenever a part of the income of the wealthier tax-payers is diverted from its natural destination of saving, to working-class consumption. Old age pensions and all expenditure on the social services are instances of this transference. We propose in Section 4 the payment, out of direct taxation, to every working-class mother, of children's allowances. This method of increasing the purchasing power of the mass of the consumers is, to our thinking, the most socially beneficial way of spending the national income. It is also free from any risk of promoting inflation. It requires no issue of fresh currency or credit. It merely effects a re-distribution of actual annual income, and would have no disturbing influence on the general price level.

The other method of increasing mass purchasing power is by raising wages. While this may be the more powerful of the two methods, it raises complicated problems, which we discuss in the later sections of this report. The obvious danger which has to be combated is that any widespread increase of wages may be wholly or partially neutralised by a rise in prices. We shall suggest several ways in which this may be obviated.

1. By the control of credit and the stabilisation of the general price level.
2. By the economy which would follow from the elimination of dealers and middlemen in the State-organised importation of staple foods and raw materials.
3. From the economies which would follow the stabilisa-

tion, both of supply and demand, in standard commodities.

But plainly, the surest way of all is to increase the output of essential goods and services, through the re-organisation of industry for higher production. There must be an increase in the total real income of the nation, while a larger proportion of it must go to mass-consumption, and a smaller proportion to rent, profits, interest and accumulation. (*pp.* 8–12)

(d) ANEURIN BEVAN. Speech on Moving the National Health Service Bill, Second Reading, House of Commons

30 April 1946

The Minister of Health (*Mr. Aneurin Bevan*): I beg to move, "That the Bill be now read a Second time."

In the last two years there has been such a clamour from sectional interests in the field of national health that we are in danger of forgetting why these proposals are brought forward at all. It is, therefore, very welcome to me—and I am quite certain to hon. Members in all parts of the House—that consideration should now be given, not to this or that sectional interest, but to the requirements of the British people as a whole. The scheme, which anyone must draw up dealing with national health must necessarily be conditioned and limited by the evils it is intended to remove. Many of those who have drawn up paper plans for the health services appear to have followed the dictates of abstract principles, and not the concrete requirements of the actual situation as it exists. They drew up all sorts of tidy schemes on paper, which would be quite inoperable in practice.

The first reason why a health scheme of this sort is necessary at all is because it has been the firm conclusion of all parties that money ought not to be permitted to stand in the way of obtaining an efficient health service. Although it is true that the national health insurance system provides a general practitioner service and caters for something like 21 million of the population, the rest of the population have to pay whenever they desire the services of a doctor. It is cardinal to a proper health organisation that a person ought not to be financially deterred from seeking medical assistance at the earliest possible stage. It is one of the evils of having to buy medical advice that, in addition to the natural anxiety that may arise because people do not like to hear unpleasant things about themselves, and therefore tend to postpone consultation as long as possible, there is the financial anxiety caused by having to pay doctor's bills. Therefore, the first evil that we must deal with is that which exists as a consequence of the fact that the whole thing is the wrong way round. A person ought to be able to receive medical and hospital help without being involved in financial anxiety.

In the second place, the national health insurance scheme does not provide for the self-employed, nor, of course, for the families of dependants. It depends on insurance qualification, and no matter how ill you are, if you cease to be insured, you cease to have free doctoring. Furthermore, it gives no backing to the doctor in the form of specialist services. The doctor has to provide himself, he has to use his own discretion and his own personal connections, in order to obtain hospital treatment for his patients and in order to get them specialists, and in very many cases, of course—in an overwhelming number of cases—the services of a specialist are not available to poor people.

Not only is this the case, but our hospital organisation has grown up with no plan, with no system; it is unevenly distributed over the country and indeed it is one of the tragedies of the situation that very often the best hospital facilities are available where they are least needed. In the older industrial districts of Great Britain hospital facilities are inadequate. Many of the hospitals are too small—very much too small. About 70 per cent have less than 100 beds, and over 30 per cent have less than 30. No one can possibly pretend that hospitals so small can provide general hospital treatment. There is a tendency in some quarters to defend the very small hospital on the ground of its localism and intimacy, and for other rather imponderable reasons of that sort, but everybody knows today that if a hospital is to be efficient it must provide a number of specialised services. Although I am not myself a devotee of bigness for bigness sake, I would rather be kept alive in the efficient if cold altruism of a large hospital than expire in a gush of warm sympathy in a small one.

In addition to these defects, the health of the people of Britain is not properly looked after in one or two other respects. The condition of the teeth of the people of Britain is a national reproach. As a consequence of dental treatment having to be bought, it has not been demanded on a scale to stimulate the creation of sufficient dentists, and in consequence there is a woeful shortage of dentists at the present time. Furthermore, about 25 per cent of the people of Great Britain can obtain their spectacles and get their eyes tested and seen to by means of the assistance given by the approved societies, but the general mass of the people have not such facilities. Another of the evils from which this country suffers is the fact that sufficient attention has not been given to deafness, and hardly any attention has been given so far to the provision of cheap hearing aids and their proper maintenance. (*Parliamentary Debates*, 5th Series, vol. 432, c. 43–5)

21

THE CASE FOR PLANNING

Socialists were so absorbed in the purely political aspects of the achievement of their aims that for a long time they ignored the technical problems. The need for public planning, though implicit in the idea of public ownership and control, was hardly noticed until the end of the nineteen-twenties, although in earlier years the analogy of scientific organisation had led a few writers, notably H. G. Wells, to point in this direction (a). The Russian Five Year Plan, and the utter incapacity of the Labour Government in 1931, suddenly drew attention to the questions of financial organisation, currency control, restrictions on the flight of capital abroad, etc. which a Socialist government might find necessary to supplement its nationalisation programme. As we have seen, only the I.L.P., in its *Living Wage* Report (20c, above), had come anywhere near what was now felt to be required. But throughout the nineteen-thirties interest in the idea of planning was *de rigeur* among Socialists, and while George Lansbury, the Leader of the Opposition, was letting his mind dwell on the prospects of a replanned countryside (b), economists were exercised to establish methods of costing and estimating demand under a Socialist system (c). Another problem for economists was to work out a financial technique to combat the periodical crises of capitalism. The Keynesian solution, propounded in 1936, was adopted by the Coalition Government during the war as the basis of future policy, and it is to this development that Attlee refers in his letter to Laski (d) as the 'doctrine of abundance'. Thus at last was satisfied one major criticism of capitalism which we can trace back through Hobson and Ruskin to the Owenites.

(a) H. G. WELLS. *New Worlds for Old*

1908

JUST as Science aims at a common organized body of knowledge to which all its servants contribute and in which they share, so Socialism insists upon its ideal of an organized social order which every man serves and by which every man benefits. Their common enemy is the secret-thinking, self-seeking man. Secrecy, subterfuge and the private gain; these are the enemies of Socialism and the adversaries of Science. At times, I will admit, both Socialist and scientific man forget this essential sympathy. You will find specialized scientific investigators who do not realize they are, in effect, Socialists, and Socialists so dull to the quality of their own professions, that they gird against Science, and are secretive in policy. But such purblind servants of the light cannot alter the essential correlation of the two systems of ideas.

Now the Socialist, inspired by this conception of a possible frank and comprehensive social order to which mean and narrow ends must be sacrificed, attacks and criticises the existing order of things at a great number of points and in a great variety of phraseology. At all points, however, you will find upon analysis that his criticism amounts to a declaration that there is wanting a sufficiency of CONSTRUCTIVE DESIGN. That in the last resort is what he always comes to.

He wants a complete organization for all those human affairs that are of collective importance. He says, to take instances almost haphazard, that our ways of manufacturing a great multitude of necessary things, of getting and distributing food, of conducting all sorts of business, of begetting and rearing children, of permitting diseases to engender and spread are chaotic and undisciplined, so badly done that here is enormous hardship, and there enormous waste, here excess and degeneration, and there privation and death. He declares that for these collective purposes, in the satisfaction of these universal needs, mankind presents the appearance and follows the methods of a mob when it ought to follow the method of an army. In place of disorderly individual effort, each man doing what he pleases, the Socialist wants organized effort and a plan. And while the scientific man seeks to make an orderly map of the half-explored wilderness of fact, the Socialist seeks to make an orderly plan for the half-conceived wilderness of human effort.

That and no other is the essential Socialist idea.

But do not let this image mislead you. When the Socialist speaks of a plan, he knows clearly that it is impossible to make a plan as an architect makes a plan, because while the architect deals with dead stone and timber, the statesman and Socialist deal with living and striving things. But he seeks to make a plan as one designs and lays out a garden, so that sweet and seemly things may grow, wide and beautiful vistas open and weeds and foulness disappear. Always a garden plan develops and renews itself and discovers new possibilities, but what makes all its graciousness and beauty possible is the scheme and the persistent intention, the watching and the waiting, the digging and burning, the weeder clips and the hoe. That is the sort of plan, a living plan for things that live and grow, that the Socialist seeks for social and national life. (*pp.* 25–7)

(b) GEORGE LANSBURY. *My England*

1934

My object in re-planning is to make England a land fit for intelligent people to live in. We must have no more of the servile spirit which says of anything "It is good enough for the workers but not good enough for the rich". Once employers lived with their people, though they never lived under the same conditions. The coming of the limited companies, monopolies, money-markets, and all the gambling in stocks and shares has changed everything. Disraeli's "two nations" no longer live together. So far as they can, the employing and land-owning classes live right away from the workers. "What the eye doesn't see the heart doesn't grieve," and the rich have settled their consciences over the question of poverty by going away where they cannot see it, and only occasionally visit the districts from which their wealth is drawn.

I should hope in time to obliterate for good and all the class distinction in houses. I would have no West Ends and no East Ends. All people should obtain housing accommodation and comfort now reserved for the few. Slum towns must be improved off the face of the earth. I would ask the House of Commons for power to set up a planning commission with authority to create new industrial areas with residential districts outside. With mechanical transport at its present state of development, there is no reason at all why workers should live where they work. No rich people do this. Why should those who produce wealth submit to doing so?

I visualise England, Scotland and Wales as a carefully planned pattern of garden land, farm land, well-defined and sharply limited industrial areas, and, in addition, huge tracts in the Highlands and Lake districts and elsewhere set apart for pleasure. When I was at the Office of Works, a Commission was set up to investigate a proposal for national parks. The report of this Commission which had Dr. Addison as its Chairman, is available, and the organisation to take charge of these national parks is obtainable either at the Office of Works or the Board of Agriculture.

Our country is not over-large, but even with our present population there is plenty of room for recreation. The Highlands of Scotland should be used for afforestation and playgrounds, not for the rich only, but for all classes; so also should the Lake and similar districts. During the summer of 1933 I saw for the first time the glories of the lochs, the Trossachs and Ben Lomond. Then I realised that modern road transport breaks down distance and all obstacles, and that here was a vast area that any minute could be turned into a national playground. Tom Johnston, when Lord Privy Seal, produced many schemes for development in Scotland, but received scanty support from the Treasury. We only need control of these watch-dogs of parsimony and make-believe economy and the work of transformation in the Highlands might begin.

So let us re-plan our ideas first of all and demand facilities for enjoying the leisure which the use of machinery can give us. In this connection also we should provide camping places for hikers and others who wish to travel on foot. Children, above ten years of age, would love to travel the Roman road from Richborough to the Wall in Northumberland. What a fine historic journey that would be! How fine if children could go round the Scottish isles and tramp the hills and valleys they read about in the stories of Wallace and Bruce! Why not use the castles and baronial halls, in which our rich can on longer live, as resting places? The Office of Works jealously guards many show places within the grounds of which shelter should be provided. Oh, yes: we can re-plan, re-discover pleasure grounds and how to use them.

You will say, "But we must find the money to do these things." Of course we must, just as we find the means to maintain and equip armies, navies, and the air forces. All we need is the will to divert that money to proper purposes. (*pp.* 59–61)

(c) G. D. H. COLE. *The Simple Case for Socialism*

1935

A PLANNED Socialist society will consider production in the light of real costs related to real human needs and wants. Up to a point, as we have seen, these needs and wants are easy to estimate, and there is no doubt to what things production ought to be directed—though there may be doubt how far it is best to provide the means of supplying wants by home production or how far by the exchange of home for foreign goods. But beyond this point, when the sheer elementary needs of living have been met, we come to a realm in which men's varying desires rather than their much less varying needs have to be supplied; and in this realm there is much more room for doubt concerning the best use to make of the available powers of production. There are so many things we could produce, and men want all of them. But we cannot produce all of them in the quantities men would use if they could be had free of charge. Which, then, of all the things we could produce, are wanted most?

That question is bound to confront a planned economy, even as it confronts the capitalist economies of today. Capitalism settles the matter by producing what the capitalists think will pay them best in the light of such knowledge as they possess of men's desires and differing abilities to pay. From the capitalist point of view, it is of no use to make things which only penniless people want; for that way bankruptcy lies. Capitalist production is doubtless directed to meeting men's wants, for unless things are wanted they cannot be sold at all. But capitalism attends only to such wants as present themselves in the market armed with the means of payment. The richer a man is, and the more money he has to spend, the greater is his influence in inducing the capitalists to respond to his desires.

Demand in a Socialist society will be differently weighted. In proportion as society gets nearer to equality in its distribution of incomes, demand will draw nearer to coincidence with real human needs and wants. There will be less inducement to spend productive resources in satisfying one man's claim in preference to another's, because there will be a diminishing difference between their several abilities to pay. Society will be organised for meeting everybody's needs and wants in a less unequal way.

But prices are a question of " costs of production " as well as of what the buyers are prepared to pay. There will have to be different prices for different things, in accordance with their varying real costs of production. But are these real costs ascertainable at all? Capitalist economists are fond of contending that they are not, and that accordingly Socialism can never work successfully, because there will be no means under it of discovering what it is best to produce. It is better, these economists argue, to stick to a system which does at least measure one money cost against another, and thus sets up a standard for deciding what to make and what to leave unmade. Money costs may not coincide with real costs, but they are at least measureable. Better stick to the imperfect measure we have than involve ourselves in a system that is bound to lack all means of measuring one cost against another.

But is it really true that a Socialist society is bound to lack the means of measuring relative costs? If no more is meant than that there is no perfect measure, we can agree: for that is true in any sort of society. But surely a Socialist society, just as much as a capitalist society, can set prices upon human labour—varying prices for labour of varying skill and scarcity. Even capitalist societies do this to some extent, on a collective basis wherever the State fixes wages; and capitalist States are in addition constantly altering the money costs of different forms of production by the taxes which they levy on commodities, land, capital or employment. A Socialist State will clearly not be without the means of fixing the levels of remuneration for different types of work, or the rents to be paid for different sorts of land, or, if it thinks fit, the rates of interest to be charged for the use of money for various purposes. But these things together make up the cost of production. A Socialist society will be quite able to price goods according to their several costs—fully as able as capitalist societies are to do this—and it will be in a position to decide what to produce in the light of the relation between these costs and the market demand which arises from the new distribution of incomes which it will have brought about. It may, of course, in fact decide to sell some things for less than they cost to produce in order to increase consumption, and to sell others for more than they cost to produce, where it holds that consumption of them ought to be reduced on social grounds. But most things it will presumably elect to sell for what they cost, in order to give the possessors of incomes the fullest possible freedom of choice between alternative products. In most things planned production, even more than capitalist production, will respond to the consumers' wants; and it will be able to respond far better out of its greater knowledge of the condition of the market. (*pp.* 129–32)

(d) C. R. ATTLEE. Letter to H. J. Laski

1 May 1944

. . . I have witnessed now the acceptance by all the leading politicians in this country and all the economists of any account of the conception of the utilisation of abundance. From '31 onwards in the House I and others pressed this. It was rejected with scorn. It is now accepted and important results flow from it. It is the basis of our conversations with the Dominions and our Allies. It colours all our discussions on home economic policy. There follows from this the doctrine of full employment. The acceptance of this again colours our whole conception of the post war set up in this country. You will appreciate that in discussions with Cabinet colleagues not of our Party the full acceptance of these conceptions concedes much of our case in advance. Take again the international field. The doctrines which we preached as to collective security, etc., and the need for world economic planning which were scoffed at by the Munichois are now the basis of policy accepted by the Government.

Take again the whole conception of State planning and the control of the financial machine by the Government and not by the Bank of England and the City. Here again I see the change since the days of 1931.

In my time in our movement, now getting quite long, I have seen a lot of useful legislation, but I count our progress much more by the extent to which what we cried in the wilderness five and thirty years ago has now become part of the assumptions of the ordinary man and woman. The acceptance of these assumptions has its effect both in legislation and administration, but its gradualness tends to hide our appreciation of the facts.

You will argue that we have not yet come to the crucial matter of the nationalisation of, say, the Mines, the Banks and the Railways. I agree, but we cannot get this until we have a House of Commons ready to pass the necessary legislation. I doubt if we can effect this until we have a Socialist majority and for that we have to wait for a general election, but it is certain that in the meantime and in the immediate transition period the controls will have to be maintained.

What then should be our tactics? I have never suggested

that we should drop our principles and programme, but it is, I suggest, better to argue from what has been done to what may be done rather than to suggest that very little has been accomplished. For myself I should on the practical side argue for our programme on the basis that the acceptance of the doctrine of abundance, of full employment and of social security require the transfer to public ownership of certain major economic forces and the planned control in the public interest of many other economic activities. I should further argue that our planning must now be based on a far greater economic equality than obtained in the pre-war period and that we have demonstrated in this war that this can be obtained.

I find intelligent Service men often of high rank and men in various walks of life who come to me and tell me that they have been converted to Socialism by what they have seen done in wartime. It is therefore in my view mistaken tactics to belittle what has been done. . . . (Kingsley Martin, *Harold Laski*, 1953, *pp.* 160–2)

22

SOCIALISM AND FOREIGN POLICY

Fabian Essays of 1889, which provided a Socialist programme to suit the conditions of British constitutional politics, failed to say anything about foreign policy. J. A. Hobson, the very unorthodox Liberal economist, provided in his book *Imperialism* (1902) an economic interpretation of world events which members of all Left-wing groups made use of, and which Lenin found valuable for his development of the Marxist attitude in his own work with the same title (1916). The extract here given to illustrate Hobson's argument is taken not from *Imperialism* but from a summary in his *Evolution of Modern Capitalism* (a). The view that the 1914 war was an imperialist struggle caused by the expansion of capitalism, and that the war effort therefore merited no support, was accepted by the I.L.P. (12g above), but not by Hyndman and his immediate circle or by the Fabians. Sidney Webb organised Fabian research on the practical problem of how to secure International Government, and Leonard Woolf's report (b) is an interesting application to the international sphere of the Fabian concept of evolutionary development. The influence of Socialist thinking on the Labour Party in wartime is shown by the *Memorandum on War Aims*, drafted by Sidney Webb (c), which emphasised the need not only for a Supra-National State but also for special protective arrangements for backward territories and for international collaboration on economic questions.

In the inter-war years pacifist feeling was widespread, and was strengthened by the Socialist criticism of imperialism, as may be seen from some of the arguments used by George Lansbury (e). The speech of Lansbury here quoted was delivered only a few months after his resignation from the Leadership of the Labour Party over this issue. The official policy, fundamentally on the lines of the *Memorandum on War Aims*, was expounded, for instance, by Hugh Dalton, a foreign affairs expert of the Labour Party in the 1930's (d), and also by Ernest Bevin in his speech just before becoming Foreign Secretary in 1945 (f). With Bevin, however, and equally with Crossman, his foremost critic (g), there are signs of the abandonment of the view that war is usually due to the clash of expanding capitalist states. More emphasis is now placed on the need to develop the resources of the backward areas of the world, and as Crossman puts it to 'civilise' the world revolution caused by the emergence of Asian and African nationalism. In this task Britain, ideologically occupying a position between Russia and the United States, the two great powers of the post-war world, is regarded as having a role of special significance.

(a) J. A. HOBSON. *The Evolution of Modern Capitalism*

1906

THE economic tap-root, the chief directing motive of all the modern imperialistic expansion, is the pressure of capitalist industries for markets, primarily markets for investment, secondarily markets for surplus products of home industry. Where the concentration of capital has gone furthest, and where a rigorous protective system prevails, this pressure is necessarily strongest. Not merely do the trusts and other manufacturing trades that restrict their output for the home market more urgently require foreign markets, but they are also more anxious to secure protected markets, and this can only be achieved by extending the area of political rule. This is the essential significance of the recent change in American foreign policy as illustrated by the Spanish War, the Philippine annexation, the Panama policy, and the new application of the Monroe doctrine to the South American States. South America is needed as a preferential market for investment of trust "profits" and surplus trust products: if in time these states can be brought within a Zollverein under the suzerainty of the United States, the financial area of operations receives a notable accession. China as a field of railway enterprise and general industrial development already begins to loom large in the eyes of foresighted American business men; the growing trade in American cotton and other goods in that country will be a subordinate consideration to the expansion of the area for American investments. Diplomatic pressure, armed force, and where desirable, seizure of territory for political control, will be engineered by the financial magnates who control the political destiny of America. The strong and expensive American navy now beginning to be built incidentally serves the purpose of affording profitable contracts to the shipbuilding and metal industries; its real meaning and use is to forward the aggressive political policy imposed upon the nation by the economic needs of the financial capitalists.

It should be clearly understood that this constant pressure to extend the area of markets is not a necessary implication of all forms of organised industry. If competition was displaced by combinations of a genuinely co-operative character in which the whole gain of improved economies passed, either to the workers in wages, or to large bodies of investors in dividends, the expansion of demand in the home markets would be so great as to give full employment to the productive powers of concentrated capital, and there would be no self-accumulating masses of profit expressing themselves in new credit and demanding external employment. It is the "monopoly" profits of trusts and combines, taken either in construction, financial operation, or industrial working, that form a gathering fund of self-accumulating credit whose possession by the financial class implies a contracted demand for commodities and a correspondingly restricted employment for capital in American industries. Within certain limits relief can be found by stimulation of the export trade under cover of a high protective tariff which forbids all interference with monopoly of the home markets. But it is extremely difficult for trusts adapted to the requirements of a profitable tied market at home to adjust their methods of free competition in the world markets upon a profitable basis of steady trading. Moreover, such a mode of expansion is only appropriate to certain manufacturing trusts: the owners of railroad, financial, and other trusts must look always more to foreign investments for their surplus profits. This ever-growing need for fresh fields of investment for their profits is the great crux of the financial system and threatens to dominate the future economics and the politics of the great Republic.

The financial economy of American capitalism exhibits in more dramatic shape a tendency common to the finance of all developed industrial nations. The large, easy flow of capital from Great Britain, Germany, Austria, France, etc., into South African or Australian mines, into Egyptian bonds, or the precarious securities of South American republics, attests the same general pressure which increases with every development of financial machinery and the more profitable control of that machinery by the class of professional financiers. To a limited extent this cosmopolitanisation of finance is a natural and normal result of improved material and moral communication between the various nations of the earth. But in large measure it arises from a restriction of home markets which must be called artificial in the sense that industrial and financial trusts, pools, and other combinations, taking out of the aggregate product a larger quantity of "profit" than they can employ for further profit in these or other home investments, are impelled ever to look farther afield and to use all their financial and political influence to develop foreign markets by such pacific or forcible means as will best serve their purpose. In every case the financier is the instrument or vehicle of this pressure; a swelling stream of investors' savings is constantly passing into the banking and financial system which he controls; in order to keep it flowing with greatest gain to himself he must find or fashion fresh investments. (*pp.* 262–4)

(b) LEONARD WOOLF. *International Government* 1916

FROM these considerations two conclusions may be suggested. All arguments against International Government based on assertions that it would endanger vital national interests should be regarded with the greatest suspicion. The most vital interests of human beings are hardly ever national, almost always international. The interests which most nearly affect a man's life are those of the international group—e.g., labor or capital, to which he belongs, not of his national group. Unfortunately, while the capitalist denies this by his words and accepts it by his deeds, the working man has accepted it in word and denies it by his deeds. Nine times out of ten in foreign politics, national interests, if analysed, resolve themselves into either the interests of a tiny class in one nation as opposed to a tiny class in another nation, or, as the interests of the ruling or capitalist class in a nation as opposed to those of the unpropertied, powerless, or working class. Take, for instance, the question of Morocco between Germany and France, which very nearly provoked a European war. In whatever way that question had been finally settled, it could not possibly have affected the lives or property, the happiness or unhappiness, the mentality or morality, of 999 out of every thousand Frenchmen and Germans. It could only have affected the purses of a small number of French and German capitalists, and, of course, that prestige of France and Germany which appears to be rather an unanalysable concept than a tangible interest. The application of International Government and organized regulation to such questions would undoubtedly seriously affect the interests of these tiny but powerful groups—which is the reason why it is so strenuously resisted. Or, again, International Government as in the case of Labor legislation, which promoted the true interests of the masses which make up the different nations, would in each nation strengthen their position in the bitter struggle which they are compelled to wage against the exploitation of capital. This is well understood by the capitalist and industrial interests which oppose International Government, not because it will undermine their position against the foreigner, but because it will undermine their power over their fellow citizens.

The second conclusion is only a development of the first. Purely national government makes no provision for the representation of vital group interests, and therefore makes it so easy for the ruling and powerful classes to delude whole nations by specious appeals to patriotism and vague references to vital national interests. A sane and practical internationalism implies the regulation of the relations of national groups through organs of government. I have had to say much in these pages against a narrow nationalism, against the deification of geography and the worship of fictitious national interests; but I have never implied that the nation and sentiments of patriotism and nationality have not their place in the organisation and society of the future. All I have tried to do is to examine the facts and to see things in their right proportions. The nation will remain the unit of international organisation, the center of the sentiments of patriotism and nationality, and the outward and visible sign that men bound together by bonds of birth, blood, or geography desire, as far as possible, to manage their own affairs in their own way. But there is no reason in the world why an international organisation which is based upon the nation as a unit should not be combined with an organisation which provides for the representation of group interests which are not national. In the international association we have already the skeleton of a social structure and organisation through which these group interests might operate. A little development, a closer association between the various organs of International Government, if accompanied by the loss of some widely held human illusions and delusions, might open a new page in the history of society. (*pp.* 354–6)

(c) *Labour Party and T.U.C. Memorandum on War Aims* presented at a Special Conference 28 December 1917

I
The War

The British Labour Movement declares that whatever may have been the causes of the outbreak of war, it is clear that the peoples of Europe, who are necessarily the chief sufferers from its horrors, had themselves no hand in it. Their common interest is now so to conduct the terrible struggle in which they find themselves engaged as to bring it, as soon as possible, to an issue in a secure and lasting Peace for the world. . . .

II
Making the World Safe for Democracy

Whatever may have been the objects for which the War was begun, the fundamental purpose of the British Labour

Movement in supporting the continuance of the struggle is that the world may henceforth be made safe for Democracy.

Of all the War aims, none is so important to the peoples of the world as that there should be henceforth on earth no more war. Whoever triumphs the people will have lost, unless some effective method of preventing war can be found. As a means to this end the British Labour Movement relies very largely upon the complete democratisation of all countries; on the frank abandonment of every form of "Imperialism"; on the suppression of secret diplomacy and on the placing of foreign policy, just as much as home policy, under the control of popularly elected Legislatures, on the absolute responsibility of the Foreign Minister of each country to its Legislature; on such concerted action as may be possible for the universal abolition of compulsory military service in all countries, the common limitation of the costly armaments by which all the peoples are burdened, and the entire abolition of profit-making armament firms, whose pecuniary interest lies always in war scares and rivalry in preparation for war. But it demands, in addition, that it should be an essential part of the Treaty of Peace itself that there should be forthwith established a Super-National Authority, or League of Nations, which should not only be adhered to by all the present belligerents, but which every other independent sovereign State in the world should be pressed to join; the immediate establishment by such League of Nations not only of an International High Court for the settlement of all disputes between States that are of justiciable nature, but also of appropriate machinery for prompt and effective mediation between States in issues that are not justiciable; the formation of an International Legislature in which the representatives of every civilised State would have their allotted share; the gradual development, as far as may prove to be possible, of International

Legislation agreed to by and definitely binding upon the several States; and for a solemn agreement and pledge by all States that every issue between any two or more of them shall be submitted for settlement as aforesaid, and that wherever necessary common cause will be made against any State or States by the use of any and every means at their disposal to enforce adherence to the terms of the agreement and pledge.

III

Territorial Adjustments

The British Labour Movement has no sympathy with the attempts made, now in this quarter and now in that, to convert this War into a War of Conquest whether what is sought to be acquired by force is territory or wealth; nor should the struggle be prolonged for a single day, once the conditions of a permanent Peace can be secured, merely for the sake of extending the boundaries of any State. But it is impossible to ignore the fact that, not only restitution and reparation, but also certain territorial readjustments are required, if a renewal of armaments and war is to be avoided. These readjustments must be such as can be arrived at by common agreement on the general principle of allowing all peoples to settle their own destinies, and for the purpose of removing any obvious cause of future international conflict. . . .

(h) The Colonies of Tropical Africa

With regard to the Colonies of the several belligerents in Tropical Africa, from sea to sea—whether including all North of the Zambesi River and South of the Sahara Desert, or only those lying between 15 deg. North and 15 deg. South Latitude, which are already the subject of international control—the British Labour Movement disclaims all sympathy with the Imperialist idea that these should form the booty of any nation, should be exploited for the profit of the capitalist, or should be used for the promotion of the militarist aims of Governments. In view of the fact that it is impracticable here to leave the various peoples concerned to settle their own destinies, it is suggested that the interests of humanity would be best served by the full and frank abandonment by all the belligerents of any dreams of an African Empire; the transfer of the present Colonies of the European Powers in Tropical Africa, however the limits of this area may be defined, to the proposed Super-National Authority or League of Nations herein suggested; and their administration under the Legislative Council of that Authority as a single independent African State with its own trained staff, on the principles of (1) taking account in each locality, of the wishes of the people, when these can be ascertained; (2) protection of the natives against exploitation and oppression and the preservation of their tribal interests; (3) all revenue raised to be expended for the welfare and development of the African State itself; and (4) the permanent neutralisation of this African State and its abstention from participation in international rivalries or any future wars.

IV

Economic Relations

The British Labour Movement declares against all the projects now being prepared by Imperialists and capitalists, not in any one country only, but in most countries, for an Economic War, after Peace has been secured, either against one or other foreign nation or against all foreign nations, as such an Economic War, if begun by any country, would inevitably lead to reprisals, to which each nation in turn might in self-defence be driven. It realises that all such attempts at economic aggression, whether by Protective

Tariffs or capitalist trusts or monopolies, inevitably result in the spoliation of the working classes of the several countries for the profit of the capitalists; and the British workmen see in the alliance between the Military Imperialists and the Fiscal Protectionists in any country whatsoever not only a serious danger to the prosperity of the masses of the people, but also a grave menace to Peace. On the other hand, the right of each nation to the defence of its own economic interests, and, in face of the world-shortage hereinafter mentioned, to the conservation for its own people of a sufficiency of its own supplies of food-stuffs and raw materials, cannot be denied. The British Labour Movement accordingly urges upon the Labour Parties of all countries the importance of insisting, in the attitude of the Government towards commercial enterprise, along with the necessary control of supplies for its own people, on the principle of the open door, on customs duties being limited strictly to revenue purposes, and on there being no hostile discrimination against foreign countries. But it urges equally the importance, not merely of conservation, but also of the utmost possible development by appropriate Government action of the resources of every country for the benefit not only of its own people, but also of the world, and the need for an international agreement for the enforcement in all countries of the legislation of factory conditions, hours of labour, and the prevention of "sweating" and unhealthy trades necessary to protect the workers against exploitation and oppression. (*pp.* 3–6)

(d) HUGH DALTON. *Practical Socialism for Britain* 1935

IF the Collective System holds firm, as a dam against war, in the critical next years, there is some chance of building solidly behind it. The next Labour Government must take the lead in organising these building operations. What do they include? First, an international convention for real disarmament; second, the creation of an international police force and an international organisation for civil aviation; third, the ending of private arms manufacture; fourth, provision for peaceful change in existing treaties; fifth, international economic co-operation on much bolder lines than hitherto. . . .

No Socialist is likely to underrate the importance of economic co-operation between the nations, and the removal of the economic causes of war. Competitive profit-seeking in the sale of arms is only one degree more dangerous to peace than competitive profit-seeking by way of concessions and loans in backward countries, or by way of cornering supplies of raw materials which all nations need. War between France and Germany all but came, in 1911, over a struggle between French and German capitalists for the possession of the iron ore in the Atlas mountains of North Africa. There are many like dangers in different parts of the world to-day. We must establish international control over such concessions and loans, and make an international plan for a fair deal in raw materials and other essential commodities. And, as already stated, we must strengthen and extend the mandatory system in Colonial territories.

Every advance towards Socialism in any national area is to be welcomed. But Socialism by national compartments is not enough. Nor can we afford to wait for its general achievement in this form. In some countries we may have to wait a very long time. We must use, without delay and to the utmost, all existing instruments of economic co-operation between nations, such as the Economic, Financial and Transport Sections of the League, and the International Labour Organisation. And we must be prepared, not only to strengthen and sharpen these instruments, but to forge new ones as well, which only Planned Socialist Communities can handle.

There is hope that, through these means, men will gradually learn the trick of working together and the lesson that private greed may be a carrier of deadly plagues.

But all such hope depends on the firm maintenance of peace meanwhile.

To-day we are all like sleep-walkers, who walk near the sheer edge of a cliff. That edge may not be quite so near as some think. But it is not far off. We must wake soon, or crash. If we let the next years slip, as we have let slip these last years, then, I fear, our feet may slip too, and we shall fall into horrors too complete and too hideous to imagine.

There is but one way back from the cliff's edge. It leads toward world government, and a worldwide plan, for justice and plenty and peace. We must step boldly away from national sovereignty and capitalism, both too weak to bear our weight much longer. Someone must lead. Let us lead. Let a Socialist Britain, by her influence and her example, help to save the world from war. (*pp.* 372, 385*f.*)

(e) GEORGE LANSBURY. Speech moving a Motion to call a World Peace Conference, House of Commons

5 February 1936

I WAS against the last War from beginning to end, as I have been more or less against every war during my lifetime, but I claim no virtue for that because masses of men—and I believe the Government of the day—thought they were doing a righteous piece of work. Millions of young men went to the trenches believing they were engaged in a great crusade to destroy militarism in every shape and form, a crusade in which they hoped they would establish democracy and build a new world on the ruins that might be made by the War. Since the War we have seen the growth of dictatorship, the growth, not of prosperity, but of poverty and degradation and destitution, millions of people in central Europe and Asia dying of famine and disease. We have not seen democracy triumph in the world. We have seen it, at any rate in Europe, rolled in the dust. Worst of all, we now have to face the fact that there is not a Government anywhere in the world which is not arming, arming, arming. We ourselves in a few days will be discussing defence plans and arguing as to the size of the gun, the strength of the ship, the strength of poison gas or the defence against poison gas.

In these circumstances I ask the House humbly, not at all as a person who thinks he has more knowledge or virtue than anyone else, because none of us has, whether they do not think that the time has arrived to make an effort on some other lines. I know that I shall be told what the League of Nations has been established to carry through, and that I have not any faith in the League of Nations and collective security. I have not any faith in any system which relies upon force, and does not at first have its basis resting upon justice and equity. The idea of the League of Nations is very fine, and so were the ideas at the Vienna Congress 100 years earlier, but unfortunately the League of Nations was founded after the Great War and after the peace, which was a penal peace and imposed conditions upon the defeated that are almost unparalleled, certainly in the lifetime of this country, with the result that the League of Nations to-day is not really a League of Nations. Japan, the United States, Germany are all outside, and, in my judgment, you cannot have a tribunal of any sort that should be first of all the judge and then the policeman. . . .

. . . Why do nations want to arm? Why do they pile up

these devilish armaments of destruction one against the other? Why do they want these things? We say, 'Because we fear attack'. Every nation says that. . . . The real thing is that each nation, first of all, wants something that she thinks she cannot get unless she fights, or, in other cases, the nations want to hold what they have got. . . . The House should remember that it does not matter what British writers say about the needs of Italy, Germany, or Japan. What has to be considered is what the statesmen of those countries have to say for themselves. We have to face the fact that those countries consider that they want to expand as Great Britain has expanded. I have read the speeches and articles of Japanese statesmen. . . . The people of the East, as a writer has said, have learnt very thoroughly how to put the case of imperialism from people like the Americans, ourselves, the French, and others. . . .

Finally, I would say this. War is futile. War is hopeless and inefficient in settling anything, because it is action against the law of morals, of religion, and of God. It does not matter how we twist it round and talk of wars of defence and wars of offence. The cold, brutal fact remains that the world has made tremendous progress along national lines. We can do things to-day that men never dreamed of centuries ago. We have all the means in the world for a full, happy, peaceful life, and the only reason that we do not enjoy these things is because we have not yet learned how to use them properly. I want us to make up our minds that we will make a tremendous effort in the field of international affairs to bring into play the principles which the workers in this country and other countries are always told they must live up to, that is, that they must preserve the peace, that they must win their way without force, and that they must depend upon reason. I want us to depend on reason, justice and equity. (*Parliamentary Debates*, 5th Series, vol. 308, c. 210–6)

(f) ERNEST BEVIN. Speech to Labour Party Conference

23 May 1945

The United States of America is a country which believes in private enterprise. The Soviet Union has socialised her internal economy. Britain stands between the two, I think, with a tremendously progressive chance towards the socialised economy we need.

Now, whoever may be the statesman who has got to weld together these different approaches and different conceptions into a world organisation to prevent aggression, he has a difficult task. You will not do it by slogans; you will not do it by saying that all the people in one country are angels and in the other all devils. You have got to do it by patience, trying to understand the other man's mind and point of view, and endeavouring to bring people together for one common purpose—that is, to maintain Peace in order that a higher standard of living can be developed, with a complete removal of fear.

It is very difficult to say what are the causes of war. Some say they are economic; some say it is traditional ambition; some say that nations get it into their heads that the only way they can get prosperous is by domination. Well, to my mind, it is a combination of all three. We, in this Government, which is now rapidly passing to its demise, have stressed the imperative necessity for the Foreign Office, co-incident with dealing with political and diplomatic measures, to proceed with economic problems as well. Malnutrition accounts, at least, for one of the fundamental cause of war. That is a terrible thing. It is mainly centred, not in the world of the industrial worker, because in most places, not everywhere, he has been able to organise into great groups to defend himself. I do not say it has always been successful, but it has modified the effect of malnutrition. The real centre of malnutrition is among the peasantry of the world, a vast body—the ordinary person who lives by his toil on the soil. The product of his labour is the source of speculation, financial manipulation, and is the prime cause of most of our depression and unemployment.

The Hot Springs Conference, therefore, was inaugurated at least in a spirit of hope. But, if it is to be successful, it needs the drive of a powerful Labour Government in this country behind it. I will tell you why. We are the greatest importers of food in the world; we can supervise prices. We can, if an international price is to be fixed, see that the price is honest and observed. We are in a better position to do this than any other country in the world. We therefore stand for a universal, but sufficient, distribution of food, and the right to take away from any middleman the power to exploit it by manipulation and gambling.

If the industrial worker in countries like Britain is to maintain a decent standard of life, then you must be just to the peasant, because he cannot buy the goods of the industrial worker unless his price is right. No one is so poor, taking the world as a whole, as the agricultural and primary producer. No one has lower purchasing power. Great Britain is a highly industrialised country, agricultural workers not being here in such great numbers. We must remember that whether it is China, India, Africa or the Colonies, or wherever you may turn, it is no use to talk about finding markets unless the standard of life of the ordinary man and the masses of the world is improved, and unless they are in a position to buy the goods produced and it is possible for them to have proper exchange of commodities.

That raises another issue: we must stand for bulk purchase. We have done it during the war. If we had not carried out such a policy, I do not know where the cost of living would have been.

We must also harmonise our position as an importing country with the growth of the organised sales method which is going on in New Zealand and Australia, and which is rapidly developing in India, South Africa, and, I believe before long, by the sheer necessity of the case, will develop in the South American countries.

We have been aiming at a minimum wheat price. I know these are mundane things, but they are very vital in foreign policy. At the end of the last war the price of wheat dropped in 1920 by 60 per cent. The international price level was broken and we had one of the greatest depressions the world has known. The farmer, therefore, must have a guaranteed price not only nationally but internationally. . . .

But one thing you must fight is the policy that went on not only in this country, but all over the world, by international combines, limiting production, and using scarcity to keep up prices. I want to add that it is essential that vital products should be grown in plenty in order that the standard of living may be raised. . . .

Therefore I would say this: the receiving end and the producing end must be brought into harmony and no agreements should be entered into internationally which seek to prevent this, at the same time leaving every State in the world to maintain their economy in their own way. (*Labour Party Report*, 1945, *pp.* 115*f.*)

(g) R. H. S. CROSSMAN. *Towards a New Philosophy of Socialism*

1952

THE revolution through which the world is passing has already ended the period of European ascendancy and substituted for a European balance of power a two-world system of politics with its capitals in Washington and Moscow. Simultaneously, the self-emancipation of the colonial peoples is undermining the traditional relationship between the highly industrialised white democracies and the producers of primary raw materials. Moreover, the overwhelming preponderance of American economic strength, now aggravated by rearmament, has destroyed any economic balance which previously existed within the non-Communist world. In these conditions it is self-deception to believe that the living standards and security enjoyed by the British people after 1945 were a *stable* achievement of socialism. Living in an age not of steady progress towards a world welfare capitalism, but of world revolution, it is folly for us to assume that the socialist's task is to assist in the gradual improvement of the material lot of the human race and the gradual enlargement of the area of human freedom. The forces of history are all pressing towards totalitarianism: in the Russian bloc, owing to the conscious policy of the Kremlin; in the free world, owing to the growth of the managerial society, the effects of total rearmament, and the repression of colonial aspirations. The task of socialism is neither to accelerate this Political Revolution, nor to oppose it (this would be as futile as opposition to the Industrial Revolution a hundred years ago), but to civilise it.

To do this we must realise that a victory for either side would be a defeat for socialism. We are members of the Atlantic alliance; but this does not mean that we are enemies of every communist revolution. We are opposed to Russian expansion, but also to an American victory. Our object is to keep the Cold War cold and, in particular, so to restrain rearmament that it remains at a level which both sides can sustain over a period of years. If this object could be achieved, there is no inherent reason why the power conflict between the two great blocs should not gradually exhaust itself during the next twenty years. The success we seek is a balance of world power, and in that balance the restraining influence of a communist China on Russia may be as vital as that of a socialist Britain on the U.S.A. If neutralism is a blind alley, ideological detachment is a requisite for those on both sides of the Iron Curtain who are seeking to strengthen the social conscience in its struggle against totalitarianism.

In the last place, we must realise that the Cold War brings possibilities of good as well as evil. Under its stress, both communists and anti-communists are overcoming antiquated forms of national sovereignty, developing new institutions of international economic planning, and accelerating the pace of social and technological change. As soon as rearmament is given an absolute priority by either side, the value of these changes is outweighed by the added risk of war and the distortion of the economy. But, while facing this danger frankly, we should not overlook the fact that the interacting pressure of Cold War (provided it can be restrained within limits) *can* create material conditions for the enlargement of freedom. The task of a socialist foreign policy is to exercise these restraints on the policy of the Atlantic powers. We must first accept the Cold War as the central fact of twentieth-century politics (just as class war was the central fact of nineteenth-century politics) and then disprove the prophets who prove that it must end in World War III. (Crossman, ed., *New Fabian Essays*, 1952, *pp.* 31*f.*)

23

SOCIALISM AND THE EMPIRE

Socialists were generally willing to accept J. A. Hobson's interpretation of the motives of modern imperialism (22a, above), and they regarded the native populations of the British Empire as fellow-sufferers from the evils of capitalism. Keir Hardie's 'Zulu Letter' was one of the early expressions of this sympathetic reaction (a). Sydney Olivier, one of the Fabian essayists, who had a distinguished career in the Colonial Service and eventually became Governor of Jamaica, expressed a rather more moderate view, though based on a similar analysis (b). It must, however, be remembered that the Fabians as a body were prepared to condone the South African War on grounds of expediency (11f, above).

Socialists readily took up the case for the independence of India. The abortive Bill proposed in 1925 by a number of Labour M.P.s (c) foreshadowed the policy of the Labour Government of 1945–50, which was successful in persuading the Indians to retain their connexion with the Commonwealth.

At the same time, most Socialists have appreciated that in the case of colonies whose peoples remain very backward and whose economic development cannot proceed without association with more advanced countries, an immediate grant of independence would have little advantage. They have therefore argued for a policy of colonial development with primary emphasis on the welfare of the native populations concerned. This policy is advocated in *Labour and the Nation*, the Labour Party's programme of 1928 drafted by R. H. Tawney (d). It has been further developed since 1940 by the Fabian Colonial Bureau and put into practice at the Colonial Office since the war by Arthur Creech Jones and James Griffiths (e), and has been accompanied by a programme of constitutional advance wherever possible, and especially in West Africa, where at least one colony, the Gold Coast, is now approaching full independence.

For other documents on the Socialist attitude to Empire, see the companion volume in this series, *The Concept of Empire,* edited by George Bennett.

(a) J. KEIR HARDIE. Letter to Mr. Bankole Bright 1906

My dear Sir,

I am obliged by your approval of anything I have been able to do to assist your race, and I regret that I cannot do more. The terrible event which happened in the Soudan the other day, with its attendant brutalities, reduces the administration of that country under British rule to the level of that of the Congo Free State, while the wholesale massacre of natives which is now going on in South Africa, under the pretext of suppressing a rebellion which does not exist, fills one with shame and horror. I hope the day will speedily come when your race will be able to defend itself against the barbarities being perpetrated against it by hypocritical whites, who regard the black man as having been created in order that they might exploit him for their own advantage. The Press and politicians for the most part keep the people of this country in ignorance of the real treatment meted out to the natives, and not until they, the natives, are in a position to hold their own can they expect to be treated as human beings.

Yours truly,

J. Keir Hardie.

(*Central African Times*, 25 August 1906)

(b) SYDNEY OLIVIER. *White Capital and Coloured Labour*

1906

It is unjust to denounce the partition of Africa and the intercourse of the White with the Black as an unmixed evil for the latter; it is unjust (in most cases) to condemn European administrators and officials as merely parasites on the countries they govern, whether India or others; but we must set out with a clear recognition of the fact that when the European colonises or annexes tropical countries the force that sets him in motion is a desire for commercial or industrial profit, and not a desire to take up the "White Man's Burden". When he really wants to do that, he becomes a missionary. There is no disparagement to the European in recognising and bearing in mind this fundamental fact. He has an undeniable right to go and peacefully seek his fortune in any part of the world without molestation. He only becomes distasteful when he begins to condemn and coerce uncivilised peoples into the mould of his personal interests under the pretext of doing them good. In hardly any nation except England and the United States is it possible, or thought necessary, that there should be a public pretence of international philanthropy in connection with Imperial expansion. Such a pretence was deliberately fomented in the United States to justify the American-Spanish War of 1898, the annexation of Porto Rico and the Philippines and the commercial annexation of Cuba into the sphere of American exploitation, and such a pretence is almost always professed in England whenever we have similar exploits on foot. If, when we have come into contact with aboriginal races through such pursuit of our interests, we so order our dealings that benefits, on the whole, result to them (which is far from being entirely or always the case), if it may really be to the natives' interest that the White man should exploit his labour, that is no reason at all for taking moral credit to ourselves for colonisation. The native (bear this always well in mind) is not deceived in this matter. Hence arises that fundamental suspicion in him that we resent as so unjustifiable and uncharitable. Hence what we denounce as his treacheries and his rebellions. Moreover, no more than the trading or settling colonists do the men who go to these colonies to take part in the government go there for philanthropy. They go, as a rule, primarily to make their living, and though they may exhibit the spirit of a devoted public service, it must always be remembered that to the native they and their dependents are merely a set of rulers, making a living out of his country and out of the taxes he pays, because they cannot make it at home, and interfering with him as a pretext for doing so. We must disenchant the facts and eliminate all the glamour which our assurance as to our own moral standards and our desire to think the best of ourselves hang about them, before we can hope to form any judgement of the aspect in which those facts appear to the African. (*pp.* 7–9)

(c) *Commonwealth of India Bill.*

1925

Memorandum

The Commonwealth of India Bill, which has been approved in substance by the Indian National Convention, purports to confer upon India the status of a self-governing Dominion, except for certain reservations as regards Defence and Foreign Affairs. The Council of India is abolished, and the Secretary of State for India will in future have the same relation to the Commonwealth of India as the Secretary of State for the Colonies has to the Governments of the Dominions. The Viceroy and Provincial Governors will have Cabinets to advise them, consisting of a Prime Minister and a number of Ministers (the minimum prescribed by Statute). The Cabinet will be collectively responsible to the Legislatures constituted entirely on an elective basis. The Constitution is of a federal type with autonomous provinces and the powers of the Commonwealth and Provincial Legislatures defined, residuary powers being vested in the former. The Commonwealth Legislature will consist of a Legislative Assembly and a Senate, while the Provincial Legislatures will be single Chambers for the present. Provision, however, has been made for enabling provinces to determine whether they will have second chambers or not. The Budgets, both the Commonwealth of India and of the Provincial Governments, will be subject to the vote of the Legislatures, except a certain minimum for Defence to be prescribed by a Commission appointed every five years, which will be an obligatory charge upon the revenues of the Commonwealth of India. The Viceroy will have full power over the defence forces of the Commonwealth, whether military, naval or air; but should the Budget estimates exceed the minimum limit, the sanction of the Commonwealth Legislature will be necessary. This reservation will disappear as soon as as the Commonwealth Legislature passes an Act with the approval of the Defence Commission, expressing its readiness to accept full responsibility for defence. The condition is attached that even in the transition period no revenue may be spent on those branches of the defence forces from which Indians are excluded in commissioned rank. Communal and special representation is abolished, but as a temporary measure the number of seats reserved for Mussalmans and Europeans will be maintained for a period of five years, to be subjected then to an enquiry by a Franchise Commission. The rights of minorities are protected by a provision to the effect that legislation dealing with such matters should lapse for the period of a year if it is opposed by a majority of the representatives of the particular interest or interests concerned. The powers over the public services in India will be vested in the Commonwealth Government or the Provincial Governments, and a Public Services Commission will be constituted to deal with all questions of recruitment, control, etc. The rights of those members who entered the public services before the constitution of the Commonwealth are guaranteed by Statute. There will be a Supreme Court of India in addition to the existing High Courts. (Bills, House of Commons, 1924–5, 287)

(d) LABOUR PARTY. *Labour and the Nation*

1928

The British Commonwealth of Nations

It is the policy of the Labour Party to take steps which would ensure closer political and economic relationships between Great Britain, India and the self-governing Dominions overseas, and the other constituent communities of the British Commonwealth of Nations. It believes in the right of the Indian people to self-government, and the policy of a Labour Government would be one of continuous co-operation with them with the object of establishing India at the earliest possible moment, and by her consent, as an equal partner with the other members of the British Commonwealth of Nations.

It would provide for closer personal contact between the Government of Great Britain and those of the Dominions and other members of the British Commonwealth, and at Commonwealth Conferences it would ensure that the British delegation should include representatives of Opposition as well as Government opinion.

A Labour Government would urge the various States concerned to co-operate in a survey of the land resources of the British Commonwealth, with a view to subordinating the private use of land to the general interests of a scientific redistribution of the population within it, and to securing, by improving the cultivation of its land, increased supplies of food for its population and of raw materials for its industries.

Migration and training schemes are part of the policy of the Labour Party. A Labour Government would see that reliable information was available for intending emigrants, and would establish centres in which suitable training for their new life could be given them. It would use the machinery of the Commonwealth Labour Conference, through which Labour in Great Britain is already in close touch with Labour in the Dominions, to establish a measure of supervision and control over their prospects and conditions.

The Labour Party views with grave concern the appalling evils produced by capitalist exploitation in certain of the tropical and sub-tropical parts of the British Commonwealth of Nations. It holds that the welfare of indigenous races, their economic prosperity, and their advancement in culture and civilisation, must be the primary object of colonial administration, to which all other interests must be rigorously subordinated. It notes with satisfaction that, where that principle has been observed primitive peoples have achieved, in a comparatively short time, results which decisively disprove the statement that they are incapable of social progress. It is determined that the fullest possible opportunities of similar progress shall be brought within their reach in all regions for whose government Great Britain is responsible.

A Labour Government, therefore, will make no compromise with policies which aim at accelerating the economic development of backward areas by methods which undermine the independence, the social institutions and the morale of their inhabitants, and which thus are injurious both to them, and, ultimately, to the working classes of Europe. It will use every means in its power to protect them in the occupation and enjoyment of their land, to prevent absolutely forced labour, whatever form it may assume, and to ensure that contracts between native workers and European employers are entered upon voluntarily and not under duress, that such contracts are subject to the approval of a public authority, and that they embody terms securing to the workers equitable conditions of life and employment. It will encourage the development of the services concerned with health and education. It will co-operate cordially with the Mandate Commission of the League of Nations, and will make every effort to strengthen and extend its authority.

In the scheme for the bulk purchase of food supplies and raw materials the Dominions and other parts of the British Commonwealth would play an important part. A Labour Government would provide facilities for overseas producers in the marketing of their produce in this country with a view to stabilising prices and eliminating unnecessary intermediaries, whilst it would co-operate in the control and cheapening of the transport of food supplies to Great Britain. (*pp*. 43*f*.)

(e) JAMES GRIFFITHS. Speech to Labour Party and Fabian Colonial Bureau Conference 23 September 1950

It is not an easy road we are travelling. It is a difficult task that we have undertaken—to guide the colonial territories to responsible democratic self-government. Democratic self-government cannot be given to a people, it must be won by them. And winning democracy means something much more—and more difficult—than overcoming oppression from outside. It means winning the battle against internal enemies—ignorance and poverty, disease and squalor. That is why we have emphasised that we regard our trust not only as that of guides to self-government, but also as partners in the task of establishing those conditions—economic, social and political, which are the prerequisites of a virile and successful democracy. And the justification for our partnership, and its continuation, is that these can best be established by our joint efforts. . . .

The Colonies are backward countries. They will, for some time ahead, need help in developing their resources and in promoting social services. They will require help of many kinds. They will need finance, capital equipment, and technical assistance. British Governments before the war neglected colonial development. Very little money was spent on it from United Kingdom funds. With but little United Kingdom Government money coming in, and with the limited resources available to the Colonial Governments, such economic development as did take place was almost entirely undertaken by private enterprise. We must recognise the benefits that have flowed from these efforts, but too often they have been accompanied by the bad consequences that flow inevitably from unplanned and uncontrolled development.

Far too many Colonies have been left with ill-balanced economies. They suffer also from the fact that far too little of the profits made were ploughed back into the development of secondary industries, and the provision of essential public services. All this led to a low wage economy that has been, and still is, both materially and spiritually, one of the greatest obstacles to progress.

There is one claim which the Labour Party can make, as its record shows: that we have made greater efforts to develop the resources and promote the provision of social services in the Colonies than any previous British Government. . . .

But—and here I come to something which is of cardinal importance—however good and extensive our policies of planned developments for the Colonies may be, they will never succeed without the full backing and co-operation of the people they are designed to benefit. We must therefore stimulate the initiative and harness the enthusiasm of the people. In every one of the territories there are educated and progressive elements who are immensely keen to improve their countries and to be given a full part in the planning of development. And at the same time there are in almost every territory the great mass of the rural population who are still slow to move and resistant to change. It is this inertia which is one of the greatest obstacles to progress. It is the legacy of bad health, poverty and ignorance, all aggravated in many cases by a difficult climate.

All these things are gradually being remedied, and we must continue and expand the positive policies on which we have embarked. But let us all realise that such a policy cannot succeed if everything is run by outside experts. A development scheme carried out on the initiative and by the efforts of the people themselves is more valuable than another scheme, even though technically better, operated entirely by outside experts. It is here, in the participation by the *people* in the work undertaken that we can find the key to the solution of many of the problems that beset us to-day. And although inertia is still widespread, we draw encouragement from the fact that where the right conditions are created, the people will respond enthusiastically and indeed will devote great efforts, sometimes without material reward, for the improvement of their own homes, their villages and their lands. This can only be done by carrying development down to the people, and by making them understand that it is by their own efforts, aided by the help we can provide, that their problems can be solved. This is the policy of mass education or community development which to-day lies at the centre of our policy for Africa. Its immense possibilities for improving the standards of the people, even in remote parts of the country, are shown by the success it has already had. . . .

We have been criticised in some quarters for going too fast politically in West Africa. It has been urged that more political experience is required and that the economic development of the territories is not far enough advanced to support the new constitutions. I do not share these fears. I believe that political maturity is best achieved by giving people real responsibility—for the essence of democracy is that democracy can't pass the buck—by asking them to become active and willing participants in the tasks of government, rather than by letting them stay outside as frustrated critics without responsibility. I am fully conscious of the need to secure that economic development should go hand in hand with political progress, and I am equally convinced of the dangers of creating responsible states without adequate economic and social foundations. But it is equally true that, unless a favourable political climate is created, economic development will be hampered and delayed at every turn.

These new constitutions are a great gesture of confidence in the people of West Africa. I believe it will be repaid many times over. I would like to address an appeal to those, particularly among the West African nationalists, who criticise us for going too slowly, even in these new constitutional changes. Now that the people of West Africa are to have so large a say in the management of their own affairs, is it not reasonable to ask those who are still impatient to be content with this great advance and to set themselves to tackle the urgent practical problems which have to be solved? Further political advance will not necessarily have to await the solution of all the practical problems, which will inevitably take time. But further political advance, whenever it comes, will be greatly assisted if the practical problems of administration, local government and social and economic development have meanwhile been resolutely tackled by the peoples and Governments. I would say to the young men and women of West Africa: "Here is your chance to serve your people, to help them forward to full and complete democratic government. Go in and take it". (Griffiths, *et al.*, *The Way Forward*, 1950, *pp.* 27*f*, 30–2, 34*f*.)

EPILOGUE

Bruce Glasier, who as a boy was employed herding sheep on the Isle of Arran, was trained as a craftsman in decorative iron work and became a keen member of the Socialist League, acting as secretary of its Glasgow branch for some time. After the League broke up he joined the I.L.P. and was for many years one of Keir Hardie's most loyal colleagues. He was chairman of the I.L.P. from 1900 to 1903, and subsequently editor of the *Labour Leader*. He and his wife, Katharine (née Conway), a Cambridge graduate, were both well-known inside the movement as lecturers and writers on Socialism. He died in 1920, but she lived to continue her propaganda work until 1950.

J. BRUCE GLASIER. *The Meaning of Socialism*

1919

COMMONLY we speak of Socialism as meaning the socialisation of wealth. It indeed means that, but by wealth it implies not only land, capital and the general means of production and distribution, but all the means and opportunities of life and happiness—knowledge, art, recreation, travel and freedom of educating our powers and practising our strength and skill.

Socialism means not only the socialisation of wealth, but of our lives, our hearts—ourselves.

In Socialist politics, it is true, the question of the distribution of material wealth, or the means of material wealth, figures as the all-important one. And indeed so it is, and must be, until such times as right conditions of wealth are established. That is not because Socialism looks upon material wealth itself as the only or even the chief object of life or means of happiness. It is because, in the first place, the possession of a certain degree of material comfort is an essential condition, not only of life and health, but of the opportunities of leisure, art and general progress; and because, in the second place, the just distribution of material wealth is the one indispensable condition, a test condition in fact, of the just relationship existing between man and man in society. It is in the justice or equality of the relationship which it seeks to constitute, rather than in the degree or quantity of wealth itself, that the essential principal of Socialism is found. Thus the great wrong of existing social conditions does not lie in the mere circumstance that many are poor while few are rich, but in the injustice and degradation, in the assertion of superiority and inferiority, in the denial of brotherhood, which these conditions imply. Were all poor alike, the poverty might not only be quite endurable, but great fellowship and happiness might be possible with it. A community in which the standard of wealth for all was not more than equivalent to that provided by an ordinary artisan's or even a labourer's wage, but in which there was complete co-operation and fellowship, would enjoy an incomparably higher degree of happiness and human dignity than would a community in which the standard of life for none was lower than that of our present-day middle class, but in which some of its members possessed vast excesses of wealth, and in which there was class separation and tyranny, selfish grabbing, and the absence of neighbourly kindness and brotherhood.

Socialism it will be seen, therefore, does not mean mere working class revolt or acquisition, though the political Socialist movement is mainly a working class movement. Socialism naturally appeals most directly to the working class, because they are the people who suffer most under the existing industrial system, and are those whose material conditions will be most beneficially affected by the abolition of capitalism and the establishment of the Socialist Commonwealth. Their emancipation is therefore the most necessary and urgent aim of the Socialist agitation. But the thought of Socialism—the desire for, and the hope and faith in the possibility of realising, a state of social equality and co-operation—did not originate in the working class. Nor does Socialist teaching to-day find less ready acceptance or excite more fervent desire among the working class than among the more thoughtful and right-hearted men and women of the "educated" and higher classes. Fortunately there are to be found as many sincere Socialists in the ranks of literature, art, science, and perhaps even of the wealthy, as in the ranks of the wage-earners.

All classes, rich no less than poor, are the products or victims of their circumstances. It is true that the rich oppress and rob the poor, but except in so far as they do so consciously, knowing they are doing wrong, they are no more culpable in the doing of that wrong than are the poor in enduring it. In precisely the same sense that we speak, as did St. Basil and St. Chrysostom, of the rich as a class being "thieves", we may speak of the poor as being unsuccessful or unlucky "thieves". For the poor are not poor because they wish to be poor, because they prefer to be poor rather than rich. They would if they could be in the lucky position of landlords and capitalists who now oppress and rob them. The trade unionist is not a worker because he desires to be a worker rather than an employer, but because he cannot help it. He does not consider (and even if he did he could never find out) whether his wage represents less or more than he actually contributes to the wealth of his employer or the nation. He simply takes as much wages as he can get. He would take a hundred or a thousand pounds a week if he could get it—get it, I mean, without intentionally or knowingly doing any more wrong than his employer realises he does when he obtains a hundred or a thousand pounds a week profit. Poor and rich, wage-worker and capitalist are in fact both of one flesh and " there is little difference between clay and clay ", as Bossuet said when applying the precept as a rebuke to the rich.

Socialism, in truth, consists, when finally resolved, not in getting at all, but in giving; not in being served, but in serving; not in selfishness, but in unselfishness; not in the desire to gain a place of bliss in this world for one's self and one's family (that is the individualist and capitalist aim), but in the desire to create an earthly paradise for all. Its ultimate moral, as its original biological justification, lies in the priniciple, human and divine, that " as we give, so we live ", and only in so far as we are willing to lose life do we gain life.

Thus, once again, we see that fundamentally Socialism is a question of right human relationship and is essentially a spiritual principle.

Socialism, therefore, is religion—not that part of religion that relates to our beliefs concerning God, immortality, and the mystery of the unseen universe, but that part, the all-essential, practical part of it, that concerns the right state of our present lives, the right state of our relation to our fellows, the right moral health of our souls.

Yet it may be better simply to say with William Morris that Socialism is fellowship, and that fellowship is life, and the lack of fellowship is death. Fellowship is heaven and the lack of fellowship is hell.

" Therefore, I bid you not dwell in hell, but in heaven, or while ye must, upon earth, which is a part of heaven, and forsooth no foul part." (*pp.* 226–30)

SOME BOOKS FOR FURTHER READING

E. E. Barry: *Nationalisation in British Politics* (1965)

G. D. H. Cole: *History of Socialist Thought* (Five vols., 1953-1960)

S. T. Glass: *The Responsible Society. The Ideas of Guild Socialism* (1966)

Alexander Gray: *The Socialist Tradition* (1946)

A. M. McBriar: *Fabian Socialism and English Politics* (Cambridge, 1962)

A. Menger: *The Right to the Whole Produce of Labour*, with Introduction by H. S. Foxwell (1899)

Raymond Williams: *Culture and Society*, 1780-1950 (1958)

A. B. Ulam: *Philosophical Foundations of English Socialism* (Cambridge, Mass., 1951)

SUBJECT INDEX